'After this book, pot-limit Omaha will never be the same.'

> Rob Hollink (the 'Chief'), *European Poker Champion 2005 ($845,190), winner of the $2,000 no-limit hold'em at the 2006 Five-Star World Poker Classic ($204,815) and winner of the €250 pot-limit Omaha at the 2004 World Heads-Up Championships ($16,240). European 'Player of the Year' 2005.*

'Rolf practises an unorthodox playing style that has his opponents complaining about his devilish luck. Those who understand the game know better. When I heard that Rolf was going to write a book on pot-limit Omaha, I knew I had to start improving my other games. Now that Rolf has decided to share his intricate knowledge of the game, pot-limit Omaha will become much tougher to beat. I can only hope that his publisher goes out of business before the book comes out.'

> Ed de Haas, *Top cash game pro who specialises in pot-limit Omaha. Winner of the $500 pot-limit Omaha at the 2004 Jack Binion World Poker Open ($100,126), and runner-up at the €500 pot-limit Omaha at the 2004 Master Classics ($45,180).*

'Rolf is a proven winner, and the strategy he writes is amongst the best in the business.'

> Ben Grundy, the 'Milkybarkid', *British top pro who finished seventh at the 2005 EPT Grand Final ($105,815), and winner of the £250 pot-limit Omaha hi-lo at the Grosvenor World Masters ($24,230).*

'Groundbreaking advice from the top PLO strategist. This book will divulge many of the secrets that until now were only known among the top pros – things that they were unwilling to give away to any other but themselves. Because Rolf has now broken with this tradition, I am certain that *Secrets of Professional Pot-Limit Omaha* will turn out to be *the* pot-limit Omaha book to date.'

> Dennis de Ruiter, *One of the best PLO cash game players in Europe.*

'When I started out on my own career, Rolf already had a well-deserved reputation of being a very big winner in the pot-limit Omaha cash games. Over the years, I've seen him beat this game with this remarkable strategy of his. Now finally, with this book, I can take a look at how he plays *exactly*. I already knew which hands he liked to play – now I guess I will also know which hands he folds. ☺'

> Noah Boeken (Exclusive), *Winner of the EPT Copenhagen 2005 ($191,355), and winner of the $200 pot-limit Omaha at the Caribbean Poker Classic ($19,830).*

# Poker books from D&B

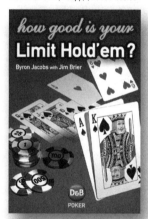

# Secrets of Professional
# Pot-Limit Omaha
## Rolf Slotboom

D&B POKER
www.dandbpoker.com

First published in 2006 by D & B Publishing, PO Box 18,
Hassocks, West Sussex BN6 9WR

**British Library Cataloguing-in-Publication Data**

A catalogue record for this book is available from the British Library.

ISBN: 1-904468-30-6
ISBN13: 978 1-904468-30-1

All sales enquiries should be directed to:
D & B Publishing, PO Box 18, Hassocks, West Sussex BN6 9WR, UK

Tel: +44 (0)1273 834680, Fax: +44 (0)1273 831629,
e-mail: info@dandbpublishing.com,
Website: www.dandbpoker.com

Cover design by Horatio Monteverde.
Production by Navigator Guides.
Printed and bound in the US by Versa Press.

# Contents

# Foreword by Rob Hollink

When Rolf Slotboom asked me to write the foreword to his book I was very flattered. Wondering why I felt like this, I came to the conclusion that this feeling of delight was *not* only caused by these human primitive instincts that automatically tell us to feel happy every time someone asks us for something that is important to them. No, it was very clear to me that I was happy that I had the chance to tell the rest of the world what kind of a player Rolf is. I have discussed his pot-limit Omaha game with numerous other players for years. The reason he was the centre of our discussion so often, was because his irritating game was extremely hard to beat. Irritating. Yes, extremely irritating, that's the way I always felt about his game. I am pretty sure that no one in the whole world was more sick about his game than I. But I knew full well that this feeling was caused by my own inability to react to his strategy in a proper way. Actually, frustration with my own limitations was what made me feel sick.

From 2001 to 2005, we played regularly in the same game in Amsterdam. Our PLO game would usually start around nine o'clock. Sometimes Rolf had already put me on tilt before it had even started. I always wanted to play, no matter who was playing or how many people were playing. I was always ready to start the game, because that was what I had gone there for: to play poker. But sometimes we would not quite have enough players to get the game started smoothly. Let's say there were four players who were all ready to start up the game, but who would only play if the game was five-handed. And then Rolf was still playing the limit hold'em game. Sometimes, I was even stupid enough to go over to him and ask if he would be willing to join us. Of course, this was always useless, because if he had been interested, he would have been at our table already. His answer was then always something like, that his short-handed game was not so good, that the potential contributors were not there, that he would probably join later, etc. So despite being the biggest winner in the whole pokerroom, he was not prepared to open his own business. Do you understand? Can you imagine how I felt about this? But the truth is, I knew he was right. This was not the composition of players he was looking for.

Then, once the table had become juicy enough for him, Rolf would come over to our game and take the seat to the immediate right of the most aggressive player, someone who was willing to gamble a lot with the worst hand. He most times bought in for the minimum, played very tight and almost never made the first raise. Hoping that the loose players would raise it up rather too aggressively before the flop so that a reraise from him would be big enough, he would have more or less all his money in the pot with the best hand – basically before the pot had even started. Sounds like a simple strategy? Well, this is a point where many discussions about his game began. Many of his opponents were oblivious to the strength of this style. Besides that you get it all-in with the best hand, you can also get a lot protection post-flop, because the big stacks can still push each other out of the pot. And Rolf always saw the river... Another advantage is of course the dead money. There were always players who paid the first raise, but were not prepared to go all the way – and this benefited Rolf.

For many opponents, he was just a lucky guy. Often he would win the pot with a backdoor flush or straight, or even just top and bottom (normally Rolf had the aces) pair. Let me give you an example how many pots of these went. Before the flop there is some raising and Rolf takes the opportunity to reraise to 270. Three players call and the four of them see the flop. The pot is 1080. Player A, in the small blind has 2460 left, holding 9♠-8♣-6♠-5♦. Player B, in the big blind has 2340 left, holding K♠-K♥-Q♥-10♣. Rolf has left 150, and his hand is A♠-A♥-7♥-6♣. Player C has 2500 left, holding 6♦-5♠-4♦-3♠.

Then the flop comes 9♦-8♦-2♣. Player A likes the flop but knows that Rolf is going to bet his last 150 for sure, so he decides to go for a check-raise. Player B is not so happy with the flop and checks. Rolf of course bets his remaining 150. Player C decides to call the 150. Now player A, with top two pair + gutshot, raises the pot to 1680 to make player C pay for his draw. Player C does not know if his weak flush draw and his bottom-end gutshot are good if they hit, so he folds, and it is just between Rolf and the strong player A now. The turn and river cards are the J♦ and the 2♣. Rolf beats player A, having just made two pair aces and deuces.

See here the strength of the post-flop protection. What actually happened is that four players saw the flop, and Rolf ended up in third place at the river. But because number 1 and 2 had already folded on the flop, Rolf walked away with a net gain of 1110. This was just an simple example how some pots went, with many people completely unaware of what had really happened.

Of course, the fact that players don't see what is really happening, is what makes poker so great. We are all making the best moves and the finest plays we can. But not many of us are aware that the capacity of our brains is limited, and that some-one else could simply be a bit smarter.

I hate it, but also *my* brain is limited. But it is good enough to recognise Rolf Slot-boom as the best short-stack pot-limit Omaha player in the world. And therefore, I am sure that all players will elevate their games tremendously by incorporating Rolf's views and insights.

After this book, pot-limit Omaha will never be the same.

*Rob Hollink is the 2005 European Poker Champion, having won the inaugural EPT Grand Final for a €635,000 first prize. He is one of the few players in Europe who excel in both cash games and tournaments, live as well as online, and he is one of the best pot-limit Omaha players in Europe.*

*For more poker info you can visit www.robhollinkpoker.com. Rob can also be found play-ing at www.robspokerroom.com under his own name.*

# Preface

What you are reading here is not, or not in the first place, a 'how to' book. What you are reading here is more than anything a collection of *my* strategies, *my* views and *my* plays. Only in the two probably most important chapters in this book, the 'Practice Hands' and the 'Hand Match-ups & Analysis' will I come up with some real concrete tactics on the way *you* could or should play. In almost every chapter I simply describe how *I* play in specific games, limits and structures – all in all, in game conditions that may not necessarily apply to the game in which *you* are playing. On top of that, most of the strategies I discuss involve feel, adjusting to tendencies and specific weaknesses of opponents, and adapting to the flow of a game – all things that are not easy to both teach and learn. So it should be clear that this book does not have a coherent game plan with easy tips that could help you get from A to Z without much thought.

What I *will* provide you with, is a detailed analysis of the various game plans I have used over the years, in order to tackle the different types of games in which I have played. This analysis starts with the game that launched my pot-limit Omaha career, the €100 minimum buy-in game in Vienna.[1] From there, I moved on to what has been by bread-and-butter game for many years: the €500 minimum buy-in pot-limit Omaha game in Amsterdam. Over a period of more than four years I played here on a daily basis with some of the best European PLO players, including Ed de Haas, Europe's Player of the Year 2001 & 2004 Marcel Lüske, and the 2005 European Poker Champion Rob Hollink. Once the money in this game

---

[1] For the purposes of this book, the €100, €200 and €500 minimum buy-in games have been converted into $100, $200 and $500 minimum buy-in games. This is simply to keep all games described in one currency, US dollars.

had dried up a little, I shifted my focus to the $2,000 maximum buy-in online games at especially Party Poker, where I spend most of my time nowadays (at least at the time of writing this book). This is a game that features not just the best Dutch or even European, but rather some of the best PLO players in the world. In the largest section on online play that I have ever seen in a PLO book, I describe the tactics that I have used and am using here in a very successful manner – tactics that have often been described by others as strange and unconventional, and that sometimes require a rather counterintuitive way of playing. Quite frankly, a manner of play that is not always appreciated or understood very well even by the better players.

For instance, in my hometown Amsterdam I used to play day in day out, and as a result I was probably the biggest winner in that game over a four-year period[2], yet almost without exception I would be called 'lucky' rather than 'good'. People would say: 'OK, so maybe you play a pretty solid and very tight game but then every once in a while come up with some strange plays that look flat-out wrong – yet you always seem to get away with them.' Now obviously, I have never explained to them the reasons behind these strategies of mine, for the simple reason that I faced these players on a daily basis and did not want to educate them – because they were tough enough opponents already. And even in all of my PLO articles[3] I have never written about them because many of these concepts are just too advanced to discuss in a two-page article. But here in this book, I will analyse every single aspect of my game in depth, with the ultimate goal of helping you benefit from this. Finally, I close off these chapters on my strategies with a special section on adjustments for short-handed online games. Even though I still prefer full-ring games, more and more online games tend to become 6-max, and in this section I will show you how you can or should adjust to this trend.

From there, we get to the parts of the book that many of you will probably find the most interesting of all: the chapters on 'Practice Hands' and on 'Hands Match-Ups & Analysis'. If I'm not mistaken, these two single chapters provide the most in-depth analysis on the play of hands that have ever been published in any PLO

---

[2] In all the games that I describe in this book I have been either *one* of the biggest winners overall, or even *the* biggest winner. While many people have attributed these results to just luck, and I have gone out of my way myself to cultivate my 'lucky' image, the fact is that in all PLO games I have played to date I have done exceptionally well over extended periods of time – usually with a game plan that most of my opponents would consider strange, unconventional or even plain bad.

[3] Especially for this book, I have re-written all of my former PLO articles that are currently unavailable. These articles were published in the now defunct *Poker Digest* magazine. Because they offer so much valuable advice, I have completely re-edited them and have changed and added many things – in order to make this 'Classic Articles' section not just an interesting, but rather a necessary part of this book. All of my more recent PLO articles that have been written for either *CardPlayer* or *CardPlayer Europe*, can simply be found on www.cardplayer.com.

book or article. I will have to warn you though: these two chapters are *not* easy reads. But I am not here to make things easy for you – I am here to help improve your PLO games significantly. If you are looking for easy answers and/or if you are someone who likes to accomplish things with a minimum of effort, then you have probably picked the wrong book, and you have *definitely* picked the wrong author. I believe in old-fashioned things like dedication, hard work, effort, discipline and a total commitment to the game, in order to play at the highest possible level. If you are unable or unwilling to come up with this effort, I would say: Don't buy this book, as quite obviously you don't belong to my target audience. But if you *are* willing to give your all, then I am certain that this book will offer a wealth of information that could lift your game to a high or even a very high level. Because I can honestly say: In this book I will tell everything I know, and I hold nothing back. I will give away every little trick I have used over the years to gain an edge, to keep my opponents in line, or to lure them into making mistakes. I will talk about all the mathematical background to my play, because obviously many of my decisions are based on mathematics. But possibly more than anything, my strategies are based on exploiting other player's weaknesses, and I will show you how I have taken this concept to a level that is quite rare even in the big games that I play nowadays.

So all in all, I guess I am simply giving away way too much information in this book, information that quite clearly could make my bread-and-butter games much tougher to beat. But I hope that in time you will thank *me* for being stupid enough to provide you with all this info, and thank D&B for being smart enough to ask me to come up with it. I can honestly say that I have given my all to make this *the* best PLO book to date – and I hope that indeed you will all appreciate it as such.

Rolf Slotboom,
Amsterdam, August 2006

# Chapter One

# My time in Vienna: A new strategy

## Introduction

Those of you who are familiar with my writing will know that Vienna has a special place in my heart. In 1997, I moved abroad for the first time in my life. I had let a former colleague of mine convince me that moving there would be a great opportunity. And not just that, she also made it clear that living over there, and working as a dealer in Concord Card Casino (Europe's biggest poker room), would be plain fun. As it turned out, we would indeed have a great time over there, not in the least because we would return from Vienna as boyfriend and girlfriend. But also because of our jobs, and the experiences we had dealing with all the different types of circumstances and people that we encountered, I can honestly say that once I finally returned home to Amsterdam, I had become a richer man.

But Vienna has also played a key role in my development as a player. When I decided to quit my job as a dealer to become full-time pro, I actually started out by playing in Vienna's low-limit hold'em and stud games. After a while, once I had proven myself in these low-limit games, I moved back to Amsterdam where I gradually moved up in limits, and became a typical example of a limit hold'em grinder. By that time, my girlfriend had come back to Amsterdam too, but after a little while she decided that she wanted to go back to Vienna once more. I joined her, and took an important next step in my poker career. I started focusing on pot-limit Omaha, a game that had just started up in Amsterdam at (for me) extremely high stakes, but which was played as a much smaller game in Vienna. In fact, lots of low-limit players over there who used to play $3-$6 limit hold'em or stud thought that the PLO games with a $100 buy-in and one $2 blind were not that much different in size from their regular game. As a result, lots of (losing) low-limit players now occupied seats in the highly skilful PLO games. Now this was of course all the more reason to jump into that game – and it turned out to be one of the best decisions I have ever made.

# Exploring the PLO games: Finding my edge

Looking back at the way this game was played back then, it was one of the easiest games in the world to beat. And just as importantly, it was perfectly suited for the abilities I had at the time. The game was played ten-handed with just one blind. In the $100 minimum buy-in game the blind would be $2; in the $200 minimum buy-in game, the blind would be $5. The fact that the blind pressure was so low was excellent for someone like me who had no problems waiting patiently for hours to find a good hand/situation to get the money in. And two more factors attributed to the potential profitability of this game. The game had a rake instead of a time collection, meaning that 5%, $3 maximum was taken out of every pot. Now, while this kind of rake may be pretty steep for a shorthanded low-limit game, for the full-ring PLO game that we were playing it was excellent – especially for an extremely tight player like me.

And things got even better because of the characteristics of the opposition. Almost without exception, people would play either a loose-aggressive or a loose-passive style of play. This meant that on the very few hands that I chose to play, I would almost always be certain of a big and juicy multiway pot – which was just what I wanted. With a style of play that I will describe in depth in this chapter, it would not be unusual to turn my $100 buy-in into $400 or even $500 on just a single hand, meaning that on some days winning just one pot in a three- or four-hour session could be good enough for a huge profit. Huge, of course, within the limits of this game – because in the eyes of those who did not know any better, we were playing a penny-stakes type of game here. But the reality was that over a period of six or seven months I played about six days a week, and easily averaged $250 a day almost free of risk. Not a lot of money for me now, but at that stage in my career it was a great way to build up my bankroll. I kept meticulous records of my play, and I had a percentage of winning sessions of just over 80% – which is incredibly high if you take into account the swings that are part of pot-limit Omaha.

All in all, the characteristics of the game as described here led to a situation that I have *never* encountered since: A situation where it was possible to *win* lots of money in relation to the size of the game, while *losing* was almost impossible. I have never again played in PLO games where I had this big an edge, simply because of these three simple factors that made the Vienna games so good:

- ♠ The characteristics of the opposition (weak, loose).
- ♠ The characteristics of the game (ten-handed, negligible rake).
- ♠ The strength of my well-defined strategy, which was entirely new to my opponents – and that they were unable to counter even until the very last day that I played there.

So, what exactly *was* this strategy that I used?

# The Vienna way

## 1) The amount of the buy-in

The casino that I played in usually had two PLO games going: the $100 minimum buy-in with one $2 blind, and the $200 minimum buy-in with one $5 blind. Whereas nowadays, almost all online games and even some brick and mortar games have a cap on the buy-in, those were two 'classical' games where you could buy in for as much as you wanted. Having said that, most people in these games were low-limit players who simply always bought in for the minimum. They would hit-and-run if they won a big pot, and when all-in they would keep out pulling $100 bills as long as they could afford it. Almost no player in this game would stay with a stack of more than four or five times the minimum buy-in.

This meant that the concept of 'covering the table' and having the biggest stack so you could break the other big stacks wasn't of much use, because a live one would *not* stay in his seat once he had accumulated any serious money. For this reason, I opted for a strategy that to some people automatically seems to imply weakness: Always to buy in for the minimum, unless by chance there *was* a live one playing a big stack. It was my view back then that in PLO you will usually want to have either the shortest stack at the table or the largest one, but not an in-between stack – and this is still my view. The advantages of short-stack play are not always seen or appreciated by the better players. But clearly there *are* some advantages to play-ing with just little money in front of you. Just the fact that you will be all-in in just one or two betting increments, could benefit you in the following ways:

- ♠ If you make a mistake, it won't be such a big one. Now I know that this may seem silly to some of you. But because a) your stack is small and b) the dead money in the pot counts for a lot and gives you much better odds than in a deep-money situation, the damage of any bad decisions you may make will be substantially limited. And for all but possibly the very best players, this is an extremely important concept that could help you play with much less fear and under significantly less pressure.

♠ You can go all-in early in the hand, thereby possibly maximising your expected value (EV), and perhaps just as importantly, taking away any implied odds your opponent could be getting (like for instance when on the flop you have a decent made hand and they are on a draw).

♠ Because the amount of money your opponents could lose to you is not that high (your stack being relatively small), they tend to fear you much less than if you are playing with lots of chips. This means that because of your short stack, they have a tendency to call you very loosely – and this is exactly what you want now that you have waited so long for the proper hand/situation to put the money in.

♠ If you win a pot when playing short money, you may very well end up with three, four, yes in very loose games even five times the amount of money that you have put at risk. Now, especially if you had the money in as a money favourite, you are playing with a huge overlay here, where the rewards can be enormous, while risking relatively little. Compare this to a situation where the money is deep. There, you may have to put $800 at risk in order to win $850 or so, whereas with a short stack you may be putting $100 at risk to win $300 or even more.

♠ Once you have moved in early, either before or on the flop, and you are now all-in, then you may very well get protection from the other players in the hand. Let's say that you are all-in pre-flop for $100 with A-A-x-x and face two opponents who are both playing a $500 stack. Let's say that one of them has a rundown hand, 10-9-8-7, while the other one is playing a K-K-Q-2. If the flop now comes 10-6-2 rainbow, the rundown hand may figure: 'Hey, I have a pair and an inside wrap. If I bet now and get the other player out, I will end up in the hand heads-up against one player. Even if this player has aces, then I am still not in very bad shape. I will have invested $100 in a $300+ pot, and obviously my chances to win here are much better than one in three. And if by chance the all-in player does *not* have a high pair but rather something like A-K-Q-J, then I may be in even better shape, where my mere pair of tens is simply the current best hand.' Many players would reason like that in this situation, and would bet big here in order to try and force the other player out and to see the turn and river card 'for free'. Now, let's say that indeed this is what happens here: The 10-9-8-7 bets the pot, succeeds in making the K-K-Q-2 fold, and now the turn or river brings another deuce, king or queen. You would have lost the pot had there been no further betting after the flop – but the fact that you have now obtained protection while being all-in means that the money in the middle is going to come your way. Or, in other words: In order to win a $300+ pot, you had invested $100 yourself – yet you had to beat just one player to get this money, not two. This is a situation with a clear positive expectation that will occur frequently when you are all-in while your opponents are not. And especially when – as in this case – you also have the best starting hand, you will be in a highly profitable situation.[1]

♠ You will not be vulnerable to any bluffs or semi-bluffs that your opponents could be making, possibly when they are taking advantage of a scary board, or when they are betting because they know that the board cards probably have not helped you much. Because you are all-in early in the hand, it will be impossible for the good and even excellent players to outplay you – for the simple reason that you will *always* reach the river, no matter what they do.

Now obviously, there are some clear *disadvantages* to playing a short stack as well. They include:

♠ You cannot break your opponents on one hand.

♠ You will not have much power/enough ammunition to pull off any successful bluffs or semi-bluffs. For instance, it will be impossible for you to fire that important 'second barrel' on the later streets, simply because by that time you will already be all-in.

♠ You will not get maximum value in those situations where you have a very good hand and are lucky enough to find your opponent with an also good, but second-best hand. Had you been playing deep money, you could have taken his entire stack, but now you will have to settle for just doubling the money that you have in front of you.

## 2) The best seating position

The second key aspect for finding the optimum strategy to beat this specific game,

---

[1] These situations where your short stack could get protection can be so profitable, that you should sometimes move in even when you suspect that you may not have the current best hand. Especially if you have a double-suited hand that has lots of potential, you will almost never be making a big mistake when you commit fully with your short stack in a multiway pot, provided that there at least two big stacks still in the hand. The reason is simple: These two players could possibly bet each other/the potential winner out of the pot – on the flop, or even at the later streets. And this, of course, will be to *your* benefit.

was choosing the proper seat. Common wisdom says that in poker you should try to have loose, aggressive and tricky players seated to your right, while having tight, passive and unimaginative players to your left. That way, you will get to see what the 'dangerous' players will do first, so you can adjust your own decisions to the actions they have made. In the meantime, you don't worry too much about the players behind you, as they are unlikely to be taking advantage of the positional advantage they have over you. Also, because the players behind you tend to fold lots of hands, you will often be able to 'buy the button', because a call or raise by you in middle/late position may lead to them folding. And because the aggressive and dangerous players act in front of you, it will be easier for you to make the correct decisions with regards to the pot odds you are getting, the possibility of isolating one or two overaggressive players by reraising them, or taking free cards later in the hand.

Whereas in limit hold'em I thoroughly subscribe to these seating rules, in pot-limit Omaha I habitually violate them. That is: I habitually violate them *when I'm playing a short stack*.[2] When playing with just a little money, as I did at least during the first couple of months of my stay in Vienna, you actually *don't* want any tight, timid or passive players behind you. Quite the contrary: You should go out of your way to get the most aggressive player in the game to your immediate left! Have you ever heard the advice that when there's a maniac in your game, you should try to have him seated to your right, because then you have position on him and will be able to isolate him whenever you've got a good hand? Well, when playing a short stack in PLO I recommend *the exact opposite*.

I have made tons of money by always picking the seat to the immediate right of a maniac – the seat that other players always tried to avoid. First in Vienna and later also in Amsterdam, all decent or good players would without exception try to move away from the seat that they considered the 'death seat': the one to the immediate right of an overaggressive player. Yet I always took that spot out of freewill! People never understood what I was doing, and both in Vienna and in Amsterdam it took my opponents months to figure out at least to *some* degree what I was doing, and why on earth I would always voluntarily pick this obviously 'bad' seat. After all, they knew that I was a winning player who was always busy exploiting edges, so they could not imagine that I would make a flagrant error like this 'by accident'.

Once my opponents finally understood it, they slowly but surely started making some adjustments. First of all, they started to instruct the maniac not to raise so often when I was also in the hand, now that they had concluded this was exactly what I wanted him to do. And just as importantly, more and more players would

---

[2] When playing a *large* stack, the recommendations above become increasingly important again. This is especially true if you also take into account the concept of short stacks to your left, and big stacks to your right. You can find much more on this big-stack approach later in this book.

start copying what I was doing. Especially in Amsterdam people were always used to buying in for lots of chips, but now they too would start to buy in for the minimum, just as they had always seen *me* do. But most of all, they too suddenly became very eager to select the seat that they had always wanted to avoid – meaning that in the end things would turn into a 'battle for Rolf's seat'. And obviously, by that time I knew I had to make some clear adjustments to my initial strategy, now that so many people were suddenly treating all these concepts I had introduced as 'gospel' – as if this was the *only* secret to success, and as if simply copying my play would automatically give them the same results. So, once so many people would think 'this is the way Rolf plays', I knew it was time to make some radical changes – and fortunately, it took my opponents another few months to again figure *them* out.

But for now, let's first focus on this short-stack, sitting-to-the-right-of-the-maniac approach. What are the reasons for picking this – in the eyes of some – strange seat, and how exactly have I turned this into such a successful approach? Well, if you do some thinking on your own, I guess it should not be that hard to find out. But here, I have done this thinking for you.

## Advantages of being seated to a maniac's immediate *right* (only when you are playing shallow money)

♠ You can always let him do the betting and raising for you. When playing a short stack, you will *never* have to put in the first bet or raise. Whenever you hold a good or even premium hand before the flop, you will simply call the initial bet. If the maniac now raises and one or two players call this raise, you can now come over the top for all your money with the probable best hand. This way, you will be maximising your wins, because with your good hands you may now be able to win two, three or even four times the amount of money that you had in front of you. When you have aces or a nice double-suited hand it will not be unusual for you to win the pot anywhere from 30 to 50 percent of the time even when you are up against three players. And clearly, taking into account any dead money, you would need to win only 23-24% of the time here to already have a positive expectation. (Do you understand why?[3]) This

---

[3] OK, here's the answer. If you and three other players each put in an x-amount of money, you would already break-even if you just win the pot 25% of the time – or one time in four. Once there is dead money in the middle from either blinds folding or from people who have first called a bet, but then have folded to your all-in reraise, they contribute to the pot without having any chance of winning. Especially when you are playing a short stack, this will improve your expected return considerably, as your expectation in the pot rises now that there's more money in the middle, while you don't have to beat any more players in order to get it. This means that 24% or even 23% pot equity may now be

means that if indeed you had the best hand going in, you will almost always have put your money into the middle with a *very* good expectation.

♠ Let's say that you hold aces and the flop comes A-9-2, or you hold kings and the flop comes K-K-7. When there is still a lot of money left to be played, you are unlikely to get serious action from the type of hands your opponents probably hold (J-9-8-7, Q-Q-4-4, A-8-6-5 etc.), other than some feeble bluff attempt maybe. But by moving in *before* the flop and having them call you, all their money is in the pot already! Also, by moving in early, you will have avoided a scenario where your opponents could obtain implied odds because they know that you probably hold a big pair, but you don't know what they hold. And finally, by moving in early, you avoid getting bluffed or semi-bluffed out of the pot by good/aggressive players, for instance when the board gets scary – simply because all the money is in already. Being seated with a short stack to the immediate right of a maniac will help you accomplish all that. In fact, by moving in early you will now win many pots on the turn or river that you would not have won with deep money – simply because you would not have called any additional bets after the flop or turn. Say the flop comes J-9-7 rainbow, you have A-A-5-4 and are up against someone holding a J-10-9-6. Against this top two pair + straight draw, you would never have called any bets with your bare aces if the money were deep. But being all-in, you could catch a seven, an ace, a running pair or possibly even a runner-runner flush to snatch the pot away from your opponent.

♠ You are playing a headache-free type of poker, where the best decisions – because of your short stack and the somewhat predictable actions of the Action Man to your left – are usually very clear. While this factor was not of that much importance in this Vienna game that I describe here, it *is* very important in the fast online games we have nowadays. In fact, because this 'short-stack/sit to the right of maniacs' approach requires so little deep thought processes, it is an excellent strategy for online multi-tablers who may not be true experts, but who still want to make good money.[4] And

---

enough to still have a positive expectation. For some thorough calculations on this exact subject, see the chapters 'Practice Hands' and especially 'Hand Match-ups & Analysis'.

[4] Obviously, this in theory great strategy is hampered somewhat by the fact that online you don't have that many options when it comes to seat selection. This is especially true on (most) sites where you are not allowed to make any seat changes, or in PLO games that have long waiting lists, meaning that you

quite frankly, by using this strategy playing on four or even five tables simultaneously, I think my number of BB/100 may be somewhat lower than most top pros who play just two or three tables
with very deep money, but my hourly rate will be about the same –
with much less risk, and much less headache.

♠ By taking this seat to the maniac's immediate right (i.e. having him
sit to *your* left), you have guaranteed that the pots you win will
usually be much bigger than if you had been seated to the maniac's
left. This arises because of the possible contribution by people who
will be caught in the middle between the person to your left (the
maniac) and you (the sandbagger). Here is an example, taken from
the Amsterdam game that we will describe later. In a $10-$10 blinds
game, you have a $300 stack and limp for $10 in early position, and
then the maniac makes his usual pot raise to $50. A late position
player and both blinds call the raise. Now, when the action gets
back to you, you simply reraise all-in to $300. A lot of good things
could happen for you now. For one, the maniac may get frisky by
reraising once more, shutting out the entire field – and he may not
even have a better hand than you to do this. But also if he just calls,
some of the players behind him may find $300 too much and decide
to fold after having invested $50 already. In fact, it would be quite
probable to get $100 or even $150 in dead money here, and even if
these initial callers don't fold but call again, you could now win a
massive pot: $1,500 total, having invested just $300, for a $1,200 net
profit. And with the quality hand you have, this can almost never
be a bad investment. But even if the initial callers fold to your all-in
raise, you are still in good shape – heck, you may even be in *better*
shape. Assuming a scenario where the maniac stays in (either by
calling or reraising) and then the others go out, there will be $150
dead money in the middle, and you will have invested $300 for a
total pot of $750. So, you would *need* to win just 40% of the time to
show an overall profit on the hand, but since you are likely to be in
there with the best hand, you obviously win *way* over 50%, making
this one of the best possible situations you could be in when playing short money.

♠ Not just will this 'bad' seat to the maniac's right secure you of
many +EV situations and/or big pots where you have the best of it,
just as importantly it will also help you to *minimise your losses* in a
situation where you don't have the best hand. Let's say that again

---

cannot easily say no to a 'bad' open seat – knowing that if you decline, you will be put at the bottom of
the waiting list again.

you have a $300 stack, as before you limp in early position, and again the maniac makes it $50 to go. Your hand is either K♠-K♥-8♠-4♦ or A♠-K♥-Q♠-J♦ – it doesn't matter which one, as your play will probably be the same. You are waiting for one or two people to maybe call the raise so that you can come out of the bushes with a well-timed limp/reraise with the probable best hand. But this time everyone else folds, and then suddenly the big blind surprises you by reraising to $170. Now, if this is someone who would not mess around in this spot, and who would only make this play with aces, you suddenly have a clear fold – and you will have lost just $10 on the hand. But had you been on the immediate *left* of the maniac and thus the maniac had been under the gun, the play would have gone like this: He would have made it $40 to go, you would have reraised pot to $140, everyone else would have folded and then the big blind would have come over the top to $470. With all this raising, even the maniac would have probably released, and you would then have had the option to fold after having invested $140, or call $160 extra and be in a $650 total pot, having invested $300 of your own, in a situation where you are probably not going to win even one-third of the time. This danger of the maniac putting you in the middle makes this 'good' seat to the maniac's left not as good as it may seem to many players – simply because it may get you in many situations where you put lots of chips at risk before you actually know where you stand. This is an important, and often underrated, aspect of being in a situation where you *seem* to be having great position over a maniac. As in this simple example: Instead of losing $10 seated to the maniac's right, you would now be losing $140 (or even end up in a situation where you are playing for your entire stack in a clearly -EV situation) when seated to his left.

♠ And finally, by choosing this seat to the overaggressive player's right, and playing in the manner I suggest, you are likely to gain protection from the other players in the hand. This is especially true in highly aggressive games with many large stacks. We have talked about this before. You will profit from being all-in because one of the remaining players who still has lots of money left could blast the other big stacks out of the pot (either before the flop, on the flop, on the turn, or yes even on the river) that in the end could very well have had a better hand than you. Furthermore, being all-in, *you* cannot be bet off the hand no matter how scary the board may look. This means that you could very well end up in a situation where you could expect to get back three or even four times the amount of money you have put in – while needing to beat just one player to get it. As you can see, a situation with a clear positive expectation.

So, what you do is play a strictly limp/reraise style of play before the flop, and a strictly check-raise style of play from the flop onward. You are taking advantage of the fact that:

♠ Your opponents will probably respect the maniac's bets and raises much less than they would respect *yours*. This means that all the sandbagging you do will result in creating bigger pots and making more money than you would have made by betting out. In fact, by doing the betting and raising yourself, a short-stacked rock like you might not have received *any* action, whereas by letting the maniac bet for you, you could now possibly win a monster pot.

♠ You will obtain very reliable information on how the strength of your hand relates to other people's, for the simple reason that you can use the maniac's raises to close the betting and put everyone else in the middle. Because all these players are put under early pressure by the maniac, it will be fairly easy for you to see where the *real* strength in the hand lies. For instance, if you limp, the maniac behind you makes it $50 to go and then a locksmith behind him with a $2,000 stack cold calls the $50 with the entire field behind him still to act, it should not be that hard to see that this person is playing a monster. So this would be a situation where almost certainly you would *not* come over the top with the K♠-K♥-8♠-4♦ or A♠-K♥-Q♠-J♦ from before, simply because it is too likely that the cold caller has aces.[5] Or, let's say that you have the Q♥-Q♣-8♥-4♣ with the same $300 stack from before, and your limp/reraise attempt has failed. So six players see the flop J♥-10♦-6♥ in an unraised pot, $60 total. Everybody now checks to the maniac, who bets the pot. Now, if there is fast and furious action behind him, you will simply choose to fold, knowing that almost certainly there are

---

[5] 'Hmm… if the cold-caller indeed has aces, why then wouldn't he reraise?' you ask. Well, quite simple. He can only reraise to $180 in this situation, which would account to just 9% of his entire stack. By revealing his aces this early in the hand, at a relatively cheap price, he is giving any other player in the hand, including the maniac, implied odds on the hand. There are two reasons for this 'implied odds' factor: a) because his opponents could induce him to fold a winner after the flop by taking advantage of a scary board, and b) they could make him pay off when his aces are clearly beat. Any time in PLO that you expose the content of your hand too soon with lots of chips still in play, you are opening yourself up to getting outplayed after the flop.

hands like sets, higher flush draws and better straight draws out there, and it is clear that there is not a single nut card left in the deck for you. But if everybody folds to the maniac's bet, or maybe just one weak/loose player calls, well then you should know that the strength of your hand has suddenly changed considerably. You may now have an excellent check-raise opportunity, knowing that with your overpair + queen-high flush draw + gutshot straight draw, you are almost certainly a clear money favourite in the hand. You know that neither one of the players needs to have much, meaning that no one may be able to call this check-raise of yours. And if they *do* call, you may even be in the excellent situation of having the best hand *and* the best draw. It is your excellent relative position that has helped you get yourself into this profitable situation.

## Disadvantages of this strategy

Now obviously, there are also some clear disadvantages to this short stack, sandbagging, sit-to-the-right-of-the-aggressor strategy. For one, it may lead to you giving free cards on those occasions when you are sandbagging a big hand, and then suddenly the maniac decides not to bet. This has happened to me on numerous occasions. As an example, say that you hold J-J-7-7 on a J♠-9♣-3♠ flop. You check, hoping that the maniac will have enough of a hand – or enough balls – to do the betting for you so that you can then check-raise all-in, but this time your opponent simply checks it back, and no one behind him bets either. Now this check of yours has given the entire table a free card. And when the turn is something like the 8♣ or even worse the 8♠, all you can suddenly beat would be just a bluff. This means that against any kind of action you will now have to lay your hand down – this action coming from players who might very well have folded to a pot-sized flop bet by you.

While this is a clear downside to the strategy I recommend, it is also a relatively minor one, for this simple reason: With a fairly short stack, you look for opportunities where you are either in a multiway pot for just one flat bet, or involved for all your money, preferably early in hand. In other words: You usually try to play for all your money, or you don't play at all. You are not too concerned about making pot-sized bets in order to defend your hand and charge your opponents for drawing out (as you would with a big stack), but rather you look for opportunities to get *all* your money in. This strategy could mean that by checking a big hand, you might let one of your opponents catch a miracle card to outdraw you. By checking, you will give them a free outdraw, and sometimes you will have no other option but to simply fold this big hand of yours on the turn – simply because it has turned sour. But the upside is that at least you have not lost any money this way, other than this small pot that you *could* have won, but didn't.

And *had* your check-raise attempt succeeded, you would have created a massive pot where you would have had all the money in with either the best hand or a premium draw – a situation that you could *never* have achieved by simply betting out. In other words: These massive pots that you will now sometimes win, and these very +EV situations that you create for yourself with this 'bag the bully' approach, will more than make up for the few times when (because of your checks) you give away a small pot that you could have easily won.

So, in my view you should always look at the big picture here, rather than focus on the two or three clear downsides to this strategy.[6] And if you keep to this strategy as thoroughly as I have always done, then you almost certainly cannot lose[7] – even when your opponents may be good or even great players, while *you* may be merely decent.

## 3) Adjustments when your stack grows larger

Even though I was very successful in this Vienna game, I was just at the start of my pot-limit Omaha career. Whereas nowadays, I have at least two different weapons in this game, both my short-stack play as well as my large-stack play, in Vienna my game was based almost entirely on playing with little money in front of me. In fact, once I had won a very large pot, it was almost always the end of my session, as I did not yet feel comfortable unless I could not get the hand all-in in just two or three betting increments. It should be clear that once the money becomes deeper, things like 'playing your hand well on all streets' and also the concept of 'outplaying your opponents' become just as important or even more important than just selecting the proper hands to play. And at that stage in my career I did not yet feel ready to play when the money was very deep.

But obviously, I would not *always* be fortunate enough to win a massive four-way pot so that I could then go home. No, quite often I would build up my initial stack to something like $190 or $220 by winning one or two relatively small pots – and it should be obvious that this had quite a few implications with regards to proper

---

[6] Another one of these disadvantages is that you let the bully pick up many small pots, while *you* won't pick up many. But again, this is not all that terrible, as your goal is to try to double or triple your stack on one hand – not to put 15-20% of your stack at risk in order to pick up a few chips. Your goal with this approach is simple: You *don't* want to take the maniac out of the lead. Quite the contrary: You want him to bet and raise you at every possible opportunity. You want to give him the feeling that he can succeed in running over you, so that he might start betting even more frequently than he already does. You let him get away with stealing two or three small pots – only to lure him into a situation where his aggression will help you win one monster pot.

[7] That is: until your opponents are starting to catch up on it, and begin to make some adjustments to their usual strategies. Once they start doing this (say, as my opponents in Vienna and especially Amsterdam did after a certain time), then it is time for you to start making some adjustments of your own. These adjustments are described in the remainder of this chapter, and also the next two chapters.

strategy from that point on. As I have said, in Vienna we would play with just one $2 blind (or one $5 blind, as in the $200 minimum buy-in game). This meant that at the beginning of my session I could simply stick to all the strategies I described in part II, because my stack would amount to less than 50 times the big blind. But I knew that once my stack had grown bigger, I could not stick to this same system, for the simple reason that after one limp/reraise or one check-raise I would *still* have quite a bit of money left in front of me. So I made some adjustments to my initial system, meaning that instead of always limping, I would now always come in for a minimum raise. This way, if the highly aggressive player to my immediate left were again to reraise the maximum, any pot-sized reraise on my part could now get a slightly higher percentage of my stack in the middle. But this was not all there was to it.

## Other advantages of the 'always come in for a minimum raise' strategy

- ♠ Even if no one reraised but just called, my raise would make the pot significantly larger than a limp would – yet I would invest just $2 extra for this. In other words: My mini-raise would work as a 'pot sweetener'.

- ♠ By always making the same size raise and by never choosing between either limping or raising any more than the minimum, I would give away almost no information as to the content of my hand, other than that I thought it was good enough to enter the pot with. This meant that I would play my aces the same way as something like an 8-7-6-5, and my opponents could never get a reliable read on me through my betting size. Had I made minimum raises with rundown hands and maximum raises with aces, then I *would* have given away a tremendous amount of information.

- ♠ Given the tendencies of my opponents, they simply disliked folding and would try to find *any* excuse to enter the pot. Making this minimum raise was the perfect excuse for the weak players to call (something I wanted them to), whereas they *would* tend to give large raises a bit more respect. This meant that an early position mini-raise by me often had the effect of dragging lots of players into the pot. As a result, it would not be unusual to see five, six or even seven players take the flop. And obviously, I chose my mini-raising hands such that I would always be in there with hands that performed well in a multiway setting. All in all, hands that had nut potential, like a big pair, a suited ace plus extra, or something like four coordinated double-suited cards. This meant that if the flop came to my liking, I would almost always have a hand of enough strength to *welcome* as many opponents as possible into the pot. This mini-raising strategy was based on a rather simple system: Either being up against as many opponents as possible for a very small percentage of my stack, or being up against just a few opponents for as much money as possible. In other words: what I did *not* want was to be up against two or three opponents for, say 7 to 20 percent of my stack. I would either want to be up against just one player for, say, 60% of my stack, *or* I would want to face a whole bunch of people when the initial costs to enter were much less than 5%.

I will illustrate this with an example. Holding aces on the button after a whole bunch of limpers, you are playing a $200 stack in a game with one $2 blind. Many players would almost automatically make a pot-sized raise here, say to about $14 or $16 or so. They are wrong. The proper way to play this is to reopen the betting with a very small minimum raise to $4, so that if someone bites and reraises this 'weak' raise of yours, you can then come over the top for (almost) all your money. And if no one bites, well then there is still no harm done. You will be in position, in a nice multi-way pot, and with a well-disguised holding – meaning that even if you manage to flop that third ace you may still get quite a bit of action. The only thing you should *not* do in this setting is to overestimate your aces after the flop if all you have is just something like an overpair + gutshot. By playing the aces 'my' way, you both minimise your losses *and* your swings, while at the same time maximising your wins if your strategy/game plan succeeds. In fact, because of this strategy you will probably give up quite a few small pots that you could have won, in order to work towards this one situation where you could be getting all your money in while having clearly the best of it. All in all, *this* is how I recommend you play your aces in the situation described here – not by making the 'automatic' pot raise that many players think is correct. This maximum raise may result in you reducing the field to probably two or three opponents – and they will all have a pretty good clue that you have aces.[8] Fur-

---

[8] Truly good players would sometimes also raise the pot in this situation with a double-suited rundown hand like J-10-9-8 or so, rather than just with aces. They do this in order to take advantage of the fact that their opponent may think they hold aces. They can benefit from this in two ways: a) by stealing the pot successfully if they flop nothing, especially if an ace flops, and b) by getting excessive action if they *have* hit a great flop, but the opponent thinks this flop cannot have helped their 'obvious' aces. Also, if by chance one of the limpers has aces and comes over the top, they would now have an easy call with their double-suited rundown, knowing that it would be almost even money against aces. In games with opposition as weak as in this Vienna game that I describe, these kinds of plays would be way over the heads of most players though. In fact, plays like that would just lead to much more risk

thermore, you have given away this information while having put in just 7 or 8 percent of your stack, meaning that your opponents will be getting considerable implied odds here. They are likely to force you to make mistakes after the flop, either by making you fold when you should have called or raised, or by making you call or raise when you should have folded – for the simple reason that they know your hand, but you know nothing about theirs.

♠ Another game-related advantage of this mini-raise strategy was this: Because most of my opponents came from a limit poker background, quite a few of them were loose-passive, some were loose-aggressive, but almost none of them knew how to handle either small or big raises well. Also, while some of them had liberal *raising* standards, a reraise would almost always be 100% pure aces. This meant that if I had mini-raised and then was faced with a pot-sized reraise, it would almost always be entirely clear to me how I should proceed in the hand, simply because I would almost always know 'where I was at'. Based upon the cost of this reraise, the size of our stacks, the (post-flop) characteristics of this specific opponent and the content of my hand, I could easily find the proper way to play my hand from that point on. Knowing that I was almost certainly up against aces, these decisions could include *folding* kings or four offsuited high cards if calling the raise would amount to a too high percentage of my stack, while *calling* with hands like 10-9-8-7 or 8-7-6-5 if there was still lots of money left to be played.[9]

♠ These minimum raises would often serve as stop raises. In this specific game that was one of the main benefits of this strategy. Many players in this game would be afraid to reraise me without aces, knowing that I could very well come over the top for all my money if *I* had them. Yet strange as it may seem, if I were simply to limp, these exact same players would not hesitate to make a big raise. So these minimum raises often allowed me to see flops cheaply in cases where I was just playing a fairly marginal hand. For instance, if you have a hand like A♥-10♥-8♠-7♣ in early position and you limp, you *don't* want to be faced with a large raise from someone behind you – as you would be playing a relatively marginal hand from out of position, quite clearly a rather bad situation. To prevent

---

and more volatility than is needed to beat this game. Therefore neither I nor any of the other players would even *consider* making this pot-sized raise with the ultimate goal of misrepresenting a hand.

[9] For the exact reasons behind this strategy, see the chapters on 'Example Hands' and 'Hand Match-ups & Analysis'.

this from happening, many players choose to simply not play the hand at all, out of fear of a big raise behind them. Yet by using this mini-raise system, I *was* often able to play these hands profitably, because people were afraid to reraise me with hands like 9-8-8-7 or Q-J-10-9 – moves that good players *would* make. Because the opposition in this game was rather weak, it was clear to me that once my stack had grown to more than the minimum buy-in, I would want to get involved with them often, especially with fairly coordinated hands. But at the same time, I did not want to pay that big of a price to reach the flop, and what I *especially* didn't want was having to pay a large price when the initial raiser had raised some of my potential customers off their hands. This minimum raise strategy accomplished all these goals to a fairly large degree, and resulted in what I wanted: Large multiway pots where many players would have invested just a slight percentage of their stack, and where I could take advantage of their specific weaknesses after the flop – like calling bets on too light values.

♠ Finally, this strategy helped me in a very simple manner: It gave me the initiative in almost every hand in which I was involved. And especially when playing a medium or large stack in big-bet play, having the initiative is beneficial in many ways – I guess I should not have to explain that.

Those were some of the adjustments I would make once my stack had grown a bit larger, say anywhere from 60 to 160 times the big blind. I would never limp but would almost always opt for mini-raises instead. With just two exceptions: When on the button I would usually just call instead of making a mini-raise, and in the big blind I would simply check with all marginal to fairly good hands. In both cases, the reasoning was clear: I simply did not want to reopen the betting.

As an example, say that you have a $120 stack and hold K♠-K♥-10♠-5♦ on the button, with three limpers in front of you. In this situation, it would be an absolutely horrible decision for you to make that mini-raise, as you are giving any of the initial limpers the chance to come over the top of you with a limp/reraise. And it should be clear that in pot-limit Omaha you hardly ever get the correct odds to call a pot-sized reraise with crappy kings if it looks like you are up against aces. (Exceptions may be in big multiway pots and/or in situations where the money is very deep.) So, if you mini-raise here, you are in danger of *raising yourself out of the pot*, whereas by just calling you would have been in a perfect situation, holding a more than decent hand in the best possible position. In addition, your mini-raise would serve little purpose here, because even if the good thing happens and everybody calls the pot will not become *that* much bigger, plus you don't need to raise to buy the button here – as you are on the button already. So all in all, with kings this would be a clear call, and mini-raising would be an awful mistake in this situation.

But with a hand like J♠-10♥-9♠-7♥, you *could* have made this mini-raise in a profitable manner, for two reasons:

1. Mini-raising is a play that you would probably have made with aces in this position. If you limp very often on the button, people will know that on the rare times that you *do* raise on the button, there's a good chance you hold aces. Mini-raising here with this JT97 could help you not just in this hand (as people may now fear you have aces, and we have already noticed before that this could benefit you in many ways). It could also help you in future hands when you *do* have aces and your opponents may decide to reraise with kings or so, because they know that on the button you could be raising with a wide range of hands. The fact that you would raise here with hands that in the eyes of some may look rather weak, may benefit you on those occasions that you *do* have aces and someone decides to play back at you.

2. Even if, as in the previous example of the K♠-K♥-10♠-5♦, someone has limped with aces, in this case you will *not* have mini-raised yourself out of the pot with this JT97 double-suited. Quite the contrary: Knowing that hot and cold against aces your hand is almost even money, knowing that you are in position, knowing that the money is deep enough, *and* knowing that you are getting implied odds, you will have an easy call even if you do get reraised here. With a double-suited medium rundown, you could easily call up to 15% of your stack if you 'know' your opponent has aces, and if you are in position you could even call up to 25% of your stack.[10]

Anyway, that's it for the adjustments with regards to pre-flop play. I will now analyse how post-flop play would be affected now that you are playing slightly more money than just the minimum buy-in.

# 4) Adjustments for post-flop play

Even though your stack has become a little larger now compared to the minimum buy-in situation from parts I and II, this won't affect your post-flop play much. Why not, you ask? Well, in contrast to the minimum buy-in scenario, you have

---

[10] Only in a heads-up situation. If a third player is also in the pot, you should be less inclined to get involved, as your cards are not necessarily live anymore. (The third player could have something like J-10-9-8 or Q-J-9-8.) This would obviously be very bad for not just your chances of winning, but also would have a negative impact on your chances of successfully (semi-)bluffing the aces off his hand because of a scary board.

mini-raised now instead of limped, and this means that in general the pots are now simply twice as big, or almost twice as big, as in the previous situation. This means that after the flop, the depth of the money is almost exactly the same now as it was before. Or, in other words: The amount of money you've got left in your stack in relation to the current pot size is about the same. Whether you are playing a $98 stack with $12 in the middle after the flop or a $196 stack with $24 in the middle, makes absolutely no difference in the way you should play your hand, as the ratios are exactly the same. This means that after the flop you can play your hand the same now as in the previous situation with the minimum buy-in and the unraised pot. Because as before you still have the overaggressive player seated to your immediate left, you *still* refrain from initiating the action yourself. As before, you simply check all of your hands to the maniac – your good, your bad and your great hands alike. That way, you will basically have secured yourself last position again, and if indeed the person to your left bets, you will have all the other players caught in the middle.

The reason why this simple strategy works so well in the long run is because of the way it looks to your opponents. What they notice is that when you check, you may fold to any bets they make six, seven, yes possibly even eight times out of ten. In their minds, it seems that you can be run over, and they may start betting with more and more hands against you. They will interpret your check for 'See, the nit is ready to give it up again' and indeed you will almost always fold. Heck, sometimes you will even fold when you think there is a good chance your hand may be good, but you decide to just forfeit the small pot to the overaggressive bettor. But then the one time when you *don't* fold, you are almost certain to more than make up for all these minor losses. Let's say that in a seven-way mini-raised pot, you again check on the flop, then the maniac bets $28 and gets called in two places. If you now come back for a pot-sized check-raise and your opponents don't hold much, you may have picked up no less than $112 in the middle without even needing to show a hand for it. (Heck, you may even have made them fold the current best hand, for instance when you decided to play a premium draw in an aggressive manner and then succeeded in making everyone fold.) And if you *do* get called, you will almost always have either the best hand or the best draw, meaning that usually you will be a clear money favourite in a massive pot.

So, your strategy consists of never making any significant investments yourself, but rather just checking or making some unusually small bets and raises, with five clear goals:

- ♠ To throw your opponents off.
- ♠ To hope to lure them into making a big mistake/suffering a big loss in a massive pot that they should not even have been in.
- ♠ To exploit their weaknesses, especially to try to turn highly aggressive players into maniacs, and turn maniacs into absolute lunatics.

- ♠ To keep initial losses very limited.
- ♠ To negate the impact of the rake, as from a rake point of view it is much better to win two $600 pots than twenty $60 pots. In the first case, we would lose $6 in rake to the house plus anywhere from $2 to $6 in tips, whereas in the second case we would lose $60 in rake plus anywhere from $10 to $20 in tips.

# Some final words

What I have described here is exactly how I played those six or seven months in Vienna, during my successful introduction into the beautiful world of pot-limit Omaha. Every day, I would be involved in just a few big pots, and usually I would win no more than just three pots of any significance during any one session. I would sit in my chair for hours just folding and folding, taking advantage of the low blind pressure, and I would never pay more than $20 rake per day. Yet at the end of the night, I would almost always quit the game with a big profit (big for the size of the game, that is), leaving my opponents wondering how on earth I had done it. Well, now they know I guess – and so do you.

# Chapter Two

# Amsterdam: Facing the best PLO players... and beating them

## Introduction

The first two years after my return to Amsterdam were the best I had ever had. I simply copied the system that I had used so successfully in Vienna, and things worked great in my hometown too. This despite the fact that many factors made it much harder to be successful here with my rather 'simple' style. To name a few of these:

♠ The players in Amsterdam were better and more experienced, meaning that there was less limping and calling than in Vienna and more folding and raising.

♠ Play was nine-handed instead of ten-handed, and rocks like me prefer as many opponents as possible.

♠ There were two or even three blinds instead of just one – and obviously, tight players don't like that.

♠ The rake was much higher.

Despite all this, and despite the fact that there were many good or even excellent players in this game (Rob Hollink, Marcel Lüske, Ed de Haas, Rolf Schreuder, Kosta Anastasyadis, as time went by also more and more players from abroad like Martin Vallo), this was actually a great game for me to make money. The reason was simple. Without exception, my opponents would play a big-stack/attacking/'macho' type of poker. They would try to cover the other players in the game so that they could break them at any time, and on a single hand. So even when in the beginning the game just had a $250 minimum buy-in, most people would have at least $1,500 in front of them, and once the minimum buy-in became $500, quite a few players would buy in for at least four times that amount. Given that the blinds were just $5-$5 (in the $250 game) and $10-$10 (in the $500 game), this meant that overall play was loose and aggressive – exactly how I liked it.

So I used the simple system from Vienna again: Try to pick the seat to the right of the most aggressive player in the game, in order to limp/reraise or check-raise him early in the hand, and thereby bag the entire field. As in Vienna, this would mean that just one or two big pots a night would be good enough for me. Especially when the game became $500 minimum ($10-$10 blinds) and sometimes even $1,000 minimum ($20-$20 blinds), I made a great living for more than two years – despite *never* winning more than five pots a night.

Now it needs to be said that I did not have the reputation of being a good or even excellent player. My regular opponents would almost without exception view me as 'lucky' rather than skilful. In fact, they viewed me as a person who would not just play too tight, but also as someone who overvalued his big pairs (before the flop), and hands like aces + nut flush draw (after the flop). They thought that I was overplaying both of these hands on a structural basis – yet got away with it on way too many occasions. Sometimes they even said it straight to my face: 'Rolf, you're not a *real* poker player. Your only strength is waiting patiently for hours for a good hand, and even then you make way too many errors in judgment to be called great. In fact, the only reason you can win is that people give you way too much action, because against any *serious* opposition you wouldn't stand a chance.' Yes, this is what I was told on many occasions – despite the fact that during these two years no one made more money than me.

So even though I hated the fact that not a single player in this game – with the possible exception of Ed and Rob and maybe two or three other players, and later to a lesser degree also Marcel – would give me any credit for my abilities, I *did* like the fact that no one really seemed to understand what I was doing. Players would *still* avoid exactly that seat that I loved the most: the one to the immediate right of any highly aggressive players. And despite the fact that they tried to make some adjustments to what they *thought* I was doing, most of them would just make it easier for me to use my simple system in an effective manner. This in turn reinforced not just my lucky image, but also my image of a 'nit' who would sit there for hours waiting for a hand, who would overestimate 'hold'em hands' like big pairs, and who thought of himself as a much better player than he really was. As I said, despite the fact that I did not like this image one bit, it *did* ensure that I could continue to use my approach successfully in the future. After all, if people didn't *understand* my strategy, then how could they possibly be able to come up with the correct countermeasures?

# Some changes

After about two years in Amsterdam, where the second year was my best-ever by a very wide margin, something happened that would influence the whole texture of the game. A likeable young man, Dennis de Ruiter, had slowly been moving up through the limit hold'em cash game ranks, and had been watching our PLO game intently for about two or three months without actually participating. He had of course heard all these stories about 'Lucky Rolf', and while he was watching from the sidelines about 30 to 60 minutes every day, it was clear that he was looking with a much clearer eye to what *I* was doing, rather than anyone else. Slowly but surely, he found his way into our game, and indeed he started out playing exactly the same way that I had always done. In addition to the fact that he played quite well even from the very start, he had some other things going for him as well. For one, he is simply a much 'nicer' guy that I am, who had (and still has) far fewer enemies than I have – and the fact of the matter is, I liked him too. In fact, we became quite friendly and talked strategy on numerous occasions, sometimes discussing hands for hours. And not just was he one of the few players that I genuinely liked, I also profited from his way of thinking. I am certain that getting to see *his* point of view on things has also helped *my* overall game a lot – so by no means was this one-way traffic.

But even with that being the case, his presence at the table was not good for me, as it hampered the effectiveness of my game considerably. Because we were both basically using the same type of system, we agreed not to get in each other's way in picking the favourite seat next to the aggressive players' immediate right. We agreed not to make this a battle, but rather he would simply get this 'best' seat one day, then I would take it the next one, etc. And as a result, we would almost always be seated next to each other – with all the Action Men behind us.

And at first, things didn't seem to have changed much. I continued to win well, and Dennis performed equally well. In fact, people started calling us the 'Lucky Guys', started calling Dennis the 'second Rolf', and things looked more than OK. The only difference was that there were now *two* big winners (instead of just one) who were using this same system – both of whom were supposed to be playing at a significantly lower level than all of these big names in our game.[1]

---

[1] By the way, don't imagine from reading this that *thus* all these big names performed badly – because they didn't. In fact, almost without exception they were winning players too. However, it was clear that many of them suffered some problems because of this short-stack/sandbagging approach utilised first by me and later also by Dennis – for the simple reason that this was a perfect counterstrategy to their skilful, aggressive, deep-stack approach. So, even though almost all these good players *were* long-term winners, they probably didn't make as much in relation to Dennis and I as one would expect based on pure skill.

And slowly but surely this led to a change in people's mindsets, in our opponents' views on the way this game should be played. Excellent players like Rob Hollink and Ed de Haas started giving this short-stack approach more and more credit, saying things like: 'Fellas, without exception you guys have always argued that Rolf was just incredibly lucky, that somehow he was just a luckier player than everyone else. Now we have a second player who employs almost this exact same system, and who *also* does very well. And, even though it is not the type of strategy that will be appreciated by many, it *does* get the job done – and thus it deserves a bit more credit.' So, the sentiment changed. Instead of just calling my system 'stupid, but lucky', some players in the game now actually started *copying* this approach. They too would start buying for the minimum, they too would start making minimum bets and raises, heck suddenly they were *all* very eager to get into that seat that for so long no one had wanted. More and more players wanted to move into 'my' seat now, and tried to copy the way I had always played, thinking: If Rolf can do it, and Dennis can do it, then why can't we?

All in all, this led to some significant changes. First of all, there was now a lot less money on the table because even some of the big players would sometimes buy in for the minimum. It also led to much tighter play, and especially now that it had become harder and harder for me to get 'my' seat, employing the Vienna System in a successful manner became increasingly difficult. This was even more true because the few (over)aggressive players that were left would get instructions like 'Don't make any raises once either Rolf or Dennis has limped.' All of this obviously led to a situation where the atmosphere became more competitive, and less 'friendly' if you will. It was a situation in which too many players were now suddenly trying to use the 'Rolf approach', while there was not enough action and not enough money anymore to use these strategies as effectively as in the past.

# Strategy changes

It was clear to me that going on in the same manner and with the same game plan was not practical, given that the texture of the game had changed so much. So I knew I had to make some clear adjustments to the strategies I had always used. In fact, it was Dennis who was much quicker to realise this than I was. Having started out merely copying some of my strengths, he had more and more incorporated new things into his game so that he would become a more 'complete' player. And now he had decided that in order to continue his good results, it would be necessary to add some new strengths, and incorporate some new weapons – simply because the game was not as soft as it used to be. When I saw *him* make these changes, I knew I had to adjust too, or else I was in danger of becoming a 'has been', a predictable player with just one strategy who had been unable to cope with the changes. Quite simply, now that my opponents had caught on fairly well to the way I played with a short and medium stack, I knew that there was one clear task for me: I simply had to learn how to also play a *big* stack well. After all, in any sport, a team can only be called great when they have a good defence *and* a good offence. And I knew that while my defence was in order, there was still lots of room for improvement with regards to the attacking part of my game.

The main reason for my success had always been the fact that I, more than any other player I knew, had been able to take advantage of over-aggression and too loose play by my opponents. But the game in Amsterdam had developed in such a manner, that play had become much tighter, and people had become less overaggressive than before – especially when they saw that I had voluntarily entered a pot. Coupled with the fact that 'my' seat was now often occupied either by Dennis or by one of the three or four other players who were eager to sit there too, I decided to develop my game in a manner that most people would not expect of me. I incorporated the following changes:

- ♠ If there were any players in the game with lots of money in front of them and they were what I considered 'potential targets', I would try to at least cover them, so that I could break them at any time.

- ♠ In that case, I would *not* try to pick 'my' seat to the immediate right of a maniac, but I would choose an entirely different one. I would try to get into a seat two or three places to the left of the person who was my target. Yes, in that case I would have the target to my *right*, not to my left as it has always been when playing a short-stack. In fact, the players that I would *now* try to get on my left were fairly tight players who would not be overly concerned about playing their position. And especially if they were playing short stacks while I had a big stack now, I wanted them to my left. I would be following the old Mike Caro principle of 'sitting behind the money', having tight short stacks to my left, and loose/weak big stacks to my right.

- ♠ Once my target was in the hand with no other dangerous players having entered yet, I would try to isolate him by raising and reraising even with fairly speculative hands before the flop. My goal would be to get the hand heads-up, in position, while being up against someone that a) feared/respected me, and b) I had good control over. So, if he were to raise to $50 or $60, and we were both playing $2,500 stacks, I would reraise it to $120 or so, knowing that my reraise would put all others in the middle. They would fear that if they called now, my somewhat overaggressive 'target' could reraise again. This meant that just about the only hand they could play comfortably in this spot was aces. And if no one had them, chances were that I could get myself into the exact situation I wanted: Heads-up against a players I have good control over, being in position, and having given away no information about my hand whatsoever. The combination of all this would lead to a situation in which my opponent would find it very hard to get a good read on me. And coupled with all three other factors mentioned, I would be much more likely to be taking his stack, than he would be to take mine. In fact, in this situation many pots would just stay small. Because I would be able to represent a wide range of hand after the flop, *and* because my opponent feared me, my pre-flop reraise guaranteed that I would simply pick up the majority of the pots uncontested after the flop – whether I actually had the best hand or not. And picking up just one or two pots a night in the $300-$400 region is *not* something to look down upon, or a minor accomplishment. Quite the contrary: This ability to pick up pots with relatively little is *the* key to successful big-stack play.

In fact, the strategy I have described here is a rather common way to play for most good PLO players – the majority of the British top pros play exactly like this. For instance, if you go to the Vic in London, you will see that almost all successful players will play in this exact manner: Covering the weaker players and trying to isolate them when in position, in order to break them on a single hand – but if not to still pick up quite a few small and medium pots uncontested. But in Amsterdam, it didn't look like it would be all that easy for me to pull this off successfully – for the following reasons:

- ♠ Because of the closing time of the casino, play usually lasted no more than just five or six hours. This big-stack approach is based on getting involved with someone in many pots, sometimes even while having slightly the worst of it, all of this in order to set up that one big pot later where you are trying to break your target and take all of his chips. But in this game, the time frame was relatively short and with no more than just 24 or 25 hands per hour, there was just not much time for successfully setting up plays for the future.

- ♠ Just as importantly, there were now always two or three players in the game who would play 'my' strategy: Waiting patiently for a premium hand in order to move in early. They knew that in contrast to how I *used* to play, I would now raise and reraise with a fairly wide range of hands in order to isolate certain players; they knew I would not need aces or kings to do that. So, if I were to reraise to isolate my target and then one of these short stacks behind me woke up with something like A♠-Q♠-Q♥-10♣ or K♣-K♦-Q♣-J♥, I knew I would face an all-in raise that I obviously did *not* welcome. So these short stacks had now become the same kind of threat to me that *I* had always been to the other high quality big-stack players.

Despite these two specific difficulties, I quickly became successful with this style too. I would not *always* use it though. Quite often, I restricted myself to my 'old' strategy, while on other days I *would* use this big-stack approach. Reasons for me to use either one of these tactics included:

♠ **My position.** If I could get my preferred position to the right of those who would play rather loose/aggressive, I would simply pick this seat and stick to my minimum buy-in, tight, sandbagging, move-in-early approach. This was the style I had developed to perfection – so if I *could* use it, I would.

♠ **Who has the money?** If the weaker players in the game did not have lots of chips in play, it would be silly for *me* to suddenly come up with lots of money.

♠ **The quality of the opposition.** As I have said, some of the players in this game were what I consider to be world-class. I can say from experience: One does *not* want to play with very deep money against top players like Rob Hollink, Ed de Haas and Marcel Lüske, and especially not if by chance they have position on you. Even though it *is* possible to sometimes take advantage of these players' aggressive moves and tricky plays, when the money is deep this is much harder to pull off. In other words: Playing with deep money when at least two of these players are also in your game is plain suicide – and thus something I would want to avoid at any cost. This meant that I would just stick to my 'normal' minimum buy-in approach, unless maybe one of them was a little hot. In that case, I *would* be playing a big stack – but only of course if I had position on them.

♠ **Full game or not?** Whereas in the first two or three years after my return to Amsterdam we would have a full, big PLO game at least five days a week, slowly but surely this became four days and then three – and often, the games would not be entirely full anymore. A large part of my successful 'Vienna' strategy had been at the mercy of being in full-ring games. But now our games would often be seven-handed, sometimes even six- or five-handed. Often one player more or less could mean the difference between starting up a game or not. Often, because the presence of some action players meant the table was expected to be juicy, I now had to say 'yes' even to the games I had never particularly fancied: short-handed games.

Now, it was clear that in short-handed games my minimum buy-in approach would not work very well – not just because the blind pressure would become too much, but also because this was a heavily raked game. In a game that is less than full, it is hard to wait patiently for a hand when the blind pressure is high, where the high rake makes playing for small pots unattractive, and where if you win the pot you still just double up – rather than triple your stack or even better, like in the multiway pot situation. Also, a large part of my successful short-stack strategy consisted of getting callers in the middle, of having someone do the betting for me, get callers in the middle and *then* come over the top. But in five- or six-handed games, almost every pot is contested heads-up, and there are rarely 'callers in the middle' in short games like this. In addition, because you cannot afford to keep folding and folding now that the blind pressure is so high relative to your short stack, you just cannot wait for too long before moving in. And knowing that very few hands in PLO are more than a 3-to-2 favourite over even a random hand, it was clear that my short-stack approach would have only limited benefit in this setting. So if the games were less than full and especially if the line-up was what I considered to be soft, I would use my 'new' system: Buying in for as much money as the weaker players had, in order to break them. And I would not be playing in a tight, defensive or sandbagging type of way. No, quite the contrary. I would use a loose-aggressive attacking approach, based for a large part on the position that I had on the weaker players. All of this was with one clear goal in mind – going after someone's entire stack, rather than just the little stabs that I used to take. The name of this approach: The 'New Amsterdam Strategy'.

# The 'New Amsterdam Strategy' in practice

With this 'New Amsterdam Strategy' that I developed, *many* things were entirely different from the way I had always played. Here are a few key points with regards to this strategy:

- ♠ Position becomes of paramount importance once the money is deep. With deep money, one of the biggest no-no's is playing a mediocre hand from out of position, especially against strong and/or tricky players. The goal with your big stack is the exact opposite: Playing *in* position, against the weak players, especially if they too are playing a big stack.

- ♠ While the quality of your starting hand is still important, of course, it is also important to realise that once the money gets deeper, a much smaller percentage of the pots end up in a showdown. There is more room than before to *represent* hands, and to outplay your opponents by playing the player: making moves specifically based on the tendencies and specific weaknesses of the person you are facing.

♠ In situations where it seems that neither you nor your opponent has flopped a really big hand, it is often the most aggressive player who will win the pot. This is exactly what I have learned throughout the years from players like Rob Hollink and Ed de Haas. While they may have had some problems coping with the ultra-tight sandbagging style that I used to employ, they *did* perform excellently against players who also had a lot of money in front of them. Because of their combination of aggression and the fact that they were very hard to read, their opponents were always very scared to mess with them. And as a result, both Rob and Ed would pick up many small- and medium-sized pots without a fight. So, I knew that if *I* wanted to employ this big-stack approach successfully, I too would have to step out of the 'safe haven' of playing only high-quality hands, and would need a more aggressive, more unpredictable and more intimidating image to make it hard for my opponents to make the proper decisions against me. If they were uncertain, this would be to my benefit because I would then be able to pick up many pots uncontested, regardless of the strength of my cards, while at the same time possibly get excessive action in a monster pot when I *did* have the goods.

# Examples of big stack/cover the table play

## Example No. 1

It is a $500 minimum buy-in game with two tight and short-stacked players in the $10-$10 blinds. One early position player with a $1,800 stack limps in, and now my 'target' with a $2,500 stack makes it $40 to go. My target is a rather loose and somewhat overaggressive player who is not all that hard to read, and on top of that someone who respects and fears my play. I am on the button with the same $2,500 and holding a rather mediocre hand, Q♠-J♥-9♠-7♦. Whereas in my 'old' strategy I would never have played this hand against a raise, in this case I decide to reraise to $120 in order to isolate my target. I know that there are many dangers here, though. If the tight small-stack players in the blinds wake up with a real hand, they will simply move all-in. And if the limper has a real hand, then *he* might come over the top. The way that the betting has gone with the target raising and me reraising, it is clear that all the other players who are still to act will almost be *forced* to either fold or else reraise the pot. They know that calling is almost not an option anymore, because that call would not close the betting, and thus the initiative would lie with the initial raiser, who could then decide to come over the top. In fact, because he is a highly aggressive player, people might think that he could reraise with a wide range of hands. And quite clearly, calling $110 extra when you don't even know whether you are going to see a flop, is not the best of propositions, meaning that very few hands would be worth playing here – except for aces of course, or some double-suited rundown hand maybe. Now, while *they* may fear that the overaggressive player may reraise even with fairly light values here, *I* know better. I know that with the money this deep, up against someone he respects (me), the initial raiser would only come over the top against me with just one hand: aces.

So what I hope to accomplish with my reraise is get past the three potential threats: the two short-stacked blinds, and the early-position limper. Once I have succeeded in doing that, 'phase one' of the hand has been completed. We can now start focusing on the target. Because quite frankly, the target is the only player that I *don't* fear in this situation. While I would absolutely have *hated* any kind of involvement from the three threats that I mentioned, and a reraise by any of them would have ranged from either *pretty* bad to *very* bad for me, my target scares me a lot less. Why? Well, because even if by chance I *am* up against the best possible hand, and he indeed holds aces, then by reraising the pot he can still only make it $390 to go. And knowing that we have both started the hand with $2,500, that I have position on him, that I have a very live hand against the aces that he probably holds, *and* that my opponent respects me, I would quite simply have a very easy call here – with excellent implied odds.

As it turns out, my target just calls and we take the flop heads-up. But before looking at this flop, let's first analyse the psychology of the situation.

- ♠ My opponent has not reraised again. While this *could* mean that he is setting up a trap with aces, it is much more likely that he simply doesn't have them. After all, if he *had* aces, taking into account the fairly large pot already, the fact that he is out of position *and* his overaggressive tendencies, he would almost certainly have raised the maximum right there and then.

- ♠ If my opponent does indeed not have aces, he might judge it very likely, or at least quite possible, that *I* have them. Even though he probably knows that a reraise by me in this deep-money situation does not narrow down my holdings as much as in a shallow-money situation, he knows that aces *are* one of the hands that I would reraise with in this spot. And while I definitely play looser in some special spots when the money is deep, it is also clear that my opponents almost without exception see me as a tight nit who has the ability to sit for hours waiting for aces – a judgment that is not going to change just because of a few more liberal raises here and there. Besides, many players actually play rather loose with a short stack and then tighten up with a bigger stack (quite the contrary from the way that I play), and in their subconscious they probably expect other players to do the same as well. All in all, in this situation, if my opponent does not have a really big hand, I am fairly certain he will give *me* credit for having one. This despite the fact that right now I am simply trying to take advantage of a potentially profitable situation, where the quality of my hand is not an overriding or even an all that important factor with regards to my decision to reraise.

♠ In poker, the person who has made the last reraise before the flop is often said to be 'in charge'. Because my opponent has not taken the opportunity to reraise when he could have done, it is quite likely that he needs at least *some* help from the board to continue with the hand, regardless of whether or not *I* have received help. There is a good chance that the pre-flop betting has paved the way for me to pick up all those pots where we both flop nothing. And this amounts to quite a large edge for me, especially because if I *do* flop help (say, with three medium cards on the board) I could get excessive action if by chance my opponent reads me for aces.

Anyway, the flop now comes A-8-4 rainbow. While I expect my opponent to just check the hand to me, he actually comes out firing, and bets out $200 into the $270 pot. A serious bet by all means, especially considering the fact that the board is not coordinated, and that there are therefore simply not many draws available.

So, considering the psychology of the situation described above, the best play should be quite obvious. Even though I have absolutely nothing, I've got a clear raising situation here. In fact, you don't even need to raise the pot here to represent the current nuts, three aces. Just a standard raise to $500 or $600 will probably get the job done. For the reasons why, it is necessary to again analyse the psychology of the situation.

♠ If I *really* had three aces for the current nuts, would I then make a maximum raise to $870? Well, probably not. Taking into account the ill-coordinated nature of the board, and the fact that it is highly unlikely that my opponent has specifically that one draw that *is* available (the 7-6-5-x nine-out inside wrap), I would probably want to keep my opponent in the pot rather than blast him out. Raising just $300 or $400 more would be the way to do that. The implication is that if I am trying to *represent* these three aces, I should also make this 'luring' type of raise rather than one that says 'I want to blast you out of the pot'.

♠ Based on the betting, it is actually quite unlikely that my opponent has any kind of hand at all. After all, if he *really* had something, wouldn't he simply wait for me to make my 'automatic' bet here? My opponent knows that once I have made the last raise before the flop, and then have the hand checked to me with an ace on the board, I am going to make a bet here close to 100% of the time – whether I actually have something or not. So, don't you think that if my opponent really had a big hand, he would have tried to give me every possible opportunity to make that bet, rather than take me out of the lead?

♠ Even if he *does* have a hand of some value, the fact that he is betting into me suggests that he is trying to win the pot without a fight. His betting suggests that he thinks his hand is not strong enough for an obvious check-raise, and that he is unwilling to put $600 or $800 at risk knowing that he *could* be up against the current nuts. So even if he does have a hand of some value like A-4-x-x or even A-8-x-x, it is clear that with the money this deep, he won't like it much being up against a tight player. And not just a tight player, no – a tight player who has made the final raise before the flop, *and* who now again raises in a manner that is consistent with the way someone would play aces. I can tell you: even if by chance he holds 8-8 for middle set, those eights suddenly don't look so hot anymore in this situation. Because the pre-flop betting has clearly suggested that my opponent is unlikely to have aces[2] while I could very well have them, raising is a no-brainer here – despite the fact that I have no pair and no draw. Even with that being the case, this raise of mine should succeed well over 80% of the time, regardless of my opponent's hand – making this a highly profitable raise.

## Example No. 2

We are in the exact same situation as before, holding the same Q♠-J♥-9♠-7♦, but this time our target *has* taken the opportunity to reraise the maximum before the flop, as we said to $390 total. I know this player very well, and as aggressive as he sometimes is, he *does* respect and even fear me. Also, I know that this player is a bit wild under normal circumstances, but once he has accumulated a rather big

---

[2] This flop betting makes it even more unlikely my opponent has aces. Given his aggressive style of play and the fact that he could have reopened the betting before the flop but didn't, I had already analysed that aces were *very* unlikely here. But even in this outside chance of him flat calling in order to trap me after the flop, it would then have to be an awfully advanced play to come out betting into me after this A-8-4 flop. While some of the best players in the world *are* capable of making this highly advanced play, it is extremely doubtful that my opponent in this hand is thinking on a level this high – meaning that the chances of him having three aces here would be slim to none.

stack like the one he has now, he tends to become slightly less 'reckless' if you will. So for him to reraise me in this spot, I would estimate that the chances of him having aces here would be *way* over 80%, with maybe 5-10% for kings or some other quality hand, and possibly 2% or so for a total bluff. In this situation, against almost certain aces, it should be clear that my very marginal holding has suddenly gained quite a bit of value. Assuming that I will choose to call here (and obviously, I do), I now have the following clear playing advantages:

♠ Since my opponent almost certainly has a very big pair, I don't need a full house or a nut straight to win the pot. If I end up with a measly two pair on the river, this is quite likely to win the pot for me.

♠ My opponent has no clue as to the content of my hand. The only certainty that he has is that I cannot hold two aces – or else, I would undoubtedly have moved in. For all he knows, I could have kings, I could have a small rundown hand like 8-7-6-5, a medium rundown like Q-J-10-8 or so, or even a two-pair hand like J-J-7-7 or 6-6-4-4 where I am hoping to flop a set. The fact that he knows so little about the content of my hand while *I* have a pretty good clue about his cards, gives me a big edge. I know with a fair degree of certainty when the flop should either be very helpful, somewhat helpful or extremely dangerous to him. This knowledge not just about his strength, but also about how he will probably respond to any bets or raises that I may make (based on how the board cards relate to his most probable holding), will give me some clear playing advantages. It should provide me with many opportunities to bluff, semi-bluff or bet/raise for value – not just on the flop, but just as importantly also on the turn and even the river. All of this assuming that my opponent is *not* the type to automatically commit himself to go all the way, that is. If he *does* think of himself as committed, this will of course provide me with lots of opportunities where I could get paid off handsomely, even though it *will* substantially limit my (semi-)bluffing opportunities.

♠ My opponent will almost certainly come out firing with a full pot bet after the flop, regardless of his characteristics, and regardless whether or not this flop has actually been helpful to him. In PLO, the person who has reraised before the flop will almost always come out with a big bet after the flop – especially if he is up against just one player. And in this case, I have a good counter-hand to his aces, a hand that has close to what we call 'maximum stretch'. This means that with that pot bet of his, he may actually be betting into a monster, or at least a hand that is much better than his two aces –

for the simple reason that I will catch *many* flops where my hand would be a clear favourite over bare aces. And when I catch one of these flops, it should be clear that I would actually *welcome* this 'automatic' pot bet of his, as it would be one of the reasons for my good implied odds here.

From this stage on, it should be quite obvious how to play the hand – my pre-flop play has ensured that post-flop the best play should be relatively easy.[3] It is the percentage of my stack that I have risked before the flop that's the key here. And with stacks of $2,110 left and just $810 in the middle, with a hand that even hot and cold is not trailing all that much against aces, it should be clear that I have good implied odds here.

OK, let's say that you are me, and with this Q-J-9-7 you have made it to the flop, just as I have. How should you now proceed from the flop onwards? Three pieces of advice here:

1. If you catch a rather marginal flop like just one pair + gutshot, you should usually *not* fold. You will almost always call the pot bet to see if you can improve on the turn – or even more importantly, to see if your opponent does *not* improve. Unless it becomes clear from the betting and/or tells your opponent may give away that he has obtained other (additional) help besides just his big pair, you should assume that your opponent is still just betting his bare aces.[4] Because *he* does not know if/when you have improved over his hand, and because *you* know that if you improve on the turn you will almost always get paid off, you can call his bet profitably – even when you have a very weak hand like middle pair + gutshot.

---

[3] If the play is not obvious, just take a look at my descriptions in the 'Vienna Way Part III', and also the second one in the series of practice hands. Both discuss situations that are fairly similar to the hand we are discussing now. One might argue: 'Well yes, but aren't the stack sizes much bigger here than in the second practice hand?' The answer is: Yes, they are. Indeed there is more money at stake, but the depth of the money is about the same – and that is what's important here.

[4] Pay extra attention to the tendencies of the bettor when the flop is two-suited. I have found over the years that people who in this situation are betting aces + nut flush draw, have a demeanour that is quite different from those who are just betting their bare aces. I cannot tell where the difference lies exactly, but I often 'feel' when my opponent has the added strength of the nut flush draw to go with his aces. And this is extremely important to know, because in this situation, you would have an easy call against bare aces – but against aces + nut flush draw, you would have a clear fold. So it is important to analyse his tendencies and his giveaways closely in situations like this, so that in time you too will develop this intangible, but incredibly important factor that separates the great players from the merely decent ones: feel.

In fact, after calling on the flop you *could* even have the correct odds to call your opponent's all-in bet on the turn as well, knowing that improving to just two pair could be good enough to win the pot. However, make sure that when you count your outs you don't make the mistake of counting all the cards that will improve your hand as full outs. So, when you err, you should err on the side of caution. This means that if you have a pair + kickers + gutshot on the turn for 15 cards that will improve your hand, you should *not* think you have 15 clean outs out of 42 cards (52 minus your four hole cards, the four board cards and the two 'known' aces). You should probably give yourself just 11 or 12 outs here. The reason for this is that your opponent could have a better hand than just one pair already, or some of the cards that you *think of* as outs may improve your opponent even more than you.

2.  When the flop comes with either an ace or a small pair, you will almost always give up. On the other hand, if the flop comes something extremely scary like K-K-Q, there may be a potential bluffing opportunity for you. However, for a bluff to work, not *some*, but probably *all* of the following conditions need to exist:

    a.  Your opponent's way of betting after the flop, the speed and force that he uses to put his chips in, and his body language in general suggests that he does indeed have the two aces that we gave him credit for, but *not* with either the third king, the Q-Q or even K-Q to go with it.

    b.  The pre-flop betting has led your opponent to believe that you probably hold a big pair or coordinated big cards, something like Q-Q-J-10 or K-Q-J-10, maybe even K-K-x-x.

    c.  Your opponent thinks that you are not the type of player to make moves, meaning that if you give him any kind of action on a flop of K-K-Q after all the strength he has shown, you *must* have him beat.

    d.  Your opponent actually is *capable* of folding his aces if all of the conditions a), b) and c) apply. After all, some players are simply incapable of this, meaning that even if they *know* for a fact that their aces have just been cracked, they still cannot fold them.

So if you have analysed that *all* of these factors apply and you decide that you are trying to snatch this pot away from your opponent, the best way to play it is by going for the *delayed bluff*. This means that you should flat call him on the flop, not raise him, with the goal of taking away the pot from him on the turn. It should be clear that if your opponent bets the pot and gets either raised or flat called by you against this K-K-Q rainbow flop, he will know that his aces just cannot be any good. He knows that you would never call or raise this big bet of his against a paired board with just a straight draw, so he knows that the minimum hand for you to hold here is three kings. However, if you raise on the flop instead of just calling as I recommend, and by chance he's got a gutshot straight draw in addition to his aces, he may reason: 'Well, with two cards to come, I will have two shots at making my aces full for a pure winner. The two remaining kings may also be outs if my opponents has Q-Q, and if I hit my gutshot and I am up against just three kings, I could win also. With two shots at hitting, I am going to gamble here, even though I am probably taking a bit the worst of it.' But if you just flat call and the turn is a blank, he will suddenly have just *one* card left to improve over you. He will reason: '$1,300 for just one card, against someone who looks like he is slowplaying a big hand. Paying this much money when I may have just two outs, or even none if my opponent is trying to trap me, and has been flat calling with quads. No, this can never be a good decision – I'll fold.' And if indeed he does fold, you will have taken the pot away from your opponent in a *very* skilful manner.[5]

3.  If you *do* flop well with something like 9-7-2 rainbow or even 10-8-6, there is no need for you to slowplay. Having put $810 into the middle already, it will be very hard for your opponent to lay down here – especially because he knows that in both situations where he faces a raise, you could be pushing a draw. (Something like Q-Q-10-8 on the 9-7-2 flop, and Q-J-9-8 or something similar with the 10-8-6.) Just raise him big when the flop has been good to you, just as you would have done if you had been semi-bluffing. Remember, you would sometimes be trying to semi-bluff your op-

---

[5] Two problems here. First, this play will only work against thinking players who recognise the strength of your flop call, and who will take this into account when deciding the proper play for the turn. If you are up against someone who simply says: 'To hell with it – I may be beat but I'll just stick it in,' and then simply bets all-in on the turn with his two pair aces over kings, well then you will simply have wasted your $810. And second, this play would work even better had the money been slightly deeper than in this example. Here the two of you both have $1,300 left, with a little more than $2,400 in the middle already. The chances of successfully making this play would go up considerably if the two of you both had more than $2,000 left.

ponent off his aces, when you have a decent draw and you know that – because of a scary board – a big raise could make him fold. The implication from this is that in order to stay credible, you should also make these big raises if you happen to flop well and think you have your opponent drawing thin. Even more so when – as in these two cases – your opponent will probably call you anyway as a big underdog.

# Final words on the 'New Amsterdam strategy'

All in all, if you want to apply this 'New Amsterdam Strategy' in the same successful manner that I have, you should always focus on these few simple things:

- ♠ Try to be aggressive, intimidating *and* unpredictable.

- ♠ Play very tight in early position, but loosen up considerably in late position.

- ♠ Try to isolate your target whenever you have a hand of at least some value, again especially when you have position on him. Don't make the mistake of just flat calling his raise if this may lead to other players coming in behind you. If that happens, you could be in danger of getting sandwiched after the flop between a loose bettor and someone behind you who may or may not have received help from the board.

- ♠ Always be aware of any tight/aggressive short-stack players that may voluntarily have entered the pot. If they have, you may need to abandon many of your positional (re)raises, as you could face a big pot-sized reraise from a quality hand, with no implied odds whatsoever (as the reraiser is probably close to all-in).

- ♠ Make certain that the size of your reraises is not so big that if someone behind you happens to wake up with aces and then comes over the top, you would be unable to call. In other words: Don't raise yourself out of the pot.

- ♠ Only reraise your target with hands that could stand, yes that would even *welcome* a reraise. This means that in some situations, you *would* reraise with hands like 8♠-7♠-6♥-5♥ or Q♣-J♦-10♣-8♦, and obviously you would reraise with aces as well, but you would *not* reraise with kings or hands like A♠-K♥-Q♣-J♦. Because with these hands your cards could be dead and/or too much in the same range of the aces that your target probably holds if he decides to come over the top of you, your reraise could then have wasted a potentially profitable situation – and have turned it into an unprofitable one.

In no time I was able to apply this – for me – new strategy in a successful manner in my Amsterdam game. With more than one good game plan to rely on now, I could adjust much better to any specific difficulties and opportunities that I saw. Also, it would be much harder for my opponents to come up with successful countermeasures now that I was able to play two or even three different systems in a profitable way.

Despite all this, the action just got worse and worse. Regular players that used to come in six days a week, now came less often because of other endeavours (Marcel Lüske), playing online (Rob Hollink, Rolf Schreuder) or simply because of losing interest (Kosta Anastasyadis). Coupled with the fact that some of the other players simply seemed to have less funds than before, this meant that much more than before the core group of players would consist of good and winning players like Dennis de Ruiter and me. It was obvious that this was not a healthy situation. Slowly but surely, I saw my bread-and-butter game breaking up, and more and more players started making the transition to playing online.

It became clear to me that I needed to make that step too. Instead of stubbornly holding on to a game where the money had dried up, I knew that it was time to focus on something new. I entered the world that I had left aside for too long: online poker.

# Chapter Three

# Moving up to the biggest online games

## Introduction

So there I was – ready to make yet another big step: Moving into online play. Frankly, I wasn't too pleased with myself about my decisions up to that point. Why, you ask? Well, because in contrast to what I *should* have done (exploiting new and profitable opportunities), I had been focusing too long on a game that had already shown many signs of being about to die out – my $500 minimum buy-in brick and mortar game in Amsterdam. But because for more than four years I had made such an excellent living playing this game, and because the casino simply felt like my 'office', I couldn't force myself to quit that game. I just couldn't imagine that in other places, in other games, or in any other way than the brick and mortar (B&M) way, it would be possible to make as much money. I didn't want to desert what I had come to think of as 'my' game, but in the end I knew I simply had no other option.

But at the same time, I knew that I was just a little too late with jumping into online play. A fair number of people were already making lots of money playing online at the time when I was just talking and teaching on the Internet – not playing. I knew I would have to start from the absolute bottom rather than jump into the big online PLO games right away, for the simple reason that my opponents would have a clear headstart on me. So I decided to work my way up slowly, just as I had done in my brick and mortar career. I wanted to make sure that I would get the most out of all the possibilities that were available to me on the Internet, whether they involved computer software, bonus deals, rakeback programs etc. It was clear to me that I was at a big disadvantage compared to those who were already used to playing online, for the simple reason that many things that were gospel to them would be entirely new to me.

But despite this, I still did not want to depend on others too much, and I refused to follow the precise example of how some of the better players that I knew did things. With all of my experience in brick and mortar play, and with all the players I had encountered over the years, there was just one, possibly two players who did things in what I view the 'correct' manner. All the other players, even if they performed well, were not people whose judgment I would trust, mostly because almost without exception they would have what I viewed as clear mistakes – either in their analysis of the game or in their actual play at the table. So my reasoning was: If there were almost no players whose judgment I would trust in B&M play, why then would I trust them when it comes to online play? I decided that the best way for me to move forward was to use the following three-step approach:

1.  First, I would try to collect all the reliable information I could find by visiting online forums and newsgroups – especially those places where the information was not likely be to 'coloured' by people who had personal interests in promoting or rejecting specific sites or products.

2.  I would stay in close contact with these one or two players who used to do things 'my' way in B&M play, expecting them to do things correctly in online games as well. Also, I knew that these players – because in the past they had benefited from me too – would not try to give me any bad advice or lure me in the wrong direction. This despite the fact that they recognised that once I did enter the big online PLO games seriously, I would probably be a clearly winning player there too.

3.  I would watch some of the big players over extended periods of time to see how *they* did things online. For instance, I have watched the big no-limit hold'em games on many occasions, when for instance Rob Hollink was there, playing against the (at that time) probably biggest online winner Prahlad Friedman. I would watch their decisions when it came to buy-in amounts, seating positions and any other decisions they made that could help *me* when moving up.

And this is what I did. In combination with the information that I obtained from this three-step approach, I would experiment with my own game, where I was playing at what many players consider micro-stakes. So it was in these very small games that I got my feet wet, playing my basic nut-peddling approach, hoping to gain experience with regards to my opponents, the game-related aspects of online play, and the technical possibilities that could help improve my game. Starting out by playing just one table at micro-stakes, I slowly but surely worked to my ultimate goal: Multi-tabling in the biggest online PLO games.

# Moving into the big game

Despite some delay because of the house I had just bought and the time it took to create my own poker corner there, it only took around a year for me to graduate from the $100 maximum buy-in games I had started at, to reach the $2,000 maximum games at the one major site that I played back then. Just as I had always done throughout my career, I decided to stick to just one place as much as possible – and in this case, this meant one site. Of course, I picked the one site that at that time a) always had many games going also at high stakes, and b) had a reputation for having fairly soft games. I logged in many hours there in order to gain as much experience as possible, and in the end I was rewarded with a successful entry into the $10-$20 blinds game. Not the biggest of all online PLO games, you may argue – and that is correct, because some sites occasionally spread much bigger games than this. But still I consider the $10-$20 blinds PLO game to be very big. And especially because – as opposed to some very big games on other sites – there were always sufficient full ring games available, I was more than happy to participate in this game, and felt no need to look much further/higher. Because in that case I could possibly end up in short-handed games against some of the best players in the world – and this is not what I wanted.

Anyway, as I am writing this I have been in this game for a little more than a year, and I am pleased to say that I have been able to become a clear winner in no time.[1] Actually, I have even made more money than I used to make in my regular B&M game in Amsterdam – something I had imagined would simply be impossible. In fact, I sometimes wonder now how on earth I could have restricted myself to playing in such a slow game for so long, when the online games had been there for me all along. I know now that playing online is the ideal solution for me, especially because of all my obligations regarding writing, reporting, teaching, travelling, and because of all the time that I spend on my TV activities and my own site www.rolfslotboom.com. Even if I wanted to, I would simply not have enough time to continue playing according to the six days a week routine that had given me so much success over the years. So yes, I am very happy that much sooner than I had expected, I have been able to become a big winner in the rather large online PLO games – while being able to simply choose my own times to play.

Frankly, it has cost me time, effort and lots of continuous analysis to get me to the point where I am probably one of the 40 or 50 biggest winners in my games of

---

[1] In fact, I have recently started playing on more than just this one site – also because of recent measures at my 'main' site, measures that make playing on more than just two tables in the $10-$20 game impossible. Fortunately, my results on these other sites seem to be in line with this 'main game' if you will. For the purposes of this book, the names of these sites are not all that relevant – especially because by the time this book is published I may already have shifted my attention to other sites and/or better, yes possibly even higher games.

choice. And in this chapter, I will give away all this information practically for free I guess, for not much more than just the honour of writing a good book. Of course, I know that by giving away all this information, I will give you a complete insight into my thought processes. I will let you follow the path that I have walked up to the point where I am now, meaning that this book could very well help to kill my current online bread-and-butter games. Because quite simply: The analysis that I will do on how to beat online PLO games has rarely if ever been done to this degree. And because I hold nothing back, it is clear that I will be at the risk of having to face a whole bunch of 'Little Rolfs' who will follow my exact rules and guidelines. This will mean that not only the games in general may become a bit tougher, but it may be especially bad for me – simply because it will be much harder to continue to use my own strategies in the same effective manner as before. So quite clearly I will need to lift my own game to an even higher level once this book has been published, now that I have spelled out to the competition what it is I am doing. People have always – and rightly! – said that one of the stupidest things to do as a poker player, is to educate the very opposition that you are up against. I guess in this book I am stupid enough to do just that.

# Rolf's rules: Beating the $10-$20 PLO games

Having looked around to see how other successful online players did things, it was clear to me that if I wanted to be a big winner at the highest stakes, I first had to get all of the conditions for playing well in order. This meant that I bought a special chair, a 21-inch monitor so that I could play four tables simultaneously with no overlap (a monitor that is already about to be replaced for a bigger one), and a double Internet connection, so that I would minimise the risk of ever getting disconnected. I purchased software and statistics programs to analyse both my as well as my opponents' games and tendencies as closely as possible. And finally, I made sure that at all times when I was playing, the TV was off, my phone was off, and there was no one else around – so that I could concentrate 100% on the task at hand, playing as well as possible. In all of my B&M years, I had been laughed at many times for my methodical approach and for taking all game-related aspects so seriously. For instance, just the fact that I would always come in at 7pm with my poker books and magazines, despite the fact that the game would not start until 8, was more than enough reason for some of my regular opponents to label me as either stupid, crazy or as someone with no life. But I have always been a firm believer in focusing 100% on preparing for the task at hand, and in conditioning both myself and my opponents that I would come to the table playing to the very best of my abilities. I think this may actually be even more important online than live. It is so easy to just make that one mouse click when it seems no one is watching, or to make this one decision that you 'would normally not make' – and therefore I try to be even more focused and concentrated online than I am live. All in all, all this preparation and analysis have led to the following approach – 'Rolf's Random Rules' for beating the $10-$20 PLO games.

## Rolf's random rule no. 1

Just as I had often done playing in brick and mortar PLO games, I started out by using the minimum approach online too. As the time of this writing, the minimum buy-in at my 'main' site for the $10-$20 games is $400, while the maximum buy-in is $2,000. (At other sites, these figures can be quite different. In particular, the minimum buy-in can be much larger there, making these games a bit more 'skilful' than the ones where you can buy in for relatively little.) This $400 minimum buy-in amounts to just 20 times the big blind, and leads to the money being extremely shallow. While this is a clear aggravation for some of the better players, I don't mind this at all – for the simple reason that I am probably one of the very best short-stack players around.

Having used – and introduced – my successful short-stack approach in both Vienna and Amsterdam, where the minimum buy-in was always at least 40 times the big blind, I knew that in this online game it should in fact be *easier* to use this short-stack approach in a successful manner. The reason was clear: Whereas in Vienna and Amsterdam I would need the help of overaggressive players to do the betting for me (or else I would not get a significant enough percentage of my stack in the pot), in this game I would not need any help. If just three players were to limp, I could raise to $130 already, making post-flop play a formality. So I would not need as much assistance from people doing the betting for me, and there would be less need to trap the maniacs. I could simply wait for a good hand to get the money in, preferably before the flop.

## Rolf's random rule no. 2

One positive aspect of this approach was that it did not require lots of advanced plays. I would not be faced with many difficult or tricky moves that are based on the weaknesses of players, or my ability to outplay them later in the hand. I could simply focus on what I am good at: Waiting for a good or even premium hand to get the money in. While it may seem a bit over-simplistic to analyse your own game in this manner, and also a bit derogatory (after all, which expert works on his game for years, analyses everything into depth, only to say after all these years of practice: 'My main strength is waiting for aces'?), it is still important to realise the basis and cornerstone of one's success.

By playing in this 'simple' manner, I could play multiple tables without losing that much information, for the simple reason that most plays were based on the strength of *my* cards, not because of a read I may have had on one of my opponents. If you are playing a large stack, it is much more difficult to keep a large edge when you play four tables at the same time, because you need to think on a very high level, and because in order to be successful, you will need to make lots of moves, plays and adjustments that cannot be made in an 'automatic' manner. Whereas a great big-stack player may make as much as 30 or even 35 big blinds per 100 hands by playing one or two tables, and a great short-stack player would be happy with 14-18 big blinds/100 in this situation. If both of these players are multi-tabling, the differences are not that big anymore. And quite clearly, the fact that the short-stack player loses significantly less edge than the big-stack player is the cause here. For this reason, short-stack players are able to play more tables simultaneously without it affecting their edge too much. And this means that while the figure BB/100 may still show a much higher win rate for the big-stack players, this difference is much less pronounced when looking at another important figure: the number of big blinds one can make *per hour*. All in all, this means that great short-stack players could average almost as much per hour as great big-stack players. In addition, they will be experiencing significantly fewer swings and also a lot less headache – simply because they won't have to face as many tough, borderline and/or crucial decisions.

## Rolf's random rule no. 3

If you get the chance, you should still try to opt for the seat to the immediate right of an overaggressive player. Although without the help of these bullies/maniacs, it is usually possible to get 25, 30 or even 35% of your stack in even when there's been no raise, it is still better to get the *entire* stack in before the flop. The maniac will help you do just that, and he may also help you after the flop by giving you protection, in the manner we discussed in previous chapters. In addition, because his raise will put everyone else in the middle on a rather structural basis, you will be in perfect position to minimise your losses and maximise your wins with your short stack.

## Rolf's random rule no. 4

In loose games, the fact that you are playing shallow money means that you will almost never be making a big mistake whenever you choose to go all-in with a quality hand. If you have a good double-suited hand and simply go all-in before the flop in a multiway pot, you will almost always be a money favourite – even if by chance one of your opponents happens to hold aces. Remember: If you are all-in in a four-way pot, you only need 25% pot equity to have a positive expectation in the hand. And with any dead money in the pot, or money you have already invested, you would need even less than that 25% to give any bets and raises from that point on a positive expectation. For instance, if with your $400 stack you are in the $20 big blind, the break-even point would be investing $380 more in a $1,600 total pot = 23.75% pot equity. This means that with just a 24% chance of winning in a four-way pot, your all-in move would already have a positive expectation – and *many* hands achieve that kind of rate. Even more so if we take into account any protection we may get after the flop from one of the bigger stacks.

# Rolf's random rule no. 5

While in my B&M game in Amsterdam I would have *two* strategies available, a short-stack and a large-stack approach, the fact that in online poker there is usually a cap on the buy-in makes the large-stack approach less attractive. The good thing about, yes the goal of playing with a large stack is that you can cover everyone at the table, so that you can break anyone on a single hand. But if you join a game and there are players with stacks of $3,000 and upwards already, you will not be the biggest stack even if you buy in for the maximum amount, $2,000. While many players disregard this and say that it is still best to buy in for the maximum, it clearly goes against my principle of 'having either the shortest *or* the largest stack, but not something in-between'. The fact that the minimum buy-in has so many advantages (easier to play well, easier to multi-table, easier to go all-in with an edge, using the all-in to your advantage by getting protection from others) means that I will usually need a clear reason to start with the maximum rather than the minimum. I do play a large stack quite often nowadays – but only in the following situations:

- ♠ When I have one or two rather tight and timid players to my left who are playing fairly shallow money.
- ♠ When there is at least one easy target to my right who is playing a large stack.

If by chance I end up in a seat like this[2], I will decide to abandon my usual short-stack approach and go for the kill instead. So, if the characteristics of the opponents to my left and right make the minimum buy-in approach unattractive, I will buy in for the maximum possible amount. Note that this in contrast to almost all good players who would *automatically* buy in for the maximum rather than just in exceptional situations.

Please keep in mind that you should buy in for this maximum amount only when you are on the button or the cutoff, *not* in middle position or so. Let's say that UTG+1 you have just lost your entire stack. You should rebuy for $400 now, not for $2,000, and you should only complete to the full buy-in once you have reached the button. Many players don't think about this at all and just buy-in for the maximum, oblivious to the fact that they could have avoided playing three hands with too much money in front of them in clearly unprofitable situations (under the gun plus the blinds). Of course, when you enter a game and have decided it is best to buy in for the maximum amount, you will post the $20 behind the button, not

---

[2] Yes, even for someone like me who pays lots of attention to seat selection, there are often limitations to what I can accomplish. This is especially true because online you are usually not allowed to make any seat changes other than by quitting the game and rejoining.

as the big blind. And finally, if by chance you had been playing a minimum buy-in approach but game circumstances have changed in such a manner that the big stack approach is best, you should wait until you get the button to complete to the maximum $2,000. Don't think that because you have analysed that 'now is the time to start using the big-stack approach' you should do this regardless of your position. In other words: Wait until the button to make your move.

## Rolf's random rule no. 6

When you are playing the short-stack strategy that I recommend, you will be employing a system that bears a good deal of resemblance to the concept of hitting and running. You wait for a good hand/profitable situation to get the money into the middle, preferably as early as possible in the hand. You immediately click on the 'Get Chips' button and enter the amount that you wish to buy in for if you lose the hand – $400 obviously. Now, once at the showdown it is clear you chips will *not* come your way, you immediately confirm the new buy-in by clicking 'OK' – this so that you will be dealt in on the next hand, and won't be forced to sit out for one or even two hands. And if it becomes clear that you *are* going to win the pot, and will be playing with more than double the minimum buy-in amount from that point, you immediately switch off the 'Auto-Post Blinds' button, so that once the big blind reaches you, you have the option to quit the game.

When playing the minimum buy-in approach (assuming we are talking about the $400 minimum game; as I have said, on other sites the minimum buy-in will be higher and this strategy is thus less attractive), you will need a *very* good reason to stay in a game once your stack has surpassed the $1,000 level. If the game is in fact so juicy that you don't want to leave, well then you should almost certainly buy some more chips and refill to the full $2,000 once you are on the button. The reason for this is that your stack has become so big already that you don't have all that many short-stack advantages anymore.[3] If that is the case, it would be better to start playing 'real poker' by buying in for as much as the site allows you to.

## Rolf's random rule no. 7

When playing a short stack in a moderately loose game[4], you should be trying to

---

[3] This is especially true when your stack has surpassed the $1,400 level, i.e., you have more than 70 times the big blind. There are almost no situations where continuing with just this $1,400 would be better than completing to the maximum $2,000.

[4] Say, with an average pot size $550 or more in a full ring game on Party, as opposed to $300/$350 in the PokerStars full ring games. Please note that at the time of this writing, not all sites have the same system to calculate the pot size, and for instance Party calculates any uncalled bets as part of the pot whereas most others do not.

create large multiway pot in order to maximise your expectation on the (few) good hands that you play. This means that as the first one in, you will rarely come in for a raise, for the following reasons:

♠ You can only raise to $70 maximum, while you are playing a stack of around $400. This is not the best way to play from a minimising losses/maximising wins point of view. (It *would* be correct with a stack of $250 or less. This way, if someone calls this $70 of yours, you know you are committed – meaning that the rest of your stack will go in, almost regardless of the flop.)

♠ You prefer to have multiple opponents in the hand, and raising the maximum will probably blast them out when you actually want them in. And raising the *minimum* with your short stack is not recommended either. What you prefer is limping, hoping that someone behind you will raise, get a few callers in the middle, and then reraise all-in. While this is obviously the best way to play if you have aces, even hands as weak as A♥-J♠-10♥-7♠ or A♥-10♣-8♣-6♥ are usually good enough to make this play profitable, provided there are at least *some* callers in the middle. If both the initial raiser and all callers in the middle now call again, you will be in a big multiway pot in which you will certainly be a money favourite, almost regardless of what you are up against, and where you could gain protection after the flop. And if someone comes over the top *before the flop*, well then you may indeed be facing aces. But at least there will be quite a bit of money in the pot then from people who called the first raise but who have now folded – thus giving you much better odds than in a situation where there would *not* have been any dead money. Quite a few people feel that if they put in $400 against just one player, they will need to win the pot 50% of the time to break even. But if because of the way the betting has gone, there is something like $200 dead money in the middle for a $1,000 total pot, you would need to win just 40% of the time to still come out ahead. And as we shall see, even if by chance you *have* run into aces, you will usually not have made as big a mistake as you *seem* to have made in the eyes of your opponents. In the next three hand match-ups, I will show that if indeed there is quite a bit of dead money in the pot, your double-suited A-J-10-7 will usually not be in that bad a shape against aces. And if by chance you are up against someone who would come over the top with a slightly wider range of hands, you may even be in *excellent* shape.

A♥-J♠-10♥-7♠ vs. A♣-A♦-9♣-4♦    38.37 vs. 61.63%
A♥-J♠-10♥-7♠ vs. K♥-K♦-J♥-10♠    43.91 vs. 56.09%
A♥-J♠-10♥-7♠ vs. A♣-8♣-7♥-6♥    62.31 vs. 37.69%

## Rolf's random rule no. 8

Obviously, you always keep the lobby open to keep an eye on (other) good games. One of the most important things here is to watch closely all the new games that are developing, any new tables that may be opening. New games are often started up by loose-aggressive players, and if you are able to jump into that game as the fifth, sixth or seventh player, you will often be able to get the exact seat that you want: to the immediate right of the most (over)aggressive player. At the same time, you should take a close look at the waiting lists for the tables you are either playing at, or are waiting for yourself. If behind you on the waiting list, you see a bunch of tight players waiting for a game that right now still has an average pot of $650 or so, it may be better to shift your attention to a six-handed game that has just started up, even if the average pot here is just $360 or so. If there are quite a few loose-aggressive players in this game, it will have the potential to become a much better game, and by taking advantage of the fact that the tight players often only look at full ring games, you will have secured yourself a good game that will probably fill up soon – a game that contains a relatively high number of Action Men. Of course, the bad thing is that many of these Action Men will probably leave once all these tight players have found their way into the game, to go and create a new short-handed table elsewhere. But hopefully you will have doubled up already before the table turns sour, meaning that you will have taken advantage of the little time that this game was actually very juicy.[5]

## Rolf's random rule no. 9

If by chance you *are* in a tight game with your short stack, you should go for the limp/reraise much less frequently than you usually would, for the simple reason that the pot may only get raised behind you when someone has a really big hand. Whereas a hand like K♠-Q♠-Q♥-9♦ in early position may be good enough for you to go for the limp/reraise in a game with aggressive players behind you, in a very tight game this won't work. In a tight game, it would be better to a) simply fold, or b) make a minimum raise to $40. If the players behind you have a lot of respect for

---

[5] At the time of this writing, a few sites have just changed their policy in such a way that there are now just two tables available at the $10-$20 blinds level. In this situation, it is impossible to start up new tables, as usually there will already be long waiting lists for the two games that *are* available. However, I don't think this situation will continue to exist for very long, as limiting the number of tables to just two doesn't seem to make much sense – neither for the sites themselves nor for their customers.

you, and would only call or reraise you with really big hands, it is quite likely that you can make everybody fold, or play in position against the blinds only – while holding the probable best hand. But obviously, if the game is this tight, you should simply leave the game when the big blind reaches you. (Unless of course there are a couple of weak players on the waiting list, in which case you should be willing to continue.)

# Rolf's random rule no. 10

In a full ring game at the level that we are talking about ($10-$20 blinds), what are the criteria to call players either tight or loose? Well, many of you will probably be using software/statistics programs to analyse not just your game, but also the characteristics of your opponents. In my book, I would rate players as:

### Loose

When they have a VPIP (percentage of the time that a player voluntarily puts chips into the pot) of 33% or more. With a VPIP of 44% or more, I would label them as extremely loose.

### Tight

When they have a VPIP of 18% or less. Good players who use my minimum buy-in approach would usually have a VPIP ranging from 14% to 17%. In fact, there are some players nowadays with a VPIP of less than 10(!)%, but they are hardly ever serious winners, simply because they miss out on too many profitable opportunities. They could only win if the opposition was truly horrible, and even then they would not win much. One final note: We have already established that there are quite a few big-stack players who beat the game for a good amount. They almost always have a VPIP of more than 18%, and usually are in the region 24-36%. Almost every player who uses a big-stack approach but has a VPIP of less than 16% does *not* beat the games. The reason for this that they play so few hands that their opponents generally can get a good line on their play and on the hands that they have. With deep money, this is a definite recipe for disaster. (More on this later.)

### Aggressive

When they have a PFR (pre-flop raise percentage) of more than 9 or 10 per cent. If their PFR is around 20% or even more, I will label them as maniacs, and I will almost always try to sit to their immediate right.

### Passive

When they have a PFR of 3% or less. Few players are this passive though, and if they are they usually won't last very long. Note that most winning players have a PFR in the range 6-12%.

Obviously, when labelling players it is also important to look at their post-flop stats: their post-flop aggression factors, percentage of the time that they reach the showdown etc. However, in the minimum buy-in approach that we are playing, it is of paramount importance how our opponents play *before* the flop, and in particular their tendencies on the turn and river are not all that important for this purpose.[6]

Let's take an example of how to use someone's stats to your advantage when you are playing a short stack. Let's say you are in the $20 big blind with a hand like A♥-Q♣-10♥-7♦. There is one weak limper, and then the button makes it $90 to go. Well, in this case knowing the pre-flop tendencies of this specific raiser is the key to making the correct decision. If this is someone who has a VPIP of 16% and a PFR of 3%, then you should simply let it go, and fold your hand there and then. This is especially true if he also has a relatively low 'attempted steal' percentage, something like 12-14%. But if this is someone with a PFR of 12% to 14%, or someone with an attempted steal percentage of 30% or more, well then your response is clear: You should reraise the maximum. The person you would worry about the most here would be the limper, *not* the button, simply because he is just too likely to be making a move.

So, even though the success of this short-stack approach for the most part depends upon the strength of your own hand, it *does* take into account relative value. This means that in special cases just a slightly above average hand can be enough to go all-in before the flop, while even a near-premium hand like K♠-K♥-8♠-7♦ can be a clear fold when a 'tightass' with a PFR of less than 3% suddenly starts raising like there's no tomorrow.

Just as in B&M play, it's about getting to know your opponents. The only difference is that online you will have a few tools to help you do just that. Having said that, you obviously should use only the ones that are accepted at the site that you play at. Just check out the site of your choice to see which programs *are* and which programs are *not* allowed. You do want to win, yes – but you want to win in a clean and honest manner.

---

[6] These post-flop stats *would* become a major issue in deep-money play of course. But in that case, I still try to rely more on my *personal* knowledge of this player's tendencies and how he will respond to *my* play, rather than on what he does in general. While I *will* analyse all of his stats in depth, I will use them merely as a guideline in this case, not as a direct reason for making a certain play or not – something that I *would* do in short-stack play.

## Rolf's random rule no. 11

When you are hopping from table to table[7], leaving when you have accumulated a decent stack to then buy in for the minimum at another table again, it is important that you have made a list of the tables that you have just left. Let's say you have just left table X with $1,200, then it is not very ethical to re-enter the game five minutes later with your initial $400. The strange thing is that some sites don't explicitly forbid this practice, even though some (most) of them do. But even on the sites that don't, it would be simple courtesy/etiquette not to go back to that table say, within 90 minutes or so. Frankly, it is my view that online casinos should simply make it impossible for someone to rejoin a game within two hours or so – unless of course he brings at least the same amount of money. But until that time, I would advise you to be ethical enough to do this even when the rules don't explicitly say so, and even when you know this will limit your opportunities to use 'my' strategy in a successful manner.

## Rolf's random rule no. 12

When you are in the big blind in an unraised pot, playing the minimum buy-in, you should usually go for the check-raise if you happen to flop something good. After all, the $10-$20 PLO games are usually played in a very aggressive manner. If it gets checked around, the person in late position will almost always auto-bet here. Most aggressive players would bet close to half the time or even more than that when it gets checked to them. You can therefore use this to your advantage by check-raising all-in or close to it – both with your decent made hands and your good draws. Almost always, this will be a profitable situation for you, especially now that there's a high probability that the bettor has very little and/or can't stand the heat.

And if by chance you had been planning to go for a check-raise with a good made hand but no one bites, well then not all is lost. Assuming that a relatively safe card comes on the turn, you can simply check it once more. Very few players in big games like this are able to withstand one check, let alone two. So, expect that after your second check someone will do the betting for you after all, and you can check-raise to simply get the hand over with (either by winning without a showdown, or by getting called when in all likelihood you have the current best hand). This play is especially successful when you have a hand like top two pair with no

---

[7] As I have said, not all that easy anymore with the recent changes of having just two tables available at the higher stakes. If when reading this book this same situation still exists and you still want to take advantage of this multi-tabling, minimum buy-in, 'hopping' approach, then you should play simultaneously at various site, rather than just at one site as I recommended. Of course, at the lower limits there are still many tables available, meaning that you can hop around as much as you want over there and exploit or practice my system to the fullest.

extras and there are quite a few draws on the board. Say you hold K-10-7-7 rainbow, the board is K♥-10♥-4♠-6♠, the pot is $60 and you are playing a $280 stack. Here the turn is an excellent time to get in the check-raise, especially if – as in this case – there has been no action on the flop. You will avoid the headache of the fact that almost every river card will look dangerous to you, *and* you will charge all straight and flush draws the maximum to try and draw out on you. Don't think: 'Hey, my check-raise attempt on the flop has failed. The board is starting to get awfully scary now, so I have no other option but to come out betting in order to defend my hand.' This is faulty thinking. With room for just about one more pot bet on the river if your turn bet gets called, you don't manage to defend your hand at all. By betting out you give your opponents excellent implied odds in two ways:

1. They can earn more if they hit their draws and you decide to pay off.

2. The betting on the turn has led to a situation where they can make a bigger bet on the river, improving their chances of pulling off a successful bluff.

In this situation, anyone who calls your turn bet can now bet either $180 on the river, or even $240 if there is also a second caller, in a situation where *any* card but the four remaining kings and tens can be considered scare cards. To avoid this tough situation where you are likely to make mistakes no matter what you do, you should simply check on the turn a second time. Not having shown *any* strength so far, your check won't scare any of your opponents. Being aggressive players, one of them will undoubtedly try to pick up the pot – and you can then come out of the bushes by check-raising all-in or close to it. This way, you will be putting in your money with the best hand, and at the same time you take away the implied odds that your opponents could be getting. In all but the most hypothetical situations (where your opponents are assigned such a range of hands that any river card except for the remaining kings and tens would beat you) you will have made a play with a clear positive expectation – simply because you had the courage to check twice.

## Rolf's random rule no. 13

When you are playing a stack of $400 or less and there is a raise in front of you, you are almost always in a reraise or fold situation: raise when you think you have the best hand, fold if you don't. Only on rare occasions should you decide to call. This could be for instance when you are seated to the immediate left of someone who has made a minimum raise to $40, and he is someone who you figure for four big cards. Let's say that you hold a hand like Q♠-J♥-10♥-9♣ here: a good hand, one that performs very well in a multiway setting, but also one that is a clear dog heads-up against probable hands for him to hold like A-Q-J-10 or K-K-J-9. Especially if you think the game is loose enough that your call could induce other hands into the pot as well, calling would be a better option than folding or reraising. Please note that if the raiser had made the maximum $70 instead of the $40 he has made it now, you would almost always have had an easy fold – despite holding a good and coordinated holding.

## Rolf's random rule no. 14

If you are on the button with a stack of less than $400 and there are one or two limpers in front of you, then whenever you decide to get involved you should either call or raise the maximum, but *not* raise the minimum. Even though the mini-raise is a tool that I use very often, it is especially useful if you have a stack in the range $1,000-$2,000, not with a stack as small as the one you have here. So, your options in this case would be limited to:

### Fold

If the situation is just not profitable enough and/or your hand is not good enough.

### Call

If you have a hand that can flop something good and/or you are in a situation where you could profitably use your good position after the flop. Please take into account the check-raise tendencies of the limpers on the flop and turn (check-raising percentages of more than 7% are dangerous), and the amount of respect that they have for you – so that you will know how much thievery you can get away with. Against people who will often check-raise, you can still occasionally bet flops like 4-4-9 rainbow or K-K-3 rainbow even when you have absolutely nothing, but you should avoid betting your marginal hands when checked to. The reason for this is that a check-raise could force you off a hand that may be best right now or else could improve to the best hand. Let's say you hold Q♥-J♣-9♣-7♠ on a flop K♠-Q♠-6♣. Five players see a flop for $20 each. When you have $360 left and everyone checks to you, this is a situation where you could often bet against people who rarely check-raise. The reasons are simple: You could win the pot there and then, you could make better hands fold and even if you do get called by what seems like a better hand, you could possibly take a free card on the turn. So betting the flop in this situation would seem like a correct decision – but not if by chance you are up against one or two frequent check-raisers. The problem is that if indeed you are faced with a check-raise, your hand will almost certainly not be strong enough to play for all your money. Yet, there is still a decent chance that against these players you either have the best hand, or a hand that could improve to the best hand – meaning that you are now losing money in a situation where you actually could have made some money in the case of a favourable turn.

### Raise the maximum

When you think you either have the best hand, or you can make everyone fold. Please note that if you get called here, you are committed to going all the way. Let's say you have raised to $110, get called by one player, and have $150 left now. There is no board that is scary enough for you to fold now. So whatever happens, all the money should go in on the flop, whether it's by you calling your opponent's bet, or by betting it all-in yourself.

# An inferior strategy?

If you thoroughly hold on to my system, you will find that in time many people start calling you names. They will tell you that it is an inferior strategy you are using, that it is not 'real' poker you are playing, etc. What is important here is that you should not let it affect you. The reason why people will complain about your style of play is that it can't easily be beaten. Because you are a) playing very few hands, and b) adjust very well to your opponents' specific weaknesses on the very few hands that you *do* play, there is just not much room for your opponents to outplay you and/or to beat your game. Don't give in to the temptation of trying to play 'real' poker too early in your career. Large parts of the strategy that I recommend are things that most 'good' players don't think very highly of: the concepts of a) keeping things simple, and b) staying out of trouble. If you hold on to my recommendations in a very strict manner, you will find that you will have to face just very few really tough decisions that rely on any expert judgment. In addition, especially when you are playing a short stack, you will find that this system will ensure that even if you *do* make a mistake, it will usually be a relatively minor one. I will illustrate this with a clear – although rather long – example.

Let's say you do things exactly the way I recommend. You have bought in for the minimum and have chosen the seat to the immediate right of a somewhat overaggressive player, someone who raises before the flop on 20-25% of all hands. You have limped for $20 with the K♥-K♦-8♥-7♣, and as expected the overaggressive player raises it up to $90. A late-position player and the big blind both call this raise, and now it is up to you. With the $380 that you have left, knowing that you are very likely to be holding the best hand, you make the obvious play of moving all-in. Now let's analyse two scenarios where you have misjudged the situation, and one of your opponents *does* have a better hand than you – aces. This is a situation that you would hate of course, because as you will see in the 'Hand Match-up & Analysis' chapter and also in my *'Defending against aces'* article, kings versus aces is one of the worst possible match-ups in PLO. Still, these examples will show that in situations like this where there is quite a bit of dead money and your stack is not all that large, you may not be in quite such bad shape as you think you are.

# Scenario 1

The overaggressive player *does* have aces this time, A-A-5-4 rainbow. He raises the pot to $1,410, and everybody folds. You have invested $400 in a total pot of $990. This means that in order to break even on this hand, your K♥-K♦-8♥-7♣ would need 40.4% pot equity. Simulations show that up against this A-A-5-4 your hand will win just 36.67% of the time. This means that in the long run you can expect to get back $363.03 out of the pot, for an average loss of $36.97. However, considering the fact that you had already made the (correct) decision to call the initial $20, one could claim that at the point when the action came back to you for $90, *that* was the real decision time. If at that point you had known you were up against aces, you would obviously have either folded and forfeited the $20, or called the $70 extra hoping to catch a good flop. So, if we analyse this situation from the real decision point on, you did not lose $36.97 on average but just $16.97 – simply because the initial $20 that you called was now considered part of the pot. Still, this is a pretty bad situation to be in, though not nearly as bad as some people would have thought. And yes, if you happen to win the pot in situations like this, people will call you lucky or even a donkey – someone who 'overplayed' his holding against the 'obvious' aces, yet in the end got away with it.

As you have just seen, even when your decision was wrong, in this bad situation of being up against aces, you still don't lose that much money on average. But if you happen to be right, and the initial raiser is in there with one of the many marginal hands that he could be holding, then you will suddenly be in an *extremely* good situation. I have simulated three of the many other hands that he could hold other than aces if he chooses to either call or even reraise my all-in raise – all of this to show the strength of this all-in reraise with my kings. This under the (reasonable) assumption that the two other players will get out of the way, regardless of whether the overaggressive player reraises again or just calls. (Note that for him reraising with a double-suited hand may not be too bad a play actually. If he figures you for aces, and if by reraising again he could shut out all others, then because of the dead money in the pot and the fact that his cards are probably live, he *too* could have a positive expectation here – knowing that he may now lose much less on average than the $90 he would have lost if he had chosen to simply fold.)

| Your hand | Overaggressive player's hand | Win percentage for your hand | Expectation out of the pot | Average profit |
|---|---|---|---|---|
| K♥-K♦-8♥-7♣ | A♥-A♦-5♠-4♣ (aces – a logical hand to come over the top with) | 36.67% | $363.03 | -$36.97 |
| K♥-K♦-8♥-7♣ | A♥-K♣-Q♥-J♦ (premium hand that contains higher flush draw, also a hand that he may be willing to play aggressively here) | 55.73% | $551.73 | $151.73 |
| K♥-K♦-8♥-7♣ | K♠-J♥-8♠-6♥ (the type of double-suited hand mentioned, where if your opponent figures you for aces, he could decide to reraise again to shut out the field and play you heads-up. Please note that against your kings he wins just 34.78% – but against aces he would have done much better) | 65.22% | $645.68 | $245.68 |
| K♥-K♦-8♥-7♣ | Q♥-Q♦-8♠-5♣ (a bad hand that he may choose to reraise you with if he figures you could also be making your limp/reraise play with other hands than just aces or kings) | 74.06% | $733.19 | $333.19 |

This table shows that because of the two callers in the middle, reraising all-in with your K-K-8-7 is clearly the correct play. This is especially true if a) the initial raiser does not need to have aces, and b) even if he does not have them, he could *still* decide to come over the top of your all-in raise and give you protection. And in this situation, both a) and b) could apply – making the all-in move with your kings a very good one.

## Scenario 2

This time the overaggressive player just calls your all-in raise (good for you, because now you know for a fact that your read was correct, and that he does not have aces), but then the first caller comes over the top for a pot-sized reraise. Bad news for you obviously, because now it turns out that someone is in there with aces after all. In fact, by playing the way he did, this person has trapped you. Because if he had reraised the overaggressive player right away to $320, you would simply have folded your kings – unless maybe you knew that this player had extremely loose reraising standards, which we assume is not the case. So, by playing 'second hand low', this person has first flat called the raise and has only come over the top after a reraise by a second player (you) – quite clearly a very good play on his part. However, a few good things can happen to you as well, as we will see in scenarios 2a and 2b.

### Scenario 2a

Even though the person to your immediate left is a somewhat overaggressive player, this doesn't mean he is an absolute fool. Once he calls your $400 raise and then gets repopped to $1,720, he knows that this pot could become awfully expensive for him. If he decides to fold (for instance because he is weak, or because he holds either an ace or a big pair – hands that perform badly against aces), this means $400 added – dead – money. You will then be in a situation where you have invested $400 in a total pot of $1,320. To break even on the hand, your kings would need to win 30.3% of the time. Assuming that you are up against the same A-A-5-4 from before, you will do much better than that, with an expectation of $484.04, and for a net profit of $84.08. Not all that bad considering that you are holding kings versus aces – conceivably one of the worst possible situations in PLO.

### Scenario 2b

Let's say that the overaggressive player does not fold against this big re-reraise, but calls. He has analysed quite clearly that the reraiser has aces, but with the 10♠-9♥-8♠-7♥ he's got an ideal hand to snap off his opponent's aces. This is especially true if both these two players happen to have very large stacks with, say, $4,000 left even after the re-reraise.

Now the flop comes J♥-10♦-6♥. Not a premium flop for the 10-9-8-7 by any means, considering that many of his straight cards are not the nuts, and because his flush draw is also just a nine-high. However, from the overaggressive player's point of view, this may not be a flop that looks all that great to his opponent if he happens to hold just bare aces with no back-up. After all, his opponent would certainly fear hands like Q-J-10-9, J-J-x-x or 10-10-x-x when bet into. Heck, even against 'just' the draw that the aces are up against here, this draw will win no less than 74.39% of the time, with just 25.61% for the aces. So, if the overaggressive player chooses to make an aggressive, pot-sized semi-bluff on the flop, there is a good chance that he will win the pot uncontested if indeed his opponent has aces without any kind of backup. This is not just good for the overaggressive player, who will pick up a $2,640 side pot while having the current worst hand – it is also good for you. Now that the aces have folded, your kings are suddenly the current best hand, meaning that even if you don't improve but your opponent doesn't improve either, you will now suddenly win the $1,320 main pot instead of losing it. And knowing that you not only have the best made hand with your kings but also the best (flush) draw, you are now suddenly in a situation where you have a huge overlay. On this flop J♥-10♦-6♥, your K♥-K♦-8♥-7♣ will beat your opponent's 10♠-9♥-8♠-7♥ a whopping 66.10% of the time.[8] This means that your expectation of the $1,320 main pot is no less than $872.52 for an average profit of $472.52 – despite the fact that when the money went in, you were in the horrible situation kings vs. aces.

## Conclusion

The thing that I like the most about the 'simple' strategy that I recommend is the fact that you will often enough be in profitable (+EV) situations, whereas you will only rarely have to face difficult situations that require expert judgment. One of my favourite soccer players used to play exactly like that. His name was Jari Litmanen, a Finnish player who was in the Ajax Amsterdam squad that won the Champions League in 1995. Jari never did anything out of the ordinary. He just came to the ball, passed it through to another teammate, came to the ball again, passed it to another player, etc. Many people said: 'Gee, *anyone* can do that, right? He never takes any chances, never goes for a spectacular dribble, nothing but these same simple moves all the time.' The fact is: He was playing at a consistently high level *simply because he knew his own limitations*. In soccer, keeping it simple is sometimes the hardest thing of all – and poker is no different in this respect. While quite possibly, the real poker experts *would* like to get involved in many tough and/or seemingly marginal situations because they could use their expert judgment, for the vast majority who do *not* perform at that world-class level it is recommended to do the exact opposite: *Avoid* those marginal situations where it is easy to make a serious mistake.

Having played professionally for over eight years, I have without doubt been one of the most consistent and most successful cash game players in Europe. Yet I *still* think that these concepts of keeping things simple and staying out of trouble are of paramount importance for me. Now if *I* feel that way, then I guess there is no shame for *you* to think highly of these things – even though as a result, you will almost certainly not receive much praise or even recognition from your fellow players.

# Starting hands in the context of 'my' system

When people who are used to playing hold'em pick up Omaha, they always seem to have trouble with one of the most elementary aspects of the game – starting

---

[8] Actually, it will win 60.61% of the time, it will lose 28.41% of the time, and the pot will be split 10.98% of the time.

hand selection. I have written a few articles on this subject that can be found in the 'Classic Articles' section, and also two that are available on my own site www.rolfslotboom.com. To expand on this, I will now analyse five different starting hands for the online $10-$20 PLO games, first in the shallow-money situation, later also in deep-money play.[9] I will not just tell you whether or not you should play them, but also *how* and *why* – taking into account the characteristics (tight/loose, aggressive/passive) of the game.

## Starting hands with shallow money ($380) in a loose game with a loose/aggressive player to your immediate left

| The starting hand | In early position | In late position |
| --- | --- | --- |
| A♥-J♥-10♠-8♠ | Good enough for a limp/reraise. (Provided it is the person to your left who is doing the raising) | After a few limpers, raise the maximum. Against a big raise by a tight player, fold. Against a raise by a loose/aggressive player (LAP), reraise all-in. |
| K♥-K♦-9♥-7♠ | Good enough for a limp/reraise. However, if you limp and a) a locksmith now raises the pot, or b) the pot gets raised and reraised behind you, well then in these cases you could have a fold. If you are not 100% certain though that you are up against aces and/or there are more than four players in the hand, then you should simply go with your hand, and stick it in. | After a few fairly loose limpers, raise the maximum. Against one or two very tight limpers, just call. Against a raise by a LAP, reraise all-in. Against a pot raise from someone with a PFR%<3, fold. |
| A♥-A♦-5♥-3♦ | Go for the limp/reraise. Had the money been slightly deeper ($1,000-$2,000), then in this position you should mini-raise with a fairly wide range of hands, and only rarely limp. Then, if someone reraises you, having mini-raised with this A-A-5-3, you simply come over the top by reraising the pot. | Always raise the maximum, regardless of the action in front of you. With slightly deeper money, a mini-raise to reopen the betting may be good. Remember though that once the money gets deeper, you will have to mix up your play, and you will especially have to avoid giving away your hand by your actions when there's still quite a bit of money left to be played. |

---

[9] As you should know by now, in pot-limit Omaha I will almost always be playing for either the minimum buy-in or for the maximum amount the site will allow me to. I almost never play an in-between stack, and that's why in this book I touch upon situations with a medium stack only very rarely.

| | | |
|---|---|---|
| 9♠-8♥-7♣-6♦ | Fold. Even double-suited, I would not usually play this hand from early position. | On the button against a few limpers, you could probably call, even though the hand is actually quite weak. The fact that it has no suits could lead to problems in this multiway pot. Against a raise, always fold. With deeper money, you could occasionally call a raise, especially when on the button, and most of all if the raiser is a weak player who is marked with a big pair. |
| J♠-J♥-7♠-7♣ | Good enough for a limp/reraise. If, after your limp, the overaggressive player raises, an absolute 'tightass' calls this raise and all others fold, then you should just call and let the flop decide your best course of action. In that case, you would probably check to the overaggressive player to let him do the betting, to see what the 'tightass' will do before committing fully. | If weak/very loose players have limped, raise the maximum. If strong/tight players have limped, just call. Against a big raise by a tight player, fold. Against a raise by a LAP, sometimes call, sometimes reraise – depending upon your position relative to the raiser. |

## A few starting hands with shallow money ($380) in a rather tight game with no overaggressive players

| The starting hand | In early position | In late position |
|---|---|---|
| A♥-J♥-10♠-8♠ | Mini-raise or fold as the first one in; both are better than calling (but only slightly). Raising the maximum is *not* good, as you may only get action from premium hands, hands that are a favourite over yours. If someone in front of you has limped, you should usually call and *definitely* not mini-raise. | As the first one in, raise the maximum. If the players in the blinds are tight (especially weak-tight), then a smaller raise may be good enough to get the job done. Against a raise from all but the very tightest players, calling may be correct – especially if you feel there is a bit of room to outplay your opponent after the flop. If not, folding is good too, especially if the raise was a maximum. |
| K♥-K♦-9♥-7♠ | Mini-raise as the first one in (but obviously *not* if someone in front of you has limped). If you get reraised by a very tight player, fold. If one or two players behind you call your mini-raise, then | With tight limpers in front of you, just call. (Don't open yourself up to a limp/reraise from a tight player with aces!) As the first one in, raise more than the minimum but less than the pot to avoid giving the blinds a very cheap |

| | | |
|---|---|---|
| | mini-bet on the flop to see what they will do – regardless of whether or not you have actually received any help from the board. Don't go for the check-raise if your opponents are timid. Against them, the mini-bets will work very well, possibly (but not necessarily) followed by a bigger bet on the turn. | flop, while at the same time not committing fully. As you can see, in contrast to very loose/very aggressive games where all my raises are of the same size (either minimum or maximum), in tight games I will sometimes vary the size of my raises based on who is in already, who is in the blinds, what I hope to accomplish etc. |
| A♥-A♦-5♥-3♦ | Often raise the maximum, sometimes raise small, occasionally limp. Because no one will do the raising for you, you will need to make the first raise – something you don't like doing. Try to be a bit creative here by not always playing your aces the same way. | Raise the maximum, regardless of the action in front of you. |
| 9♠-8♥-7♣-6♦ | Fold. | As the first one in, and up against very tight or weak-tight players in the blinds, raise more than the minimum but less than the pot (a 'cheap steal'). In all other cases, fold. |
| J♠-J♥-7♣-7♣ | Usually fold, sometimes raise small, occasionally call. | After tight limpers, call. Against a raise, fold. As the first one in, raise anywhere from the minimum $40 to $55, depending upon the characteristics of the blinds. |

**A few starting hands with deep money ($2,600) in an average game (with at least *some* rather good, big stack players), holding position on your 'target' – the one you are trying to break**

| The starting hand | In early position (assuming your 'target' is under the gun) | In late position |
|---|---|---|
| A♥-J♥-10♠-8♠ | If target has called, raise to $50. If target has raised to $40, reraise to $100 or $120 or so. If target has raised to $70, reraise the minimum to $120 to face the field with a raise plus a reraise, while still not giving him enough room for a massive reraise if he happens to have a big hand. If target has | If target has made a small raise to $40 or $50, reraise to about $120. If target has just called, and there are also other callers who are not habitual limp/reraisers, raise to about $60 or $80, but not more than that. Don't forget your goal here: You want to keep your target *in* the pot – not blast him out. |

| | | |
|---|---|---|
| | folded, you will fold as well, because despite the fact that you hold a more than decent hand, you don't want to play this hand out of position against good players who also has a big stack. | |
| K♥-K♦-9♥-7♠ | If target has called, raise to $50. If target has raised to $40, reraise him the minimum. If target has raised to $70, just flat call, as by reraising you could possibly be raising yourself out of the pot. | If target has raised small, either call or reraise small, depending upon whether there are other players in the hand who could be limp/reraising with aces. If target has raised big, just call but don't reraise. Keep in mind that there are many hands and situations in deep-money play where you can take an aggressive posture. But K-K is one of the few hands that I will sometimes play in a fairly passive manner, simply because I want to reach the flop with the hand. Also, I don't want to make it too easy for tight players who happen to hold aces to have their ABC play rewarded with a big and/or easy pot. |
| A♥-A♦-5♥-3♦ | If target has called, raise to $50. If target has raised to $40, either reraise him the minimum or else make your standard reraise to $120, the raise you would also make with your 'other' hands. The goal of the minimum reraise is to lure someone into making a third raise so that you can then come over the top (remember, no cap on number of raises in big-bet poker!), while if they *don't* bite, you still have not given away the content of your hand. If target raises to $70 or $90, either flat call (in order to go for the 'second hand low') or better still, make the same minimum reraise that you would also make with double-suited rundown hands like J♠-10♥-9♠-8♥. | If target has called, raise to $50. If target has raised to $40 or so, either make a normal raise to $120 (the one he would 'expect' from you in this position), or sometimes make the minimum reraise. (As you can see, I almost *never* raise the pot before the flop when there is still a lot of money to be played!) Almost never flat call with aces here as a 'second hand low' attempt. Because you would reraise here with a wide range of hands *representing* aces, you should also reraise when you finally get them. If both the target and some other players have just called, just make the standard raise to about $80. |

| 9♠-8♥-7♣-6♦ | Regardless of what target does, you should fold here. When the money is deep, this is not a hand you want to play from early position, and it is not a good enough hand to isolate the target with. | If target has called, possibly with one or two other limpers, just flat call on the button. Because one single raise will not get out many players, it may be better not to escalate the pot at this point with your rather weak holding. However, if your target has raised and no other dangerous players are in the hand yet, you should reraise – either to $120, or else the same minimum reraise that you would sometimes make with aces. (This to keep your opponents off-balance, and to make it more difficult for them to make correct counterplays to your strategy.) Your goal is to play heads-up, in position, and against your target, while holding a hand he probably doesn't expect. This way you may get bluffing opportunities on, in particular, flops with one or two big cards, but get excessive action when you have caught an – unexpectedly – good flop. Still, a double-suited 9-8-7-6 would have been much better for making an aggressive play than the no-suits hand that you have here. |
| J♠-J♥-7♠-7♣ | If target has called, raise to $50. If target has raised, usually just flat call him. This is a hand where the flop should make quite clear where you stand, and also a hand that should be fairly easy to play even from out of position, for instance when you flat call a raise and players behind you come in as well. However, your hand is not great by any means, so don't stand *too* much heat with it. If target has folded, don't be too eager to get involved. | If target has called, make your standard raise to $50, and adjust to $70 or $80 if one or two weak or loose limpers are also in. If there are tight limpers who could be trying for a limp/reraise with aces, you should just call – especially if they are playing short money. If target has raised, just call. You don't mind him keeping the initiative, holding a hand where you will probably need to flop a seven or a jack to continue. And if you flop that seven or jack, you *want* your target to keep betting at you. So, this is a hand where you can finally give your target some leeway, some breathing room where for once you |

| | | do *not* try to take him out of the lead. If your target has folded and only fairly strong players are in the hand, you should usually just call. No need to build a big pot when the person you are aiming to break is out of the hand. This would be a situation where I would be trying to play for a small pot, rather than a big one, and where I would like to see a flop before investing a lot of money. |
|---|---|---|

# Playing with deep money

In this section we wll examine strategies for when you have more than the $2,000 maximum buy-in in front of you.

When you are using the 'second' strategy in your arsenal, the strategy where you are playing a deep stack and are trying to break one or more very weak or predictable players to your right (your 'targets'), then things are quite different from the short-stack approach we have discussed before. You will now be trying to get yourself in a situation where you have good position in a pot that has been raised or reraised by you, in either of the following two situations:

1.   Holding a quality hand, preferably a *coordinated* quality hand where all four cards work together – so that if the flop comes pretty good, you could have a very powerful holding.

2.   Up against weak, loose and/or predictable players who are also playing a big stack. Of course, in this scenario you would want to have position on your targets.

## Tight or loose? And just as importantly: How aggressive?

Those who have paid attention to my comments earlier in this book know that in contrast to the way most people play, I do not tighten up considerably once my stack has suddenly become large. (Or better: I do not *loosen* up as much as most people do when they have a *short* stack.) Quite the contrary, I often play *looser* with deep money than with shallow money! The reason should be obvious: When the money is deep, there will be more opportunities to make plays based upon the situation and the person(s) you are up against, rather than just play according to the strength of your cards. This is a luxury you don't have when you don't hold all that much and are playing with little money in front of you – for the simple reason that the likelihood of getting called is too high now that you don't have enough ammunition to put pressure on your opponents.

But it is important to realise that you can only loosen up in *specific situations*. Because obviously, if your overall play becomes too loose and you start raising somewhat indiscriminately, you will begin to face many problems that you never had to face in your short-stack approach. When playing deep money, you will have to take into account and be aware of at least the following possible dangers:

♠ You need to realise what a radical shift you have made in your overall strategy. Whereas in your short-stack approach, you would almost always have the current best hand or the best draw once all the money went in, in this new situation this is not necessarily the case. In this deep-money situation, you will have many reasons other than the quality of your hand to make bets and (re)raises. To name but two: a) securing yourself the button by trying to raise the people who sit behind you out of the pot, or b) isolating one of your targets so that you can play him heads-up, in position, in a situation where you could possibly break him. This means that a rather large percentage of the time, your bets both before and after the flop will be bluffs or semi-bluffs. Only very rarely will you have the hand you are representing, in contrast to the short-stack situation where you would almost *always* have the big hand that was suggested by your betting. It is important for you to realise that a much smaller percentage of the time you will now actually have a real hand whenever you choose to bet or raise. And just as importantly, you should know that after a while your opponents, who had always seen you as a true rock, will *definitely* realise this. This means that the fact that they know you are more likely to make 'moves' now will change their perception of you, and it will change the way that they will respond to your bets.

♠ The fact that you now sometimes invest $50, $80 or $120 before the flop may not be that big a deal for you, as even this $120 would almost certainly account for less than 5% of your total stack. But it *could* be a big deal for your opponents! Especially if they are playing 'your' old system of keeping a short stack and waiting for a premium hand to move in, this $120, yes even this $50 would amount to a significant percentage of *their* stack. You need to realise that while *you* are focusing on the best way to break your prey and to take his entire stack on one hand, these short-stack players will now see *you* as *their* prey. They will be hoping to double through you, now that they have noticed you will often make raises with fairly marginal holdings. Things will be exactly the same now as I described earlier in this book, when I explained how I was able to beat truly great players by just using a very simple system. And how did I do that? Well, quite simply by taking advantage of their over-aggression, and the fact that the small stack that I had did not pose any real threat to them. While *they* were aggressively trying to get themselves into situations where they could break the weak player, *I* was sitting there with my short stack waiting to take advantage of a situation where people would make bets and raises with just marginal hands. But now that the situation has changed and *I* have become one of these big-stack players, it is entirely possible that good short-stack players are now lying in the bushes, hoping to trap *me*. And this is something you obviously have to take into account when you are playing deep money. Even though making positional and strategic moves is part of successful deep-money play, you do not want to get yourself too often in situations where you clearly take the worst of it (i.e. where you face an all-in reraise by a short stack and either have to fold there and then or call as a clear dog). This means that you should now pay proper attention if any tight/aggressive players with a short stack have voluntarily entered the pot. If they have, you should often refrain from raising even with your above-average hands, because you do not want to give them an opportunity for a limp/reraise and let them succeed with the simple system that they are using.

♠ Now that you have a stack of more than the maximum buy-in, you will obviously be trying to accumulate as many chips as possible. The goal: To become the biggest stack at the table, or at the very least have enough funds to cover the weak players in your game. Even though a style that leans towards a somewhat loose-aggressive approach is the way to do this, you should not take this concept too far. You should not take any unnecessary risks to reach that goal, or get involved *too* often in situations that are clearly –EV. The fact of the matter is that online things just change very quickly. If a weak player has $4,600 and you have just $2,400, you could feel that you should maybe push things a little to get yourself in a situation where you have as many chips as he does – so that you can break him. However, you should realise that every time you make a –EV play, you are losing money. The nature of the Internet is such that you don't know whether or not the possibility will ever arise to recoup these losses. After all, the player that you are planning to break could be gone in 20 minutes from now, he could go broke by losing his money to someone else – heck, the entire table may break up before you even get a *chance* to go after his stack. So, don't make too many gambling plays now in the hope of maybe gaining a big edge later, unless you are absolutely certain that the person you have labelled as your target will stay in his seat for a very long time.

So, when you are playing deep or very deep money, it is important not to make the mistake that many players make: Only looking at the amounts that they stand to win, while neglecting the amounts of money that they put at risk for this. Also, even more than with short-stack play, it is important that at all times you are aware of the costs of calling versus the potential reward, and the percentage of the time your hand will win against the various types of holdings your opponents could hold. In the 'Hand Match-ups & Analysis' chapter, you will see many examples of one's chances of winning in common situations. Make sure you develop both your analytical and your mathematical skills sufficiently before moving up to deep-money play. If you habitually make some mistakes in short-stack play because you don't know exactly where you are in a hand, you could still be a slight overall winner. But in big-stack play, you will get *creamed*.

## Two specific situations when playing deep money

Anyhow, with these recommendations in mind, let's move on to some specific situations which show how you could get the most out of this deep-money approach, and also the kind of thinking that is required in order to be successful. Included in this analysis are correct countermeasures you should make to the adjustments that your opponents will have made, now that they have noticed the significant changes in your overall strategy. In both situations, you will be in the $10-$20 game mentioned, with a $2,700 stack.

### Situation 1

You are in the $10 small blind. Everybody folds to the button, the person who is your 'target': the exact person you are trying to break. He raises to $70. You hold the 8♥-8♦-5♥-4♦. What do you do?

Well, the answer is quite simple in my view: You fold. Even though you want to get involved with this person that you have labelled as too loose/too weak, when playing deep money you usually want to have position on him before going to battle. Here, your target has position on *you*. In order to call from out of position, you would need not just a hand of some value, you would also need a hand that is *easy to play well*. Even though this 8-8-5-4 double-suited *does* have some value, it is also a hand that is not all that easy to play well after the flop. Quite the contrary: It is a hand that could cause you a lot of problems, for instance because you could be receiving a lot of problem flops that give you a second-best hand or even a second-best draw, or you could end up getting involved in other situations where you don't know where you stand. This carries the danger of winning lots of relatively small pots uncontested (when you successfully check-raise him on the flop to make him lay down), while *losing* every time that the pot becomes big. This may be, for instance, when your target plays back at you and you are too committed to fold now, but also when you check-raise your target and then the big blind check-reraises. In fact, the big blind is the other problem here. Had you been in the big blind against the target's $70 total raise and the small blind had folded, then you could possibly have called, because you would then be closing the betting and be up against just the one person on whom you have a good read. But being in the *small* blind, you also have the big blind still to be heard from, and if he also calls this could lead to you being in a bad spot after the flop.

So, in the case of you being the *small* blind I would say you have an easy fold, while being the *big* blind you could possibly have called. But let's now change the scenario to your target being the *cutoff*, with you on the *button*. If now your target had made this same raise to $70, you would almost certainly have reraised him to $140 or so, in order to shut out the field, and to play him heads-up, in position with a well-disguised holding. So, you would be *reraising* with this hand while in position, having invested nothing yet, while *folding* the exact same hand from the small blind, with some money invested already. Strange, yes – but undoubtedly correct.


### Situation 2

Again, you are in the $10 small blind. There are two limpers with $1,200 stacks, and now the same person as in the previous situation – the one you have labelled as your target – makes a raise, this time to $50. You decide to flat call with the K♠-K♥-8♠-7♦. Why just flat call, you ask – wouldn't reraising be better? Well, there are two reasons for taking the conservative approach here:

1.  In this hand, there are two relatively tight early-position limpers, both with a stack of just $1,200. You know that if you make your standard reraise now, say to about $120, you give them a perfect opportunity to come over the top for more than one-third of their entire stack if they happen to be in there with aces. You don't want to give them this opportunity, because if that happens you will either be forced to fold after having invested $120, or you will call in a situation where you may be a clear dog, with not much in the way of implied odds either. But if you just call now and then one of these players goes for the limp/reraise, they can only make it about $240 or $260 to go – say, just 20% of the money they have in front of them. Especially if your target then calls this raise (as he probably will), you can then take a flop and hope to catch a big hand. You

will also be in decent position here, knowing that if for instance you flop a king, you can simply check to the limp/reraiser, who will certainly bet this hand for you. You will then put your target in the middle, and if he calls, you can surprise him with a well-timed check-raise. Now, while this scenario does not happen often, if it *does* happen it will be so profitable that you are willing to 'gamble' $250 before the flop with a hand that in all likelihood is not currently best. But had you gone for the aggressive approach of reraising to $120, you could very well have raised yourself out of the pot, and you would have turned a potentially profitable situation into an unprofitable one.

2. If you decide to make a pot-sized reraise from out of position (say, more than the $120 mentioned above), you are simply putting a big sign on your head saying 'Guys, I have a big pair'. While this is not so bad if you are almost all-in, it *is* bad when (as in this situation) you still have about $2,500 behind. This will give some clear playing advantages to all of your opponents including your target, simply because they have a good grasp of the texture of your hand whereas you don't know much (if anything) about theirs. To avoid this, it is better not to let the cat out of the bag just yet. In fact, I would not even have reraised the pot here with aces, meaning that I *definitely* won't do it with kings. You are up against three players (the two limpers plus the pre-flop raiser) who all could have aces, and who would be ecstatic if you were stupid enough to make a big reraise with kings here. Usually, you would only make pot-sized reraises with aces, or with rundown hands like J-10-9-8 or 8-7-6-5 double-suited – but not with kings. This is especially true in a situation like this where a) the money is deep, b) you are out of position, and c) you are up against players over whom you have good control, meaning that you don't want to give them the chance to win a big pot in an easy manner.

To cut a long story short, you decide to flat call the $50 raise, the big blind folds and the two limpers call. Pot size: $220. Now the flop comes J♠-5♥-3♠. You have flopped an overpair to the board + king-high flush draw. Not a bone crusher by any means, but definitely a hand that you would like to play against the person you have labelled as too loose, too aggressive, too predictable, too weak. So, a check-raise would seem like the correct play here, right? After all, if everyone checks to the pre-flop raiser, he will almost certainly bet $220. And you can then check-raise to $880 with a hand that could be best, and if not will have a lot of outs to *become* best. Right?

Well, not really. While in general I like to check-raise often, and especially against people whom I know will do the betting for me, in this case there are more factors to consider. In fact, there are two clear reasons why I think that in this situation the check-raise would *not* be the best play:

1. You will have to think about the two other players in the hand, the two initial limpers. These two players are also likely to be bagging the pre-flop raiser. If they catch a good flop, then based on their position in the betting, the pre-flop actions and the relatively small size of their stack, it should not be that hard to see that the check-raise will be the best play by far. And if they have flopped either a set like J-J-x-x or else maybe something like aces + nut flush draw, they could certainly try and take advantage of the button's aggressive tendencies by bagging him. But if they do, they will be bagging you as well! This means that if indeed you go for the check-raise to $880 and then get check/reraised to $1,160 all-in, you will of course have to call – but you would have invested an awful lot of money while having clearly the worst of it. You would probably have either a maximum of ten outs twice (eight flush cards plus two kings, if you are up against a set, and provided all the cards you need are still in the deck) or even just two outs twice (the two kings, if you are up against aces + nut flush draw).[10] Obviously a rather horrible scenario.

2. Your stack is probably just a little too large to make this play. If you check-raise to $880 here and your target calls you, you will still have $1,780 left on the turn – meaning that you are still faced with a very meaningful decision there. This is not what you want when you don't know exactly where you stand, and don't know whether or not you actually want to catch a spade on the turn – a turn where many scare cards are possible. With this type of holding you want to make the critical decision on the flop, with two cards to come, meaning that any turn play becomes 'automatic'. That's why the check-raising play would have been much better with stacks in the region $800-$1,800, not necessarily with the $2,700 that you started the hand with.

So what I would do in this situation is make a very strange play that very few players I know would even *think* of making here. I would opt to *bet through* the

---

[10] Of course, you would have a few more outs than that because of backdoor potential. You could catch things like runner-runner straight, r-r two pair, or r-r trips to improve your situation somewhat. For more info on how bad an overpair + flush draw fares against a higher overpair + bigger flush draw, see the chapter 'Hand Match-ups & Analysis'.

two initial limpers, but not with a standard pot or even half-pot bet, but rather with an unusually *small* bet. I would bet $30 or $40 into them, a bet that will undoubtedly surprise them. After all, lots of players (myself included) become quite confused when a bet comes from a different corner than they had anticipated. If indeed I opt for this strange play and bet small into them, the two initial limpers will probably see this situation as follows:

♠ If they have one of the strong holdings I just mentioned, hands that they would be willing to play for all their money, they won't like this bet of yours one bit. They will fear that if they decide to just call with their strong hand, this bet from a good/dangerous player like you may stop the button from making his 'expected' big bet or raise. And thus, they may fear that if they don't raise now, they could give everyone in the hand practically a free card to outdraw them, for instance by catching a gutshot. This means that if they have a big hand they will fear that their check-raising opportunity could be gone, and they will almost certainly raise the maximum now. If this happens, you will have dodged a bullet because of your clever play. Instead of having invested $1,160 extra in a situation where you are probably a big dog, you will now simply fold and have lost just the $30 or $40.

♠ If they *don't* have a big hand but just something very marginal, they will dislike this little bet of yours just as much. Tight players hate it when they first have to put in money with a marginal holding, and then be forced to fold because of a raise behind them. In view of the fact that they could get sandwiched now that you have bet into them, with the aggressive pre-flop raiser still to act, they will probably fold a rather high number of hands here, rather than first call your bet and then *still* not be certain that they are going to able to see the turn card.

All in all, what you hope to accomplish with this unusual bet is to expose the tight players early in the hand, and make them reveal their true strength before you have invested any serious money. If they fold and then the overaggressive player raises you after all (for instance, because he doesn't take this 'non-bet' of yours seriously), well then you are basically in the exact situation where you wanted to be. You can now reraise the maximum without facing the risk of running into the traps that the tight players have set for you. And yes, of course it *is* possible that your target has finally picked up a big hand as well, and that you are trailing here. But that's just the chance you take. Because he is often aggressive with little, he *could* pick up a big hand every once in a while to take your entire stack. But especially now that you have a two-way hand, you almost certainly aren't taking *that* much the worst of it, even in the unlikely case of being up against a set for instance. So, by making this strange flop bet you are first trying to get rid of the two players you fear – and only once you have got rid of *them*, do you start messing with the person you are *really* after.

'But hey,' you ask. 'Why shouldn't I just bet the pot into the field then, rather than this seemingly silly bet. Wouldn't that work much better?' Well, the answer is: No, it wouldn't. Your real goal is still to induce the late-position player to make a big bet or raise on the flop while holding a hand that does not warrant this aggression. But if you bet full pot, your target will almost certainly take this as proof that you are seriously interested in this pot – meaning that most likely he will only play back at you when he does actually have the goods. With a decent, but not great, hand he may simply call you now. And this is an action that you *don't* want to see, as you will have no clue whatsoever what your opponent could be holding, and also because so many turn cards will look scary to your vulnerable hand. In fact: Only the two remaining kings and the A♠ will give you the nuts; with all other cards, the best play on the turn will not be automatically clear. To avoid this situation, you want to get the money in on the flop, rather than be out of position on all streets with lots of money still to be played. By making this strange small bet that your target may either not take seriously or else read as a stop bet, he may still raise you. And that is exactly what you want – but only *after* you have managed to get rid of the two dangerous players who are likely to be sandbagging.

So, what is this strategy exactly? Well, quite simply: First you eliminate the real threats, then start 'gambling' a bit with the loose guys. This in short could be the exact description of successful deep-money play, and a clear example of how almost all the good big-stack players think. And if you are good enough at this, you will find out that with all this 'gambling' that you do, you will have the best of it surprisingly often – at least 'surprisingly often' in the eyes of your opponents.

# Some final words

That's about it for now regarding the large-stack approach in the big online game. Please note that both this large-stack approach and the big online game will play a prominent role in the chapter 'Practice Hands' – where you can analyse your own knowledge in this respect.

# Chapter Four

# Playing online: Adjusting to shorthanded play

## Introduction

At the time of this writing, I am still making my money playing the $10-$20 online PLO full-ring games: 9 or 10 players maximum. Frankly, that is the way I prefer it, because full-ring games suit my personality fine. I like to be playing in games with relatively little (blind) pressure. This way, I can take my time to either a) wait for a premium hand to get my money in with a clear edge, or b) look for opportunities for a profitable situation to present itself, regardless of whether I have a strong hand or not. But it should be clear that both these situations do not occur all that often. Big hands don't grow on trees. And situations where it is possible to out-play opponents or steal some pots don't come up all that frequently either – especially not for players like me who like to enter very few pots. For me it is nice if I have a little time to wait for these profitable situations. So quite clearly I am very happy with the way things are now: In a situation where I can multi-table the $10-$20 full ring games with relatively little stress, and with not much pressure to have to get involved frequently.

## Impact of the rake

Frankly, I don't expect things to stay that way. Right now, the majority of the smaller PLO games are already 6-max, and I expect that in time almost all the bigger PLO games will become 6-max as well. Even though the rake has a bigger impact in short-handed games, it seems that most players don't care much about that, and at the higher stakes people *especially* don't care about that.[1] But in short games, the rake *does* become an issue, because most sites take up to 5%/$2 maximum, and some even take more than that. This despite the fact that there are just six players or even less in the game. Let's assume a five-handed game on average (there is always someone sitting out, right, or someone who is not back in time, or is all-in, etc.), with about 50 raked hands per hour x two dollars. This means $100 per hour leaves the table – or $20 per player. This would be $40 per 100 hands, equalling no less than two big blinds per 100 hands. Now, even though a good player will make *much* more than that, it shows that even in this big game the rake *is* an issue. This is even more so because in shorthanded play, as opposed to full-ring, you cannot afford to keep waiting and waiting for very long. This means that in short games, you will often be forced to play:

♠ More hands (and this equals paying more rake).

♠ In heads-up situations, rather than in the multiway pots that sometimes occur in full-ring games. Heads-up means less dead money, and it also means risking more money to win the same or even less than in multiway pots.[2] This leads to a proportionally higher rake, now that the rake is divided among fewer players than before.

♠ With a smaller edge than in full-ring games – maybe not in the long run, but definitely in individual hands. After all, in short games you cannot afford to keep waiting for aces, or else you will be blinded to death. So quite often you will and should be involved with hands that are not much better than your opponent's. You may still have an edge because sometimes you *play* your hands better, but based strictly on hand values you often don't have much edge – if any. And in situations where your edge is smaller than usual, a bigger impact of the rake certainly doesn't help.

Having said that, even with this slightly higher impact of the rake, one can still make an awful lot of money in shorthanded games, obviously. This is especially true if you are playing against weak and/or predictable players. You will now have many more opportunities to butt heads with them than in full-ring games, where you would often need a very good hand before going to battle, and where a higher percentage of the pots ends up in a showdown. But because in shorthanded games there will be many opportunities for you to outplay your opponents, your results in shorthanded games should actually be *better* than in full-ring games, not worse.

---

[1] There is still a common belief among high-stakes gamblers that a) bad players pay the rake anyway, and b) the rake is negligible in relation to the size of the pot.

[2] Of course, you would also have a better chance of winning the pot.

# Changes in stack size/buy-in strategies

As should be clear by now, in pot-limit Omaha I often buy in for the minimum, waiting for an opportunity to get the money in while holding a good or even premium hand. This could be in a heads-up situation where I hold aces or kings against just one player, but it could also be a multiway pot where I am 'gambling' by moving in with a nice double-suited hand. It should be clear though that in 6-max games this minimum buy-in strategy is much less effective, provided we are talking about a game where the minimum buy-in is just 20 big blinds. (Some sites have a minimum buy-in of 40 or even 50 big blinds.) Assuming again a 6-max $10-$20 game with an average of five players, you will pay $6 per hand on average as a blind bet. This means that if you buy in for $400 and you don't find any hands good enough to move in with, your stack will be down to just $340 or even less after only 10 hands. This means that if you double up on the 11th hand, you will probably have about $700 or so. Despite the fact that you have doubled, you have *not* doubled your stack compared to your initial starting amount. And probably, on that 11th hand you weren't even much of a favourite either – simply because in Omaha it is hard for *any* hand other than aces to be more than just a 3-to-2 favourite against a random hand.

Now obviously, this is not the optimal way to play in 6-max games. Therefore, if I cannot count on my 'safe haven' of a full game, I will adjust my usual buy-in strategies in the following two ways:

1.  If I get a seat to an overaggressive player's immediate right, I will again buy in for less than the maximum, with the same goals as before: hoping to trap the person to my left by limp/reraising before the flop, and check-raising afterwards. However, in this case I will *not* buy in for the minimum $400, but rather anywhere from $700 to $900. If the person to my left often makes *small* bets and raises, then I will buy in for about $700. However, if he has the common habit of making many large and/or pot-sized bets and raises, then I will buy in for $900. The goal is always the same: Hoping to get as much money into the middle as possible, with one difference compared to the full-ring situation. In full-ring games, any limp/reraising that I do will almost always be with big pairs or premium high cards, situations where I almost certainly have the current best hand and thus would like to be all-in before the flop is dealt.

    But in shorthanded play, things are a bit different. Here, you don't have many multiway pots and thus you don't get protection as often as in full-ring games, meaning that there is a bit less value in going all-in early. What's more, in a shorthanded setting with fairly short money, your limp/reraises will often be done on much lighter values now. In fact, if the person to your left is overaggressive enough, even hands as weak as 10♠-10♥-8♠-7♣ and A♠-10♥-9♦-6♠ may be good enough for you to go for a limp/reraise. However, because in this situation you cannot expect your edge to be this large if both of you get to see all five cards, you hope that you will have just enough room for one pot-sized bet on the flop. Because you are *representing* aces, your opponent could now fold many hands on the flop that he *would* be correct in calling with had he known your actual holding.

Let's say for example that you limp, your loose/aggressive opponent raises with A-Q-J-7 single-suited, everyone else folds, and then you reraise to $300 total with your opponent calling. We'll assume that you have either one of the hands mentioned above, the 10♠-10♥-8♠-7♣ or A♠-10♥-9♦-6♠, and the flop now comes 7-2-2 rainbow. Had you been playing just a $600 or even $400 stack then your opponent would have a rather automatic call, even if by chance he *does* give you credit for a big hand. But if instead you are playing the $900 stack that I recommend, you would have just enough room for one pot-sized bet of $600. This bet would almost certainly be just big enough to make your opponent fold, when either he had the proper odds to call but didn't know it, or even had the current best hand but didn't know it. Because in shorthanded play you will *represent* hands more often than you do in full-ring games, you will have to make certain that you adjust the size of your buy-in for this specific purpose. In other words: If you know that your game plan for 6-max games consists – at least for *some* part – of making power plays every once in a while, then you should ensure that you will have some ammunition left to bet after the flop. This is also true in situations where you decide to buy-in for less than the maximum – meaning that if you follow my guidelines, you will almost never start with a minimum $400 buy-in.

2. Just as in full-ring games, you should often adjust the size of your buy-in to your relative position at the table. For instance, if seated to your left are one or two tight players with little money, and to your right one or two weak or predictable players with a big stack, well then it should be quite obvious that this is a situation that calls for a *maximum* buy-in. Especially because we are now in a fairly short game, we are now getting nearer to what I would call 'real poker', rather than the 'showdown poker' that has helped me make so much money. What you are doing now is *not* just waiting to get all your

money in on those occasions where either you have an edge or the probable best hand. No, you are actively trying to find situations where you can go after the weak players' entire stacks, *even when your own cards are not that good*. You should actively be looking to isolate the weak players by making strategic bets and raises, for instance from the cutoff – hoping that you can get rid of the button and thus will have the best position throughout the hand.

Now that you have bought in for the maximum (instead of the $700-$900 that I recommended earlier or the $400 that should be often used for full-ring games), you should change your strategies drastically. You are no longer focused on the short-stack concept of 'play for your entire stack or don't play at all'. No, you start doing the exact opposite now. Instead of waiting patiently for a good hand, you are now pounding on the weak players, hoping to win many small and medium pots uncontested. Note that your 'targets' are *not* limited to just the overaggressive players anymore: They now also include weak-tight players, or simply those players over whom you have good control and that you can read very well. Here's an example of how to play profitably in these situations. A weak player limps for $20, you raise to $70 from the cutoff, and everybody folds to the weak player, who calls. On the flop the weak player checks, and you bet half pot. Your opponent folds and you now pick up a pot regardless of the quality of your starting hand, and regardless whether the flop has actually helped you or not. Keep in mind that your goal is *not* just winning many of these small or medium pots uncontested. Your goal is *also*, and perhaps even more importantly, to work towards the climax of breaking the weak player in one big pot.

What do I mean by this – and how could these two seemingly conflicting goals be combined into one proper strategy? The answer is this: You know that if you keep pounding on the weak players long enough, at some point they are going to become fed up with the fact that you are always taking control, and just keep on taking the pots away from them. You know that at some point, they are going to play back at you. Now, if your timing is right, you will have this one big hand (either before the flop, on the flop or even on the later streets) exactly at the time that they decide to take a stand – and you will be able to take their entire stacks there and then. So, if things work as planned, you will have won many small pots while holding absolutely nothing, to pave the way for that one big pot where you *do* have the goods – and are able to break your opponents, who have decided to make a stand right at that point. Quite frankly, this is exactly the way some of the best PLO players in the world play. And if they happen to pick up that one big hand exactly when their opponents don't believe them anymore, these players are always called lucky. But beating the game in this manner has nothing to do with luck. It has to do with getting yourself in a situation where you have manipulated your opponents' thoughts in such a way, that your opponents think you are just a maniac who is *always* betting and raising with nothing – only to find out too late that those times when all the money goes in, you are loaded for bear.

# Dangers of the big-stack approach

Of course, this is the way you *want* to play with a big stack. But naturally things are not always this easy. A few clear dangers of the big-stack approach include:

## Danger no. 1: The swings

The nature of Omaha is such that even in the extremely big pots you will often see a lot of 60-40, 55-45 and even 50-50 situations. For instance, if you have a set and your opponent has a pair + wrap + flush draw (or the other way around, with your *opponent* having the set), then it is quite likely that all the money is going into the middle when no one has a really big edge. This means that in a situation where you are trying to bust a weak player, it is also possible that *you* will be the one who gets busted. And if by chance the two of you both have over $3,000 or even $4,000 in front of you, this could mean that it is actually the *weak* player who ends up with this massive pot. Heck, he could even leave right after that pot, taking *your* money to another table! So it should be clear that unlike in no-limit hold'em, where it is often somewhat easier to put yourself in situations where you have a big edge, PLO will have quite a few situations where you don't have that much of an edge. This is especially true in situations where the draws have not yet been completed – and quite obviously, those are the situations where monster pots are most likely to occur. So you would need a fairly large bankroll and quite a bit of stamina to withstand the swings that are part and parcel of PLO. And those who think that in shorthanded situations where you often play this big-stack approach, they could get away with a bankroll of just $30,000 or so, these players will have to be either very good or – more likely – very lucky *not* to end up on the rail.

## Danger no. 2: Not adapting well to the effect that your game will have on the other players' mindsets

With shorthanded big-stack play, it is *extremely* important to pay attention to the atmosphere at the table and to your opponents' states of mind. Because you are so busy now running over the table, isolating people etc., this may start to irritate the other players. It may start to irritate not just the weak players that you are trying to isolate them all the time, but also the players to your left who hardly ever get to see any cheap flops, who are always raised off their button, etc. This means that at some point, they may decide to take a stand and come over the top of yet another one of your raises. *Don't automatically think that you are up against a big hand in a situation like this: Your opponent may simply be fed up with you.*

Here is an example. I have raised from the cutoff on four consecutive occasions, in all cases making it $90 to go. All these times, I succeeded in making the button fold, and in isolating the weak player. Now, the fifth consecutive time this weak player again limps, and again I make it $90 to go. My hand: Q♠-Q♥-9♥-8♣. This time, the button comes over the top with a reraise to $320. Everybody folds, and it is up to me, playing a $2,200 stack. Well, in this case, most people would reason: 'I have only queens and face a pot-sized reraise, in a fairly deep-money situation, up against a player whom until now has always folded to my raises. So I must be up against a bigger hand here. And being out of position with fairly big cards, I don't have any implied odds either, making my hand a clear fold.' While most players would reason like this, in reality the situation is almost certainly quite different. In fact, the button is probably thinking: 'This *schmuck* keeps raising me off my button with garbage all the time. I cannot let him succeed in doing this every time, so I am simply going to fight fire with fire here. The first time I get just the *semblance* of a decent hand, I will simply reraise him the pot to put him to the test there and then. Then we will see how hot he *really* is.' If you judge it likely that your opponent is in this exact frame of mind, there is just one way to play your hand here: reraise the pot once more. Then, if your read is correct and you indeed have the best hand, you could win the pot there and then – netting you $370 without even needing to see a flop. Or you could get called by a hand that is either a slight or a big dog to yours. For instance, the times that you will get called by hands like J-10-9-7 and Q-J-9-8 (hands that are massive dogs to your hand) more than make up for those times where you have misjudged the situation and *are* up against aces or kings. And if indeed you get called by a worse hand, you will have put yourself in a highly profitable situation with a hand that is not really *that* good – but simply because you have analysed the psychology of the situation well.

## Danger no. 3: The problems you face because of bigger stacks than yours that may be out there

While all the time we are talking about 'big-stack' play here, the fact remains that even your $2,000 maximum buy-in does not automatically need to qualify as 'big'. One or two of the weak players whom you are eager to break may already have stacks of $4,000, $6,000, yes even $8,000. And unlike B&M play, in online games you can't reach into your pocket to take out as much money as you want in order to cover them. Yet your goal *is* to go after their entire stacks and break them. In this situation, quite a few good players take a few more chances than usual in order to accumulate chips, to build their stack to about the same level as the stacks of the weak players. While I reason a bit like that myself, it should be clear that this situation carries quite a high degree of risk. Because even if we manage to complete phase one successfully (building our stacks enough so that we can cover our 'targets'), we still have phase two to complete. And the following things can go wrong here:

♠ In online games things can go very fast. Unlike B&M play where you can often make an educated guess, online you almost never know how long people are intending to stay. For one thing, the weak player with the big stack may reason: 'I have just won quite a few pots by getting lucky. No need to push my luck here. I am simply going to hit and run.' Or he may decide to stay until 'the tide turns'. This means that by the time that *you* have built your stack, where strictly speaking you had taken way too many chances, *he* may have left the table already. What this means is that as a result, you will simply have made too many –EV decisions (a clear downside), while the upside of these decisions does not even exist: Your target has already left the table before you have even had the *chance* to take his entire stack.

♠ At high-stakes play, and especially at *shorthanded* high-stakes play, tables often consist of quite a few good and knowledgeable, winning players, and just one or two weak players whose money they are after. If a table has just one or two soft spots and exactly those players decide to sit out for a while, some of the good players may follow suit by sitting out as well, waiting for the contributors to return. Usually the end result will be that you either continue to play heads-up against a strong player in order to keep the game alive (which, if you are not that good at heads-up play yourself, could prove to be a *very* costly decision), or else the table will simply get broken. Now if you just have been 'gambling' a little too much in order to be able to cover these weak spots, but then the table is broken, this will be a horrible result for you. This is even more true because at any other table you will now go to, you can only start with your initial starting amount again, $2,000, not with the entire stack that you may have built.

What you want is to build a big stack and have this table last for a very long time, so that at all times (barring unusual and unwanted developments) *you* will be the one who covers the table. But because of the fast-changing nature of Internet games, this strategy has some clear drawbacks as well. This means that you should usually try to increase your stack size *only* by making +EV decisions, and that the concept of 'taking a few chances now in order to reap the benefits later' does not have all that much going for it.

# Some final words

Fortunately for me, there are still enough full-ring games available right now for the stakes that I like to play. But at the lower stakes, where many PLO games are 6-max, I have already put these strategies I have just described into practice, and in a pretty successful manner. This way, I know that once this 6-max virus has found its way into the bigger games too, I will be well prepared to cope with these changes. And probably just as importantly, I may be able to surprise my regular opponents by using some strategies that they have never seen me use before. Not because I didn't *know* how to use them – but because there were always better strategies available, and thus there was no *need* for me to use them.

# Chapter Five

# Classic articles

## Introduction

Over the years, I have written many articles about pot-limit Omaha that are still of decent, yes sometimes even good quality. Many of them appeared in the now defunct *Poker Digest* magazine, and have therefore been unavailable to the public for quite some time. A while ago, I put them back in the spotlight through my own site www.rolfslotboom.com, and in no time, they became the most requested feature there. Now, especially for this book, I have re-edited these articles, making them not just a valuable but rather a necessary addition to the text in this book. I have rewritten entire passages and have added lots of text, so that every recommendation resembles the game plan and the strategies that I recommend throughout this book. Please note that even though they are re-edited, these articles all originate from the period 2000-2003, which means that they discuss times and situations where some things are sometimes be quite different from the way they are now. Enjoy!

## Specific aspects of pot-limit Omaha

### Aspect No. 1: The impact of bluffing

In pot-limit Omaha a lot more bluffing is possible than in most other types of games or betting structures, but it's still more of a *semi*-bluffing than a bluffing game. In this game it's often the big draw that becomes aggressive on the flop, rather than the made hand. (In fact, if the flop comes J♥-9♦-3♥ and the J-9-x-x faces a huge bet by K♥-Q♦-10♦-8♥ and then the bettor shows his hand to him[1], the J-9 is going to fold without a shred of doubt even though *he* has top two pair and the bettor only king-high.) Because draws can be so powerful in this game, playing like this is barely even regarded as semi-bluffing anymore, let alone bluffing. Bluffing on the river is possible every now and then, although in the big pots one or all of the players involved will be all-in on the flop or turn most of the time, and decisions are therefore made early in the hand rather than at the river. If the money is deep, a big bluff on the river is possible however, even if you suspect that your opponent has a very good hand.

## Example 1

Flop K♥-10♣-3♥, your opponent bets the pot, you (in early position) check/call with A♥-J♥-x-x. Turn: J♦. You figure your opponent for a very good hand – top set, three kings – but decide to represent the nut straight you might very well have – after all, you must be in there with something to call a pot-sized bet on the flop, right? – and bet the pot. After some hesitation, your opponent calls. If the board rags on the river, a good-sized bet might very well win the pot for you – despite the fact that you are obviously up against a very good hand, top set. But every time the nuts need not be out there, your bluff could have a good or even very good chance of success, especially if you are known as a tight, solid player who is not out of line very often.

## Example 2

Another example of a bluff that might very well work in pot-limit Omaha is the 'bare-ace play'. The flop comes three of a suit (or even better, two of a suit, you bet, get called and on the turn comes the third card of that suit). If you have the lone ace of that suit you might be able to win the pot on a pure bluff because in this game people know better than to call with a non-nut flush. (You, of course, should know which players *are* and which players *aren't* capable of folding the king-high flush). Don't overdo this play, however, and better still don't let people even *think* you know of its existence. This play works best when you've also got a set or two pair in addition to your lone ace. Then, if someone decides to call you down with a non-nut flush, you could still be able to win the pot by improving to a full. In fact, you would be semi-bluffing here, rather than bluffing.

---

[1] Assuming deep money and relatively little dead money. If the J-9-x-x has made a bet already, if there is any dead money in the pot or if the money is not that deep, then folding could be a mistake, obviously. In that case, it could be better to simply flat call the flop bet (rather than fold or raise) and wait for a safe turn card before committing fully. What this example shows though is that a premium draw can be a clear favourite against even a hand as strong as top two – and *all* good PLO players know this. For example, with this premium draw up against the J♠-9♠-5♣-2♣, the draw would be no less than a 68.54-31.46% favourite. Now, I bet very few of you would have thought the difference was *this* huge.

### Some words of caution

A few words of caution are necessary here. First, you should always be aware of your and your opponents' stack sizes. If some of them – or you yourself – are playing short money and are about to go all-in, no one is going to fold a decent, but possibly second-best made hand, and you're basically giving away your money. Also, you've got to be a hell of a guy, a real strong character, to pull off a big bluff on the river. It can be tough for you when you try to bet your opponent off his great-but-non-nut hand, and he starts staring you down for a long time, trying to figure out if you *are* strong or are in fact only *representing* strength.

## Aspect No. 2: The power of draws

Pot-limit Omaha is the ultimate drawing game. If the flop is K♥-10♥-2♦, you have A♠-A♥-Q♥-J♦ and your opponent, holding K-10-x-x, figures you for the hand you have, then he is going to fold the current best hand without a shred of doubt. That's right: *you* have only one pair of aces (plus a premium straight – and flush draw) whereas *he* has top two for the current best hand – yet he's still going to pass. In Omaha, the draw is king. On the flop, the drawing hand can be a (slight) favourite over the temporary nuts, even when the nuts is as strong as top set or a made straight. Draws can and should often be played aggressively, especially if you suspect that there is no set out there.

### Straight draws

Still, don't overestimate the power of straight draws, because they sometimes look better than they really are. Someone may have the same straight draw as you (so you might make your hand and have to split the pot – heck, if someone has a bigger / higher straight draw, you might even make your hand only to find out that it is second-best) or a flush may be completed on the turn or river (so you could make your hand but still lose).

### More key aspects with regards drawing hands

- ♠ Pot-limit Omaha is a game of implied odds, where your decisions on the flop and turn should be dictated by opportunities and potential profits on the later street(s). You've got to know exactly where you stand in the hand, and you've got to know exactly what you have to beat, since this will decide which strategy is best (push or pull).

- ♠ If you're relatively new to the game, be very careful about drawing hands that may be second best if you make them. The king-high flush is a hand that can in fact be very profitable, if you know how to play it; if the novice player gets any action when holding this hand, he will most likely lose his entire stack.

♠ In Omaha it's important to know *exactly* how many outs you have. (For example, if your opponent has a set and you've got the nut flush draw, you usually have eight outs, not nine. And on top of that, your opponent could hit a redraw on the river even if you make your draw on the turn. That is: Completing your draw is not the same as winning the hand.) Only if you are able to calculate your outs quickly and without mistakes, and of course if you are able to read your opponent's hand well, is it possible to know for sure if you belong in the pot or not.

♠ Make sure you've got good computer software available to you, so that you can simulate interesting hands that have occurred. This will help you to get better at calculating your drawing odds, and in time will play a better game overall. The calculations in this book are done through www.twodimes.net, but there is also a useful odds calculator at www.cardplayer.com, and Wilson's software programs have excellent simulation tools as well.

## Aspect No. 3: The importance of position

Position is one of the most important, yet one of the least understood aspects in poker. A lot of players don't even think about their position relative to the button; they think about their cards only and don't adjust their decisions (whether/how to play) to their position in the betting. Another group of players talk about position all the time; they play hands 'because they are on the button', they bet 'because they always bet when they are last to act' or make remarks like: 'I don't play cards. I play position.' The first group of players doesn't make the adjustments necessary to become a winning player and is often easy to play against. The second group seems to focus on one aspect of the game only and tends to forget that (especially in limit poker, but also in pot-limit games – especially PLO games with relatively shallow money) card selection might be even more important, because most of the time you're going to have to show the best hand to win the pot.

Nevertheless, position is a very important factor in poker. Both hold'em and Omaha are positional games: the closer you are to the button, the better. You might occasionally play hands that are slightly below your usual standards. You might decide to become a little bit more aggressive with your hand because you're last to act or try to steal a pot because of the weakness the other players have shown by checking. However, if you overdo this you'll find your edge might decrease instead of increase. People might start check-raising you because they know you are going to bet whenever it's been checked to you; in fact, even tight, solid players like myself are going to (semi-)bluff check-raise you (and the other opponents) out of the pot.

## Position in pot-limit Omaha

In pot-limit Omaha, compared to limit and maybe even pot-limit hold'em, position is of paramount importance. Because in PLO so many turn or river cards may cripple your hand, people are reluctant to give free cards. Therefore, if it's been checked to you, the odds are against anybody being in there with a real hand, and a good-sized bet usually has a good chance of winning the pot right away. Even if people suspect that you are stealing, they still tend to give up the hand. Pot-limit players don't like to battle for small pots with less than premium hands, even if they believe that the bettor doesn't need to have a premium hand either. Often the person who makes the first bet is able to pick up the pot, and therefore it might just as well be you who does the grabbing here. But once again, be careful that you don't overdo it. If you try to pick up pots too often when the action gets checked to you, people might start check-raising you with hands that they would fold against other people. If you bet a marginal hand in late position that you will have to give up against a check-raise (for example, an open-ended straight draw when there's a two-flush on the board), then it might be better not to bet at all, since you can just check it back and perhaps make your hand for free. In fact, if you get check-raised here, you are losing money on a hand you actually could have made some money with.

## Position and aggression

In general, I like to play for the big pots in Omaha. If there has been no raise before the flop and the hand gets checked to me, I often check my marginal hands back. I don't want people to think I'm trying to pick up pots all the time. If on the other hand the pot *has* been raised before the flop and the money is deep, I might become very aggressive when I'm in position and I suspect that there are no great hands like top set or some kind of monster draw out there. I try to use my tight image to represent the temporary nuts (most often top set) and if someone decides to play back at me, all the money is going into the middle. If I get called, I will almost certainly have a lot of outs regardless of what my opponent has. (In Omaha, you hardly ever bet or raise without having outs because people may be in there with all kinds of hands, and therefore the likelihood of getting called is high.) If you bet or raise on the flop with a fine draw like a wraparound straight and/or a big flush draw and your bet gets called, then it's up to you whether or not to bet the turn as well. Against most players I have the tendency to keep putting as much pressure on them as possible if I think they're in there with something like top two pair or a small set, to try to make them fold their hands. If the player is unlikely to fold even after a second pot-sized bet (either because he's a really bad player or simply because he doesn't respect my play), then I will just check it back and try to make my hand for free.[2]

---

[2] This example shows the importance of position in pot-limit poker. Against a player who doesn't respect you, you could simply take a free card on the turn when you have position on him – so you could

One more thing: While in general you can become more aggressive with your hand the closer you are to the button, sometimes the opposite is also true. If you flop a very good draw in early position, you might decide to go all-in on the flop by check-raising or betting out yourself, whereas you would have just called a bet (rather than go all-in) in late position. The reasoning is this. By check-raising all-in from early position, you try to get maximum value out of your hand. If you just check-call a bet when you're out of position and then you make your hand on the turn, the original bettor might fold if you come out betting and if you check, he might simply check it back. But if you are last to act, the original bettor will most of the time be forced to pay you off anyway, since he may feel his check could have induced some kind of bluff. So you may make just as much money here as in the check-raise all-in from early position situation – but you could *lose* less in case of an unfavourable turn.

### Some final words on position

Your position in the betting is always an important consideration in poker. Still, you shouldn't make decisions based on position alone but use your position in combination with all the other important factors: Is the opposition likely to be weak? What do I think I'll have to beat? If I bet will they suspect me of stealing? Does the board make it likely for someone to be checking a monster? Are there any habitual check-raisers anyway? Etc. If you are able to combine all those factors with your position in the betting process[3], then you should be able to make (or save) a lot of money, just because you're last to act.

# A few pot-limit Omaha starting hands

In my first ever article, *'About pot-limit play and table image'*, I gave a few general

---

make your draw on the river and possibly break him *then*. But if you are out of position, then you are probably not going to reach the river, simply because you cannot give yourself any free cards here. If you check on the turn, or even if you bet small, your opponent may read you for being on a draw – meaning that he is probably going to bet or raise you off your hand.

[3] In pot-limit poker, there is also another important positional consideration besides position in the betting process and that is position on the pre-flop raiser. If there has been a late-position raise and you are on the button, your position is in fact rather vulnerable. People might check their good hands to the raiser on the flop, expecting him to bet (which, even in Omaha, will happen quite often) and thereby bag you as well. If the pre-flop raiser *doesn't* bet, it is by no means certain that a bet by you will win the pot because someone might be lurking in the bushes. On the other hand, if you're on the big blind and there has been an under-the-gun raise, your position may not be as bad as it seems. When the flop is favourable, you just check and if the pre-flop raiser bets, you might be able to bag the entire field, or induce some kind of (semi-)bluff by someone who is trying to pick up the pot because there has been no action yet.

guidelines about how to approach most pot-limit Omaha games.[4] I will now discuss some of the most profitable specific starting hands in this game and a few suggestions about whether and how to play them. When reading this, keep in mind that in pot-limit mixing up your play is *very* important. Some of the easiest opponents to beat are the ones who play in predictable patterns, so you should fight this tendency in yourself. Some basic knowledge about the value of Omaha hands is assumed for this article. If you are not sure about your hand selection, even in limit Omaha where a few more hands can and should be played, I suggest reading Bob Ciaffone's '*Omaha Hold'em Poker*' or taking a closer look at Michael Cappelletti's point count system. (I also suggest using Wilson's software on Omaha poker for that matter.) That being said, let's take a look at some Omaha starting hands and how to play them, before and after the flop.

### Big pairs (aces or K-K-A)

A few pot-limit Omaha players use the simple system of raising the pot every time they get aces, regardless of their other two cards, their position or the size of their stack. More experienced players often limp in with aces, trying to reraise some pre-flop raiser in order to win the pot before the flop or to make it a heads-up contest, thus maximising their chances of winning. In the first case, the players doing this basically reveal their hands to everybody and therefore will not get any action after the flop unless they're beat. In the second case, most players don't pay enough attention to their (and their opponent's) stack size. If the reraise leaves the players with, let's say, 85-90% of their stacks left, the implied odds for the caller will be huge, since he knows what he needs to hit to beat the reraiser, whereas the reraiser only knows his own hand but nothing about his opponent's. The pre-flop caller may flop the nuts or close to it with the aces (or kings) unknowingly paying him off, or the big pair may be (semi-)bluffed out of the pot because of the texture of the board. Therefore, the 'reraise-the-raiser' strategy is useful only if you can get your opponent all-in or close to it, that is if there's only enough money left for just one bet on the flop.[5]

---

[4] This article is available in edited form at www.cardplayer.com, as part of the article '*A hard day at the office*'.

[5] For this strategy you don't necessarily need aces. Against an overaggressive opponent – beware of limpers – kings or even queens with suits and/or an ace may also do. (The ace being very important, because most players will give you credit for three aces when an ace flops and fold their – made – hands, but if they decide to try to make some kind of draw against you, you'll still have a pair of aces with a good kicker). In fact, you might even try this play with four double-suited high cards if the situation is right. However, keep in mind that if you hold a K-K-A-x type of holding, you need to be *very* certain you are not up against aces before coming over the top. Because if by chance you *are* up against someone with A-A-x-x, then you are in one of the most unprofitable situations there is in Omaha. You will not be just trailing a little – no, you will be a huge dog.

## Two-pair hands

Two-pair hands are more valuable with the pairs being close in rank, for example Q-Q-J-J as opposed to Q-Q-7-7. However, under most circumstances this second hand is certainly playable (being in position adds some value, as does being suited). I will sometimes raise before the flop with these types of holdings. Heck, I might even call a reraise with them if the reraiser is somewhat predictable (and therefore marked with aces) and the money is deep, trying to flop a set and take his entire stack. The reason I play these hands in raised pots is that whenever I flop a set I want to be able to protect it when a straight or flush draw flops, so that I can gain control over the hand. However, if the flop doesn't help me and may have in fact helped others, I will almost always just give the hand up. Always keep in mind the *reasons* for playing a hand or not: a K-K-10-10 hand is virtually always playable, hands like 7-7-3-3 almost never. Remember, this is pot-limit Omaha where you *don't* want to make bottom or even middle set, especially not if the money is very deep.

Also, you should be aware that in general you should not become *too* aggressive before the flop with hands like Q-Q-7-7. Yes, a small raise could be OK, but if your raise is *too* large, you may be opening yourself up for a reraise that (if the money is relatively shallow) you cannot call.[6] So, you should know why you are raising here: To create a multiway volume pot so that you could win a big pot if you happen to catch a lucky flop.

## Rundown hands

Four connected cards (preferably, but not necessarily, suited), when played under the right circumstances, can be a very profitable starting hand. The goal with these hands is to flop a big wrap most of the time, or something like pair + wrap or two pair + open-ender. (Position is very important here; big draws in position make *a lot more* money than when out of position.) If your starting hand is a quality one like Q-J-10-9, this means that when the flop is favourable, you will have a two-way hand (for example, two pair + straight draw) or even a three-way hand (if you flopped a flush draw also). Big draws can and should often be played aggressively after the flop, depending on what you think you have to beat. (And even then, if you are up against a quality made hand like top set, the draw often has a lot of value and could even be a small favourite).

---

[6] The same goes for making a small raise after a group of limpers. If any one of the limpers is playing relatively shallow money, you should refrain from making this raise, because you are opening yourself up to a limp/reraise from someone with aces. Let's say that *you* are the one playing shallow money here, holding Q-Q-7-7 after a bunch of limpers with a fairly short / medium stack: In that case you should either flat call (if you suspect someone has aces) or raise the maximum (if you think your hand is probably best), but *not* make a mini-raise that accomplishes nothing – and that could very well lead to you raising yourself out of the pot.

I like to play the smaller rundowns also – once again, especially in position. I even raise with them pre-flop occasionally, as I might get paid off very well in case I flop something good – simply because opponents may figure me for big cards rather than the relatively small ones that I actually have. By doing this I try to mix up my play and add some deception into my game. There are a few players who just love to play these hands, also – and especially – against someone who is marked with aces. They might call *very* large raises with them, being only a 3-to-2 dog most of the time. These plays can be dangerous, however, especially if the aces are quality (double-suited) aces *and* simply because there are still two unknown cards in the raiser's hand.

Rundown hands may be some of the most profitable hands in pot-limit Omaha, *if* you know how to play them, and provided that the circumstances are right:

- ♠ Out of position these hands – especially the small rundown hands – can prove very costly: whenever you miss your draw on the turn your opponent may charge you, and whenever you hit he might release. Your best option, when out of position, may therefore be to try to go all-in on the flop, which gives you better odds than waiting for the turn. However you usually have no chance of winning the pot *without* making your hand (by semi-bluffing your opponent out of the pot on the turn, or even bluffing him out on the river). This is simply because your all-in (check-)raise semi-bluff on the flop is likely to be called now that there are still two cards to come – and even more so if your stack is not all that big.

- ♠ A hand like 9-8-7-6 is a lot better than 10-8-7-5, although to many players they seem almost the same and they will therefore play them the same way. Always take a close look at where (if any) the gaps in your hand are. A hand like J-10-9-7 is *much* better than a J-9-8-7. In the first case you'd be delighted to see an eight flop, because you would have hit the key card to your hand. But in the second case a ten won't thrill you as much, since higher straight draws might be possible, and thus any straights that you make now may not be the nuts.

- ♠ A hand like A-K-Q-J may seem like a monster, but it isn't much of a hand if pre-flop action suggests someone might have A-A or if a few tight players have indicated strength.

### Some final words

In pot-limit Omaha starting hands, a suited ace or a big pair is worth a lot, of course, but with nothing else to go with it these hands are hardly ever profitable. A hand like A♥-7♥-9-8 is a lot better than A♥-7♥-Q-3, because of the possibility of flopping a flush *and* straight draw. A hand like Q-Q-K-J is much better than Q-Q-K-7, because whenever you flop a set in the first case you might flop a straight draw also (plus some of the cards your opponents may need to beat you are in your hand), whereas in the second case you will just have the set. In some of his books T.J. Cloutier warns against playing 'dangler' hands, three cards that fit together plus one that does not. Whenever you start playing for higher stakes, you'll see it's often the *extra outs* that make hands profitable; it takes a very good player to turn a less than average hand into a money maker. Therefore, if you pick up this beautiful game, selecting only the quality hands we've discussed here might not be such a bad idea. This will mean that you avoid the trap hands, because that's what they will most likely be to you: traps.

# The importance of playing quality hands

People who have played with me know that I play very tight in just about every poker game. When I started out many years ago (playing limit hold'em) my play could have even be labelled *extremely* tight. Only in time, once my knowledge of the game and judgment of various situations improved, did I start adding a few extra hands to my starting requirements, learnt how to steal an occasional pot, and also discovered how to play my *opponent's* hand rather than my own.

Nowadays, I play mostly pot-limit Omaha, a beautiful and exciting, but also extremely complicated game. Unlike limit hold'em, where patience is rewarded and tight/aggressive players take the money, some of the best PLO players play rather loose. They play lots of hands and like to pump up the pot before the flop, using their (expert) judgment later on – when there's a lot of money in the pot already and their decisions therefore really matter – as to whether or not (and how) to continue with the hand. People who have played with me know that I'm as aggressive as anyone in this game, and that whenever I think my hand is good or my opponents might be weak all the money's going into the middle; still I'm considered to be one of the tightest players around because I fold so many hands before the flop. It takes a lot of discipline to keep folding hand after hand, especially when you know you might be able to outplay your opponents after the flop and therefore lowering your starting requirements a little might seem like a good idea. It is my opinion, however, that in pot-limit Omaha too (where it may often seem like it's all just luck, because you'll see people come in with the strangest holdings to win huge pots) waiting patiently for a good hand will be rewarded, *if* you know how to play well after the flop. Let's take a look at two flops and how the quality of your starting hand can be of influence in making the correct decisions later on, and how extra outs (redraws) can be very important when both you and your opponent have flopped the same hand.

# Flop A: 9♥-8♦-2♠

### Hand #1: 9♠-8♥-4♦-4♣

If you hold Hand #1, you have flopped top two pair, always a dangerous holding in pot-limit Omaha. Against this particular board, your hand is extremely vulnerable. If both you and your opponents have a lot of money in front of you, it's unlikely you will win a big pot with this hand; if the pot gets big (that is, you get a lot of action) there will be so many draws out against you that it is unlikely your hand will hold up. Almost every possible turn card will be dangerous to your hand, assuming it's still good now. Any Q, J, T, 7, 6 or 5 might make someone a straight, and every ace or king might give someone a higher two pair or even a set; only the remaining nines, eights, fours, threes and deuces can be considered 'safe' cards to your hand (although the fours, threes and deuces might also create a backdoor flush draw for your opponents, in addition to the draws they already hold). And if in fact your hand is *not* good on the flop when you think it is, well then you're in even worse shape. You will probably lose quite a lot of money with a hand that has only a few outs (when you're up against a small set) or even none (when you're up against top set). Since you cannot see your opponent's hole cards, it is often hard to tell if someone is betting a made hand or is pushing their draw, and it takes very good judgment to know how to play your two-pair hands in cases like this. For most players, simply folding the hand on the flop would often be the best option.

### Hand #2: 9♠-8♥-K♦-K♣

If we take a look at Hand #2, your situation looks a little better. There are some more 'safe' cards to your hand now (in the quite probable case that indeed you've got the current best hand on the flop). These safe cards are the two fours that were part of your holecards in Hand #1. If you're up against somebody who is holding the same hand as you (98, top two pair), any deuce or running pair might now win the pot for you, giving you kings up, and a king might even leave your opponent drawing dead. When you think your two pair nines and eights are good on the flop but they aren't (that is, you're up against a set), you might get lucky, catching a king on the turn or river to break your opponent.

### Hand #3: 9♠-8♥-K♠-K♥

Hand #3 offers even more possibilities, as any heart or spade on the turn will give you a backdoor flush draw which will most likely be good, so that even if your judgment has failed (you thought your hand was good when it wasn't) you've still got some chances to win the pot on the river: any king or heart/spade without the board pairing. This doesn't mean you should always play top two pair in cases like this; it just means that with a quality hand you will often have some 'escape hatches', a few chances to get lucky and win the pot, even if your judgment regarding your opponent's hand was incorrect.

# Flop B: 9♥-8♦-7♠

In pot-limit Omaha, it's rather common for someone to flop the nuts. Especially when the board is coordinated like in this flop, it's quite likely that the nuts is out there; since most players tend to play coordinated high cards, it's even possible for more than one player to hold the temporary nuts right now. People who have read about pot-limit Omaha may know that it's sometimes correct to fold the nuts on the flop in this game. There are some players who overdo this, wanting to impress other people with their ability to fold a hand that is best at the moment. For a fold to be correct, at least some of the following statements have to be true:

- ♠ There isn't a lot of money in the pot yet.
- ♠ You and the other players involved still have a lot of money in front of you, meaning that the money is deep.
- ♠ The temporary nuts is rather fragile; it's quite likely that the hand that is best now won't be best on the river.
- ♠ Someone else may have the same nuts as you (possibly with a redraw as well), so that even if your hand holds up you will have to split the pot.

Now, let's take a look at three hands and see how they relate to this flop.

### Hand #1: J♠-10♥-6♦-5♣

With this hand, you will probably be thrilled to see this flop, because it's about as good as it gets for your hand. As we shall see, however, if you're up against either Hand #2 or Hand #3, you are in trouble, and in danger of losing your entire stack.

### Hand #2: J♠-10♥-Q♦-5♣

Hand #2 may not seem that much better than your Hand #1, but any of the remaining tens or jacks will give your opponent a higher straight (redraw). If all the money goes in on the flop (which is quite likely, with both players holding the nuts), then the best possible outcome for you is a split pot and Hand #2 is freerolling: he is certain to get half the pot, plus he might even take the entire pot if he receives help.

### Hand #3: J♠-10♥-Q♥-9♠

Against Hand #3, your Hand #1 is in even deeper trouble. Not only will any ten or jack cripple your hand, any heart or spade will create a backdoor flush draw, and any nine or queen creates the danger of your opponent improving to a full. If you are Hand #1 and suspect that you might be up against a hand like this and there isn't much money in the pot yet, well then simply folding the hand on the flop might be your best option. If there *is* a lot of money in the pot already, then it's almost impossible to get away from the hand, even though you suspect your opponent to be freerolling. (But then again, how could the pot possibly be that big already, with you holding such a poor hand?)

## Some final words

In pot-limit Omaha, it's often the *extra outs* that count. Therefore, make sure to only play quality hands: you will have to rely less on your judgment when it's not clear who's holding what and you will be able to play more according to the strength of your own hand. In addition, you will have the chance to 'get lucky' once in a while – by making a hand you weren't initially drawing for.

# A few misconceptions in Omaha

A while ago, I wrote the articles *'A few misconceptions in poker' (1) and (2)*. I described some ideas, thoughts or statements that are considered to be 'true' by a large group of players; ideas that *seem* OK, but that in my opinion are not completely accurate or may even be flat out wrong. In this article I'll discuss some misconceptions regarding my favourite game, pot-limit Omaha, in the context of two kinds of hands that seem quite easy to play but are in fact often misplayed: straight draws and the underfull.

## Misconception 1: 'I had an open-ended straight draw on the flop. I had to play.'

An open-ended straight draw isn't always a hand to be thrilled about. If in pot- and no-limit hold'em you've got a seven in your hand and the board shows 9-8-6, there's no reason to get involved too much. Some other player may have the same straight draw, have made a straight already or make a higher straight (with the Q-J or J-7 for example, in case a ten comes up, or the Q-10, if a jack falls).

In Omaha, when there is J-10 on the board and you've got Q-9, then you *don't* have an open-ended straight draw. The only outs that are relevant here are nut outs. When the K comes up and you get any substantial action, you can be sure your Q-9 is no good; that is, you might *lose* a lot if you make the hand you're drawing to, rather than win. The odds of making your hand if you are drawing to a straight are almost always worse than they seem, because of the possibility of making your hand and then having to split the pot with one of your opponents. In Omaha an open-ended straight is by no means a premium draw. Your opponents may be in there with some kind of wraparound straight draw (that is, they've got the same draw you have plus some extra outs), so you might not be able to win the whole pot, even if you make the hand you're drawing for. Even worse, in

Omaha flushes are all around: if on the river a flush is *possible*, it is *likely* to be out there, even if the flush has been backdoored. If in Omaha you have an open-ended straight draw on the flop but two of the flop cards are suited, then in general you shouldn't invest *too* much money in your hand. Straight draws are vulnerable hands for the following reasons:

♠ Your opponents may have the same (or even better) straight draw.

♠ Your drawing odds are therefore not as good as they seem. (Are all your outs nut outs?)

♠ You might make your hand and still lose: a) the cards that make your straight also make somebody else a flush, b) the card that makes your straight creates a new (backdoor) flush draw or higher straight draw that might be completed on the river, c) you make your straight on the turn but the river completes the flush draw that had been possible from the flop onwards (or the board pairs and you lose to a full house).

Does this mean that you should never play an open-ender in Omaha? Of course not. It all depends. Just remember that in Omaha you want to play wraparound straight draws, preferably with some kind of (backdoor) flush potential. Open-enders give you eight outs maximum, and even if you make your hand it's by no means certain that the pot will be yours in the end.

## Misconception 2: 'I have a full house. How can I pass?'

In *limit* Omaha, a small full house can sometimes cause you some problems. That is, if you're up against a bigger full you might lose quite a few bets. In *pot-limit* Omaha, you might lose your entire stack. If you get any serious action after you've bet your underfull, especially on the later streets, well then you shouldn't expect the chips to come your way. Just to be sure, the underfull is this: the board shows J-J-6 and you have two sixes in your hand, rather than J-6. Now let's say this J-J-6 is the flop in a pot-limit Omaha game. You're in early position (you're one of the blinds) with your sixes and there are three or four players behind you still to act. If you're playing a short stack, you've got no problems: You could just go all-in, and you would probably get played with by one (or two) of the jacks. If they hit one of their kickers, they win; if they don't, they don't.

But if you (and your opponents) are playing a big stack, things are a little different. A lot of players come out betting and raising big with their underfull both on the flop and turn, and sometimes even on the river as well, and quite often they get away with it. The problem with this hand though, is that you never know whether your opponent has hit his kicker or not. (Assuming, of course, that he does not have four of a kind. If you bet out on this flop and are called in two places, then you know your hand is likely to be good at the moment.[7]. If you get only one caller, it is much more likely that you may in fact be drawing dead). If you come out firing on the turn as well, when your opponent in fact *has* hit his kicker, the hand is going to cost you a lot of money. Now let's say he *hasn't* hit on the turn just yet, but he calls your bet on the turn anyway, and then the river comes with yet another one of his possible kickers. How are you going to play your hand *now*? It should be clear by now the implied odds in this hand are with your opponent:

♠ When you bet on the turn or river and he hasn't improved, he might fold.

♠ When you check (or bet small) and he hasn't improved, he might make a big bluff at you and make you fold a winner.

♠ When you check (or bet) and he raises when in fact he *has* improved, you might decide he's bluffing, pay him off and lose a bundle.

Contrary to what most players do, I often *don't* bet my underfull on the flop, even in late position. If I bet, I'll only get called by someone with the third matching card (the jack, in this example), making the pot big when I don't know where I stand. It's hard to create a big pot with the underfull and then *win* it when the money is deep (that is, when there's enough money for bets on the flop, turn *and* river). It's not that bad to just check the hand down on the flop and possibly the turn – and then maybe try to win some money on the river if you think your hand is still good, or possibly induce some kind of bluff because of all this checking. A problem with this strategy of checking the flop is that the turn or river may make somebody else a *higher* underfull, meaning you will now *lose* a small- or medium-sized pot instead of picking up (winning) a small one. But if this person is a reasonable opponent, he won't be too thrilled about *his* hand when he gets action on the river, after the hand had been checked on the flop and the turn as well. After all, with a small full house that does not contain any jacks, the first thing *he* will probably think if he suddenly gets action late in the hand, is that *you* may be in there with a slowplayed top full or quads – so, he may fear a slowplayed big hand

---

[7] Even then, with two callers, you seriously have to consider the possibility that one of the callers has not just the jack, but specifically J-6 – leaving you drawing dead. Especially the first caller could have been smooth-calling with J-6 for the current nuts. The second caller, after all this action, is a lot less likely to be holding specifically the J-6 here, because after all this action he would probably have raised to protect his current nuts against an outdraw. Still, because the card combination J-6 cannot transform as easily into a playable starting hand as combinations like J-9 or J-Q can, I would not be *that* terrified of specifically J-6 in this case – even more so because with two sixes in my hand, there is just one six left in the deck for my opponents.

as much as you do! This means that even in this case where your flop/turn check has given a free outdraw, the pot that you will lose will almost certainly not be a very big one.

Another problem of not betting the flop is that someone may bluff you out of the pot on the turn now that 'clearly' no one has much. But even then the harm done is relatively small, as there is not much money in the pot yet.

There are, as always, exceptions, but in general you should not make many large bets or raises when you flop a hand like this and the money is very deep. This is especially true because if someone is in there with a third jack, the money may go in anyway, and in that case *he* would be doing the betting rather than you. Because he would be putting in chips with a hand that *he* thinks is probably best, it may now be much easier for you to decide (by his body language and/or his betting amounts) whether he is still betting trips or has already improved to a full. And because it is another player rather than you who has the initiative here, and thus it is more likely that he could be giving away the content of his hand by his actions, it should now be easier for *you* to take the correct countermeasures, either by maximising your wins or – just as importantly – by minimising your losses. Beware of the underfull!

# Adjusting your strategy to game conditions

In some of my articles about pot-limit poker, I have written about the optimum strategy to beat most games. I have advocated a tight but aggressive strategy and stressed the importance of having more chips on the table than any other player (especially the ones you expect to make money from). For the past couple of months I have been playing pot-limit Omaha in Vienna. Compared to the places I usually play, the ante pressure is relatively low. The game is ten-handed and there is only one blind (usually, pot-limit poker is played nine-handed with two or even three blinds). Since playing extremely tight gets rewarded in a structure like this, this is just what I've done. I also decided to buy in for the *minimum* when I started playing rather than for a large amount. Because of the game conditions over here (low ante, negligible rake, people buying in for the minimum all the time until they are up – in which case they leave – or are broke – in which case they *have to* leave – lots of calling but not much raising before the flop, and in general rather passive and predictable play), I have found it to be a better strategy to *build* my stack than to buy in for a large sum. In quite a few of my articles, I have described how to play the game with a big stack, facing other big stacks. Today, I will give a few suggestions how to build your stack, after having bought in for the minimum.

### About rake, ante structure and stack size

Most of the time I play poker in Amsterdam. Over there the pot-limit Omaha game is nine-handed, there are three blinds ($5-$5-$10), the minimum buy-in is $500 and the rake is relatively high (5%, maximum rake $20). Under these conditions I play *very* tight, but when involved I try to build a monster pot – as by winning only small pots it is very hard if not impossible to beat the rake. Buying in for the minimum isn't such a good strategy here. It's hard to double or triple your stack when the ante pressure is relatively high – as just one round of play costs $20, or 4% of the minimum buy-in. Also, the effective rake is at its peak in small pots, but significantly smaller when the pots get bigger than a certain amount ($400). So, if you're a fairly good player, the best strategy here is to buy in for a healthy sum and try to break the weaker players/other large stacks in a monster pot.[8] Most of the time I only play three or four big pots an evening in this kind of setting. If I win two of them I figure to make a nice profit, but if I don't a big loss is possible; that is, the swings can be huge.

Since my girlfriend got the offer to work as a dealer in Vienna this winter, I left Amsterdam to stay there with her. Vienna can be considered Europe's poker capital; there are eight 24-hour casinos or card rooms where the game is spread. Most of the time low-limit poker is being offered, with an expensive rake plus money taken out of the pot for jackpots, high hands etc. It's pretty hard to beat those games, or rather they don't offer enough expectation to the serious player who makes his living out of the game.

A few pot-limit games are also being offered, however. No jackpot drops are taken here[9]; the rake is pretty easy to overcome and the players are rather inexperienced and (thus) play very loose, although the ante pressure is low. In games like these, buying in for the minimum *can* be a good strategy. Since the blinds don't affect your stack size a lot and the impact of the rake is negligible, it can be good strategy to try to build your stack by winning some large multiway pots with your premium hands. People will give you action anyway, your small stack being no real threat to them. Of course, it's not easy to win a five- or six-way pot, but when you stick to playing premium hands and try to go all-in before the flop, you're in good shape. That is: you might lose one or two hands playing like this, but when you do win, you might be able to win three or four times your initial buy-in. You've got to be *very* patient, however. You must have the discipline to fold for hours *and* still be able to get some action when you do play. Plus you've got to be immune to people criticising your ultra-tight play.

---

[8] I still think this is the 'best' way to tackle this game, albeit by playing a bit looser than I recommended in this article. Of course, after this article had been published in *Poker Digest* magazine, I ended up having considerable success with my short-stack approach even in this game, despite the fact that not all game conditions in Amsterdam were as favourable for this approach as they were in Vienna.

[9] This situation has changed in most Austrian casinos since I wrote this article. Most casinos *do* now have jackpot drops of about $1 in most PLO games.

Of course, when you've finally won that first pot, you can't keep using the same strategy you used when you were short-stacked. What are the differences?

### Short-stacked/minimum buy-in strategy

The following strategies apply when you have a stack of less than 40 times the big blind:

- ♠ Play very tight.
- ♠ Never make the first raise before the flop, but try to reraise a raiser to get maximum value out of your premium hand.
- ♠ Stick to high pairs, big cards and double-suited quality hands. Try to play them either for a single bet or (preferably) for your entire stack.
- ♠ Avoid hands like 6-5-4-3, Q-Q-7-4 rainbow and 10-8-7-6 single-suited in all positions, except maybe in multiway, unraised pots on the button. But even then, they are marginal – so, even on the button you should only play them when the opposition is rather weak.

### With a medium stack (after having won the first pot)

- ♠ Play tight, but not as tight as in the short-stack approach.
- ♠ Play your position more.
- ♠ Whenever you play, always come in for a small raise (also with hands like 9-8-7-6) to avoid giving away information about your hand. Also, when somebody reraises you when you've got a premium hand and by reraising again you can get yourself all-in (or close to it), you might win the pot right away or play heads-up, all-in with a hand that figures to be best. (Don't always use the limp/reraise strategy with a medium stack when you've got aces. Re-raising a raiser may only get a *small* percentage of your stack in, thus giving your opponent implied odds).
- ♠ Play the rundown hands as well (especially in position), even the small rundowns.
- ♠ Use the check-raise a lot, especially when you flop big draws (semi-bluff all-in raise) or have a multiway hand (for example: two pair + straight draw or overpair + nut flush draw, especially when you think there's no set out there).

### With a big stack (after having won the second pot as well)

The following strategies apply when you have a stack of more than 120 times the big blind.

♠ Play very tight when out of position. When in position, loosen up both the calling *and* raising requirements considerably – especially if weak/predictable players with large stacks are in the hand.

♠ Avoid confrontations with other big stacks when out of position, especially if they are playing well post-flop.

♠ Make sure your big pair hands are *quality* hands. That is: You should avoid playing hands like K-K-8-4 rainbow to just try to flop a king, especially when you are out of position. (On or near the button, these types of hands could be playable, especially against weak or predictable players who also are playing a large stack. But even then, hands like K-K-9-8 single-suited are *much* better than the K-K-8-4 rainbow that we have here.)

♠ Be careful with the small rundown hands. When the money is deep, you might not be able to go all-in on the turn when the board is favourable. If the river makes a new nuts possible (higher straight/-flush/full), this will give your opponent the chance to bluff you out of the pot when your hand is in fact still good, or you might decide to pay him off when the river *has* improved his hand over yours.

♠ On the flop, bet out (rather than going for the check-raise) with your good hands, and your good draws as well. Try to get someone to play back at you, so that you might be able to build a monster pot on the flop with a hand that figures to be the favourite. Do go for the check-raise on the *turn*, when you're up against an aggressive player who doesn't respect a check by you. Don't make the mistake of getting 20-40% of your stack in on the turn when you are out of position and there are straight- and flush draws everywhere – for example, the board is 10♠-7♦-5♠-2♦ and you've got wired tens. The reason for this is that on the river any good player will put you under tremendous pressure if a scare card comes (whether in fact he has made his hand or not), because *he* knows what *you* have, but you don't know *his* hand. If you could get yourself in the favourable situation of check-raising all-in on the turn (holding the nuts, taking away your opponent's implied odds), then you might still lose the hand if you get called, but at least you got your money in as the clear favourite.

♠ When there are some experienced and highly aggressive players in the game with big stacks also, you should quit! Playing pot-limit poker requires *a lot* more skill than playing limit poker; playing a large *stack* in pot-limit a lot more skill than playing a short stack. It is especially dangerous for you if the good players with the large stacks have position on you. In that case, they are much more likely to take *your* stack than the other way around. (Unless of course you are an expert big-stack player already – but I will assume this is not the case.)

## Some final words

The strategies I've described have given me some very good results. Having said that, playing like this requires a *lot* of discipline, and it requires the ability to recognise the situation you're in, knowing if your kings are good enough to reraise before the flop or require a pass, etc. When the opposition is rather weak, you might as well use the 'normal' strategy of buying in for a lot of chips to try to win someone's *entire* stack, rather than trying to build your own stack in a very gradual manner.

I have always considered some of my main strengths to be my patience, my discipline, my image (I somehow manage to get a lot of action when I'm involved with my premium hands; and when I'm only semi-bluffing, I seem to be able to make people lay down their hands), and my ability to handle a short or medium stack. This means that for me this special strategy can be very profitable, even if it *can* be tough to sit there for hours with just a few chips in front of you. So if you're the kind of player whose ego suffers when people see you sitting at the table with just a short stack, then this strategy is not for you. But then again, if you're the kind of player who lets ego take over, rather than trying to find the optimal strategy to beat the game you're in, then I guess playing poker for a living is not for you.

# Just another day at the office

Playing poker for a living can sometimes be just like work: tedious, dull and boring. But just as often, you'll find there are lots of exciting things happening during the course of just a single session. A couple of days ago, I was playing pot-limit Omaha in Vienna. The game was lively, the players were nice and lots of remarkable things happened. In this particular session, I managed to book a nice win. However, people who believe that poker is purely a game of skill should have been there that day. People who believe that poker is all luck should certainly have been there. And people who routinely play small pairs in Omaha to try to flop a set, should *definitely* have been there. In the space of just thirty minutes, we had four set over set situations, and one set over set over set. People who are familiar with pot-limit Omaha, know that in cases like this everyone's money is most likely going to be in the middle. Let me tell you about the most remarkable hand I witnessed.

## A remarkable hand

### Pre-flop

There was a small raise by a player who isn't usually very aggressive before the flop, a rather predictable player who therefore most likely has aces, kings or four premium high cards. As it turned out, he had kings… and he was in for an unpleasant surprise.

### Flop: K-9-2 rainbow

When the flop hit the board, I was watching the pre-flop raiser. His reaction came right out of Mike Caro's *Book of Tells*. He looked at the flop, and when he saw the king he looked away immediately. Obviously, the opponent to his right wasn't familiar with Mike Caro's book. He bet the pot into the pre-flop raiser, who groaned, sighed and then called (same book, different chapter), and then a third player decided this pot was well worth going for and also threw the money in.

### Turn: 9

It was up to the flop bettor. He thought for a while and then checked. This player is known to slowplay his very good hands and I thought he was doing this right now. To tell the truth, I figured him for quads. He doesn't come out betting on the flop very often, and certainly not into a raiser. He will only bet if he has a strong hand but *not* the nuts, since in that case he would check most of the time. That is, considering the board, he must be in there with nines, deuces or K-9. Since he checked the turn, I thought his most likely hand was quad nines. The pre-flop raiser (the guy I figured for kings) checked also, probably already counting the money that he was going to win on this hand. The third player also checked. It seemed like he suspected what was going on, and wouldn't fall for the trap of betting a marginal hand or running a bluff because it had been checked to him.

### River: 2

The flop bettor came out betting an unusually small amount, acting a little weak (yeah, I know, the book). The pre-flop raiser thought it was time to let the cat out of the bag and raised his bet four times. Then player no. 3, someone who can be labelled weak-tight, came over the top of his raise. Now, what was going on *here*? If I had analysed the situation right, he could only have one hand… quad deuces. The initial bettor shoved his entire stack in, as did the pre-flop raiser. He did indeed have top full… and finished third-best. The guy I figured for the nines had the deuces instead, but his four of a kind didn't win either. The guy who had checked the turn in late position came up with the nines and won an amazing pot. Three sets on the flop, top set finishing last, quads beating quads… amazing hand.

## Good things are on their way for me

While this was certainly a remarkable hand to watch, the evening wasn't over yet. In fact, good things were on their way for me, since I was going to win two pots in a row and book a large win. But have you ever heard people mentioning the luck factor in poker? Have you ever heard anyone say how thin the line between winning and losing is? Well, here's a story about lucky me. I had been playing ultra-solid poker all evening, like I always try to. I had been successful in building my stack (using the strategies I described in my article '*Adjusting your basic strategy to game conditions'*), and I was in front for what could be considered a standard win. I hadn't played a hand in two hours and was actually thinking about heading home, as I had been playing for fourteen hours already. Then I got aces double-suited on the button, A♣-A♦-9♣-6♦. Someone had made a small raise, there were a few callers and with my relatively large stack I reraised small (like I often do in this particular game, not just with big pairs but also with rundown hands in position). Had someone reraised me back, most likely I would have gone over the top, but now we took the flop seven-handed(!) and I was in position with a high-quality hand. The flop came 10♣-8♥-7♣, meaning that I had flopped the second-highest straight + nut flush draw. Everybody checked to the player in front of me, who bet out half pot. He didn't have a lot of money left and since I thought it was unlikely that the J-9 was in his (or any other hand) and he only had a short stack, I raised him all-in. The hands were shown down, I won the pot and my image of 'not involved a lot, but when involved winning' was strengthened a bit further. Most players at this table respected my play anyway, and this hand just confirmed the feelings and opinions they already had.

## Lucky me – narrow escape

Then, on very next hand, I got A♦-Q♥-J♥-10♥, a hand that *looks* very good but is in fact rather marginal. Still, I decided to make my standard raise (three times the blind) here, and people, still thinking about the last hand, said things like: 'Ooh, beware. Aces again!' Again, we took the flop seven-handed (yeah, this was a juicy game), flop A♥-6♥-5♦. Everyone checked to me and since people figured me for aces anyway, I decided that I might as well become aggressive with this hand; in fact, a little more aggressive than the quality of my hand warranted. I bet the pot and was called in two places. I thought that if any picture card were to come on the turn, the pot would probably be mine. If a 2, 3, 4, 7, 8 or 9 were to come, I might have to give up my hand and if a heart fell... well, that's what actually happened: turn 4♥. The first caller bet the pot instantly, my other opponent folded and it was up to me. This particular player often likes to use the 'bare-ace play' – or, in this case, the 'bare-king play'. That is: Bet a large amount without the nuts, but with the one card in his hand that *would have made* the nuts had a second card of the same suit been in his hand as well. He is especially likely to make this play when he bets full pot rather than some smaller amount and when he acts very strong, which was just what he was doing now. Still, what other hand but the king-high flush could he have? What else could he have to call a pot-sized bet on the flop with? Anyway, I called his bet instantly. On the river the board paired, he checked and I bet, representing aces – and he folded immediately, showing the K-9 of hearts.

### Analysis

I had been very lucky here. Although I had used my strong – tight – image on the river correctly, I might have lost my entire stack with the second-highest flush (which often happens to inexperienced pot-limit players) had the river not been so helpful. Instead I managed to win a big pot and people looked on in awe as I raked the chips. Right after this hand I left, having won big and having people compliment me on my play once more. Still, I knew better. The line between winning and losing *can* in fact be very thin and I had most of all just been very lucky. Just another night in the casino – just another day at work.

# Snapping off aces

In pot-limit Omaha, one of the most profitable situations for the professional player is being up against someone who plays in predictable patterns. A rather frequent occurrence in this game is the following: there has been a small raise before the flop and a locksmith reraises pot. If the reraise leaves him (or you) close to all-in, you should not give him any action and simply fold your (even very good) starting hands. Why play kings or four high cards when you're up against obvious aces? Quite often, players will reraise with aces just because they have aces – they don't think about either their or the other players' stack sizes. If you and the reraiser are both playing a large stack, you are getting implied odds on the hand. Since you know his type of hand but he doesn't know anything about yours, it's unlikely you will lose any more money after the flop because you know whether the board might have helped him or not. At the same time, if you receive help, he may unknowingly pay you off or, if the board looks scary but hasn't in fact helped you at all, you might be able to bluff him out of the pot. There are some downsides to this strategy, however:

1.  Since you don't know which aces he holds, you might lose a lot of money if he becomes aggressive against a flop with two or three of a suit, when in fact he has the ace plus another card of that same suit in his hand.

2.  You know he's got aces, but you don't know his other cards. If you hold 8-7-6-5 (a nice hand if you try to snap off aces) and the flop comes 7-6-5, you might be thrilled about your hand, bet like there's no tomorrow, only to discover that his side cards were in fact an eight and a nine, giving him the nuts.

Still, once in a while a potentially profitable situation may arise when your opponent basically reveals his hand by his betting actions, when you've got a good hand to play against his high cards (four connecting medium cards, preferably, but not necessarily, suited), when there's a lot of money left to bet *and* you are in position. In this article, I'll discuss two hands I played recently in Vienna and the thought processes involved.

# Hand #1

**Pot-limit Omaha, minimum buy-in $100, one blind ($2), ten-handed.**

When this hand came up, I was playing a medium stack (in fact, I was up quite a lot, having built my stack using the strategies I described in my article 'Adjusting your basic strategy to game conditions') and hadn't played a hand in three hours. Most people in the game respected my play and thought of me as a super-rock already, but the current situation (not having had a good starting hand for a long time) had strengthened this image even further. Then I got 7♣-6♥-5♥-4♠ on the button, a hand that I might fold for just a single bet if I think the situation is not right – but this hand was different. There was an under-the-gun raise to $5, there were a few callers and then the player on my immediate right reraised pot. This player hardly ever raises before the flop and his reraise could only mean one thing: aces, or – less likely – kings. I figured the original raiser for high cards only (if he has aces he raises the maximum most of the time, which in this case would have been $6), but even if he had aces and were to pop it again my hand wouldn't be in terrible shape. I called my opponent's reraise immediately, which caused quite a stir, since I hadn't played a hand for such a long time and now I called not just a single, but a double raise. (The reraiser himself exclaimed: 'What's happening *here*?') Everyone else folded, and we took the flop heads-up. The flop was 10♣-5♣-4♦. The pre-flop reraiser bet the pot, I raised him the maximum, and he quickly called all-in. I didn't like the fact the flop was two-suited (if he was betting an overpair + nut flush draw, he would in fact be in pretty good shape), and when on the turn an ace fell and on the river a club, I thought I was beat for sure. He was shaking his head, however, showing the only possible hand I could beat: K-K-A-x with the bare ace of clubs.

In this hand I was able to take my opponent's stack because of his predictability. He had revealed the nature of his hand while having a lot of chips left and on top of that I had position on him. Of course, I was lucky to receive a flop this favourable (bottom two pair + open-ended straight draw) and even more lucky to win the pot after the (from my perspective) horrible turn and river cards. Still, I played the hand like I was supposed to. Most players don't expect someone who folds hand after hand for just a single bet to pay off a pot-sized reraise before the flop with a hand that according to all point systems is trash. (Since you fold so often, they expect you to play aces, kings and high cards only.) But if the situation is right, you shouldn't be afraid to get your money in in a high-risk situation like this. In fact, I was very proud of the way I had played this hand. It was already clear to most players I knew how to play the big cards, but now they saw I was also able to *beat* them.

# Hand #2

**Pot-limit Omaha, minimum buy-in $100, one blind ($2), nine-handed.**

While I was rather proud about the way I had played Hand #1, Hand #2 was a lot less glamorous. In fact, I made one of my worst calls before the flop I've made in a long time, with a hand that looks pretty good, but in fact is considered cheese by experienced pot-limit players. I was on the button with A♥-J♠-3♠-2♥, a hand that is worth playing in hi-lo and maybe even in limit Omaha, but in pot-limit Omaha high is nothing to be proud of. There had been a raise to $5, which I called, and then the under-the-gun limper reraised pot to $40. Three people called the reraise and I decided it might be worth the gamble, even though I didn't have a really good hand to play against the reraiser's obvious aces (because I had an ace myself). The flop came 7♦-3♦-2♠, and – as happens quite often here when someone is aggressive before the flop and then the flop comes with rags – the reraiser came out betting the pot ($175), making him almost all-in. The guy who had made the first raise before the flop called him, the other player folded, and it was up to me.

I had bottom two pair, not a hand to be thrilled about in pot-limit Omaha and certainly not against a two-suited flop, but I knew what I was up against. The bettor had aces with possibly the flush draw to go with it, but most likely just aces. The caller probably had the flush draw, possibly (though not likely) accompanied by a high pair. That is: my hand was vulnerable, but probably good at the moment. I decided to call as well, rather than fold or go all-in. I wanted to see the turn card before committing any further.

The turn was an offsuit 4. The flop bettor declared all-in, the flop caller called and even though the guy with the aces might very well have made a small straight, I had my opponent for the side pot beat for sure, so I bet all-in ($300), which he called. The river was a black eight and when no one wanted to open his cards, I knew my two pair was good. I had been very lucky here (in fact, I can't remember ever having won a pot this big when I had to show a deuce and a three to win) but once again, it was the predictability of my opponents that gave me the chance to win it. My play had been dangerous: had a diamond come on the turn, I would have had to fold after having invested more than $200 in the hand, and had the turn been a picture card, I might very well have been drawing dead for both the main and the side pot. As it turned out, my opponent for the side pot was just going for the nut flush; he was playing four high cards only. The pre-flop reraiser had the aces I had expected, no diamonds.

## Some final words

The possibility to snap off aces doesn't come up very often. In fact, the situation is hardly ever perfect. You've got to know for sure what your opponent holds[10],

---

[10] Which is extremely hard. For instance, take Hand #1, the hand that I said I was so proud of. Well, had the flop been K-5-4 instead of 10-5-4, I might have lost my entire stack, figuring my opponent for aces rather than top set, three kings – meaning that I would have assumed a much higher chance of winning than I actually had. So, in most cases 'knowing' that someone has aces usually means no more than just 'being quite certain' he has them.

you've got to have a quality hand yourself, you've got to be in position *and* you must be able to make the right decisions after the flop. Having said that, it's nice once in a while to be able to beat a good hand by playing skilfully, rather than the usual situation of people trying to snap off *your* quality hand with rags.

# Defending against aces (a few simulations)

Having a pair of aces as your starting hand is good in almost any poker game, and pot-limit Omaha is certainly no exception. But if you aren't able to get a decent percentage of your stack in before the flop, you will probably have to catch an ace to continue, or get a small pair on the board so that you can win with aces up. In Omaha, it's rare to see aces win unimproved (like you will often see in limit hold'em), and even more so in multiway pots.

If I'm playing a small or medium stack in pot-limit Omaha, I always look for opportunities to go all-in before the flop with aces. (In some of my articles here, I have discussed the best strategy how to accomplish this. The best strategy is *not* raising the pot before the flop every time you get aces. For more discussion on this subject, see my articles '*Adjusting your strategy to game conditions*' and '*A few pot-limit Omaha starting hands*'). Quite often when you raise all-in before the flop with aces, you'll get called by someone with a high pair or high cards, unable to let his hand go – and this is great for you, of course. Most good Omaha players know that having a high pair yourself isn't a good thing when you're up against aces; they know that rundown hands (especially the smaller rundowns) do better against them. In this article, I'll discuss a few simulations I made, using Wilson's *Turbo Omaha High for Windows* software (100,000 hands), matching aces against both high pair and rundown hands.

## A-A-K-2 offsuit vs. Rundowns (no gap)

A-A-K-2 vs. 7-6-5-4 (both offsuit) 56.8 vs. 43.2%

A-A-K-2 vs. 8-7-6-5 (both offsuit) 55.4 vs. 44.6%

A-A-K-2 vs. 9-8-7-6 (both offsuit) 57.7 vs. 42.3%

A-A-K-2 vs. 10-9-8-7 (both offsuit) 57.7 vs. 42.3%

## A-A-K-2 offsuit vs. Rundowns (with gaps)

A-A-K-2 vs. 10-8-6-4 (both offsuit) 56.4 vs. 43.6%

A-A-K-2 vs. J-9-7-5 (both offsuit) 57.2 vs. 42.8%

Looking at these figures, it seems like 8-7-6-5 is the best hand to defend against aces, better than 9-8-7-6 for example. However, one of the side cards of the aces (the king) might have something to do with this: any Q-J-10 coming on the board would make a straight for the 9-8-7-6, but a bigger straight for the aces. Therefore, I have done some extra simulations, matching rundown hands not against A-A-K-2, but against A-A-3-2[11]. The figures also indicate that you don't necessarily need to have a quality hand to defend against aces. You're not out there trying to make a straight against the aces, you want to make two pair. Four different cards having maximum stretch (J-9-7-5, 10-8-6-4) fare relatively well against aces, although they are in fact poor starting hands.

## A-A-3-2 offsuit vs. Rundowns (no gap)

A-A-3-2 vs. 8-7-6-5 (both offsuit) 54.9 vs. 45.1%

A-A-3-2 vs. 10-9-8-7 (both offsuit) 53.9 vs. 46.1%

A-A-3-2 vs. Q-J-10-9 (both offsuit) 58.9 vs. 41.1%

Now that the aces don't have the king to go with them, the 10-9-8-7 hand has become almost even money. The figures here show that the fine starting hand Q-J-10-9 in fact does a lot worse than the smaller rundown hands, because the smaller rundowns have maximum stretch whereas the Q-J-10-9 does not. Now, let's take a look at how the big-pair hands fare when facing aces.

## A-A-Q-2 rainbow vs. Kings or other hands that contain pairs

A-A-Q-2 vs. K-K-8-3 (both offsuit) 76.3 vs. 23.7%

A-A-Q-2 vs. K-K-J-J (both offsuit) 65.9 vs. 34.1%

A-A-Q-2 vs. 8-8-7-7 (both offsuit) 60.0 vs. 40.0%

It should be clear that you should not try to crack aces while holding a high pair yourself. Even the high-quality hand K-K-J-J does very poorly here (winning only 34.1% of the time) and the smaller two-pair hand 8-8-7-7 in fact does significantly better. If you're playing your kings and are facing an all-in reraise by what looks a lot like aces, it seems like folding the hand is recommended most of the time (unless maybe there are also other players in the hand, there is a lot of dead money in the pot and/or you figure it might be good to try to build a side pot).

---

[11] An even better way to do this match-up would be to simply create a hand 'ace-ace-random-random'. This is because we assume two aces, but don't know the two cards to go with them. The A-A-3-2 and A-A-K-2 I have picked here may overestimate the strength of the draw somewhat, because these two A-A hands a) give the opposing draws maximum strength and b) don't include blocker cards to any of the opposition's holdings from this example.

So far, all these simulations have been done without suits having any effect on the outcome. However, it should be clear that in pot-limit Omaha you like your hand to be suited. In fact, I don't particularly like to go all-in even with aces when my hand is not at least single-suited. (This is especially true if I suspect that the pot could be multiway, and even more so if I think there is a reasonable chance that one of my opponents could have aces too.) When matching A-A-3-2 against 10-9-8-7, the aces were a small (53.9 to 46.1%) favourite; now how does being suited influence these figures?

## Impact of being suited

A-A-3-2 (double-suited) vs. 10-9-8-7 (offsuit) 60.3 vs. 39.7%

A-A-3-2 (offsuit) vs. 10-9-8-7 (double-suited) 47.0 vs. 53.0%

A-A-3-2 (double-suited) vs. 10-9-8-7 (double-suited) 54.2 vs. 45.8%

As you can see, being suited in Omaha is very important. The aces' win rate increases more than 6% when double-suited compared to offsuit; the small run-down double-suited even becomes a small favourite against the offsuit aces. If *both* hands are double-suited (of different suits; say, Hand #1 is double-suited in spades and hearts, Hand #2 in clubs and diamonds) the results are about the same – 54% to 46% – as when they were both offsuit.

## Some final words

Just as in any other poker game, hand-reading abilities are very important in pot-limit Omaha. If one of your opponents makes an aggressive move before the flop (reraising all-in), you should know with which kinds of hands he would do this. There are players who make this play only when holding aces, and there are other players who move in with a wide range of hands. Knowing if your kings might be good enough for an all-in reraise or should in fact be mucked requires a lot of experience (and a lot of feel for the game). If you know your opponent has aces and it looks like the hand is going to be played heads-up, calling with your small run-down hand might (because of the dead money and/or the money you've already put into the pot) be the right decision. You will probably be a small underdog to win the pot, but you'll be a money favourite – and that's what's important here.

# An interesting hand (1)

I began playing pot-limit poker in the winter of 1999. For the previous two years I had been playing limit poker exclusively, and even though my results were better than I had imagined possible at the limit I was playing ($10-$20), I decided to take up pot-limit poker, since this was becoming increasingly popular in The Netherlands, France and Austria and I wanted to see if I could also beat these (tougher, more dangerous, more skilful) games. People in Vienna and Amsterdam knew me as a super-rock back then, and that's exactly how I played during my first couple of pot-limit poker sessions. I wanted to get used to the flow of the game without it costing me a lot of money, so I bought in for the minimum every time, played only premium hands, read and reread all the books and articles I could find about big-bet poker, and even had some good results during this period, because my good hands held up more often than could normally be expected. I had just become a little accustomed to the specific characteristics of the pot-limit Omaha game itself and the betting patterns of my opponents, when the following interesting hand came up.

Having just doubled my stack, I got involved with Kosta[12] (a Greek local, a very creative and deceptive player who rarely has the hand he represents), Greg (a somewhat loose Australian player who likes to draw for straights and non-nut flushes) and Marcel (a good and aggressive player, who often raises pre-flop and then usually bets the flop regardless; one of the most talented players there is, and a proven tournament champion). When the hand was over, I was criticised by Kosta (who shook his head as he lost the pot to me, as if to say 'how could you get so lucky') as well as by Ed (someone whose PLO play I respect very much and who claimed that I had overplayed my hand, since I didn't have the nut flush draw). I thought their reaction was mostly caused by their surprise that I was willing to risk my entire stack on a draw, because I believed at the time that I had made the right play. Here is how the hand developed:

## The game

Pot-limit Omaha, minimum buy-in $250, blinds $2.50/$2.50/$5, nine-handed.

## The situation

Kosta small blind, Greg early position, Marcel middle, me (Rolf) button. Greg call $5, Marcel raise $25, two callers, Rolf button call, Kosta and the blinds call, Greg call. We take the flop six-handed, pot size $155. My hand: **10♦-9♥-8♥-5♦**. The flop: **7♥-6♦-2♥**. Kosta bets $100, Greg calls $100, Marcel folds as do the two other callers. Stack sizes: Kosta $485, Greg $1000, Rolf $525. My play: raise pot all-in.

## Motivation:

- ♠ Greg might be on a higher flush draw or possibly a split pot straight draw. He most likely won't be able to call my raise.

---

[12] In the year 2002, Marcel Lüske, Ed de Haas, Kosta Anastasyadis and I all became part of Holland's national poker team, *The Dutch Poker Police*.

♠ Kosta doesn't need to have a premium hand. True, he bet into the pre-flop raiser (Marcel), but Marcel would have bet the flop anyway. Had Kosta flopped a set, he would, considering his stack size, probably have check-raised Marcel all-in with possibly a few callers in the middle. Kosta has a hand for sure, but in my opinion a flush or straight draw is more likely than trips or two pair. It seems unlikely Kosta will have the right odds to call my raise against the hand he thinks I most likely have – top set – since he would need a wraparound straight draw or a flush draw with extras for this (say, the hand I actually do have). An open-ended straight draw *or* the bare nut flush draw are not enough to call my all-in $485 if he thinks he is facing a set ($385 more for Kosta, total pot size $1205 after rake $20). If he does have a set or two pair I'm still not an underdog with my wraparound straight + flush draw. (See the calculations later on.) That is: If Kosta has a set, I may have as much as eight heart outs, three fours, two fives, three eights, three nines and two tens = 21 outs twice! If my opponent also has a straight draw, I probably have a bigger wrap because of the five and the ten, and I also have a backdoor flush draw, which will most likely be good.

♠ My hand does well heads-up anyway, that is to say, I have a lot of outs no matter what hand my opponent has (but I don't like playing the hand against two opponents, where one opponent could have the same kind of wrap that I have, and the second one a higher flush draw). Had I just called on the flop, Greg might have stayed in and I would have set myself up to be bluffed out on the turn. After all, my flush is non-nut and if the board pairs and someone bets, I'll have to pass. In addition, if I hit one of my outs on the turn, I might not get paid off, or – in case of a straight – I might have to split the pot.

♠ Conclusion: I don't want to play guessing games. The odds are against my opponents being able to call my raise and if they do call, I still have a lot of outs (even though I don't know exactly which).

## End result

Kosta calls my all-in raise with A♣-J♠-9♣-8♦ (no hearts), Greg folds. Turn 6♣, river 4♦. My straight wins.

## The odds:

Kosta made it seem like I got lucky. But did I?

| If turn is: | Result: | Odds: | Redraws river: | River outs (40 cards) Rolf – Split – Kosta: |
|---|---|---|---|---|
| 3♥-4♥-5♥-6♥-10♥-J♥-Q♥-K♥-A♥ | R flush | 9/41 | - | 40-0-0 |
| 2♦-3♦-7♦-J♦-Q♦-K♦-A♦ | R backdoor flush draw | 7/41 | hearts (9), diamonds (8), fours, eights (2 each), nine (1), split: fives, tens (2 each) | 22-4-14 |
| 4♦, 4♠, 4♣ | R nut straight | 3/41 | split: fives, tens (2 each) | 36-4-0 |
| 9♦, 8♠, 9♠, 8♣ | R nut straight | 4/41 | ten for nuts K (2) | 38-0-2 |
| 5♠, 5♣ | R & K both nuts | 2/41 | hearts (9), eights, nines (2 each) | 13-27-0 |
| 10♠, 10♣ | R & K both nuts | 2/41 | eights, nines (2 each), for nuts K, hearts (9) for R | 9-27-4 |
| 2♠-3♠-6♠-7♠-Q♠-K♠-A♠, 2♣-3♣-6♣-7♣-J♣-Q♣-K♣ | K in front | 14/41 | hearts (9), fours (3), eights, nines (2 each), split: fives, tens (2 each) | 16-4-20 |

All this data combined shows that Rolf will win the hand 63.54% of the time, Kosta 24.02%, and that the hand will be split 12.44% of the time. (High speed simulations on Wilson's *Turbo Omaha High* software and also www.twodimes.net give the same results.)

# Analysis

Was Kosta right in calling my raise when his total chance of winning was only 30.24% (24.02% + 0.5 x 12.44%)? Well, let's see. If he folds, he loses $125 ($25 pre-flop plus his $100 bet). If he calls, his expectation is 30.24% of the $1205 pot = $364.39. He had to call $385 more, so he lost just $20.61 on average making the call. As you can see, the dead money in the pot made his call almost correct – despite being a serious dog.

In this case I had the best of it, both percentage- and money-wise. But what if one of my opponents was in there with a set or the nut flush draw instead of just an open-ended straight draw?

If I'm up against a set with no extras, it is clear that with my premium draw I am in good shape. In their fine book *Pot-limit and No-Limit Poker* Stewart Reuben & Bob Ciaffone (p. 210) state:

| | |
|---|---|
| Set vs. 13-way Straight + Flush draw | Draw is 1.11 Favourite. |
| Set vs. 17-way Straight + Flush draw | Draw is 1.23 Favourite. |

Simulating my 10-9-8-5 double-suited against the A♠-K♣-7♠-7♣ for top set with no blocker cards, my hand wins no less than 56.59% of the time. And even in the worst-case scenario of being not just up against top set but also a higher flush draw (something that, based on my read, seemed truly out of the question), my hand *still* wins one third of the time. (To be exact: 33.41% against the Q♥-J♥-7♠-7♣). So, it seems that even if I'm up against a set, I'm still in pretty good shape, especially if my flush draw is good. How about when I'm up against just the nut flush draw?

When the nut flush draw is around and I raise all-in, my opponent probably suspects a premium draw or (more likely, considering my image) a set. Is he right in calling with the nut flush draw if he fears a set?

| | |
|---|---|
| Set vs. Overpair + Flush draw | Set is 1.97 Favourite. |
| Set vs. Gutshot Straight + Flush draw | Set is 1.91 Favourite. |

It seems that if an opponent has the nut flush draw and fears a set, he doesn't have the right odds to call my raise. If he calls anyway, he's got only seven flush outs (I've got two hearts in my hand) against my wraparound straight draw. Still, this is one of the worst possible situations for my hand. When up against a hand like A♥-K♥-5♣-3♠, for example, simulations show that my hand will be a winner only 43.17% of the time. But even in this (for me, pretty bad) situation, my decision to move in on the flop would not be as 'bad' as some of my opponents made it look like. That is because (as in the original example) I would still expect to get back $520 out of the $1205 pot. And combined with the $40 that I would still have left after Kosta's all-in call, my stack size after the hand would be $560 on average – considerably more than the $525 that I had left on the flop, when all the decisions took place.

## Conclusion

Although I was by no means an expert pot-limit player when this hand occurred, I think all the decisions I made could be justified, and I still like the way I played the hand. I'd like to hear your comments if you disagree or if you think the call before the flop was wrong (which may be true). Anyway, I hope that the people who are used to limit/no-limit hold'em terms like 'having the best hand stand up' see that pot-limit Omaha should be played with a different mindset, and that the power of draws should not be underestimated here. In this game, you should be willing to back your good hands with your entire stack if the situation calls for it. Just keep in mind that 'good hands' don't necessarily mean good *made* hands.

# An interesting hand (2)

In the previous article, *'An interesting hand (1)'*, I analysed a hand that occurred when I had just picked up pot-limit poker. In that hand I decided to go all-in on the flop with a good draw, which was unlike the way I usually played back then (very solid; never betting without a very strong made hand; buying in for the minimum and then try to build my stack by becoming aggressive before and on the flop with high quality hands). A few weeks later, another interesting hand arose at a PLO game in Amsterdam. This time, the blinds were $5-$5-$10, the minimum buy-in $500 and once again, the game was nine-handed. After an hour of play, the following hand developed:

## Pre-flop situation

Small blind one: Rushdie, a very tight player. Small blind two: Ed de Haas, a very good pot-limit player, who had just won a big pot about 10 minutes previously. Big blind: Belinda Blokker, a former poker pro, and a very dangerous and tricky opponent. She was the one who had just lost that pot to Ed, and had to buy in for another $500, of which she had about $380 left now. In addition to the three blinds there were three (somewhat loose and passive) callers on my right when the action came to me. I was on the button with A♥-8♦-7♥-6♦. I liked my hand, knowing that I can flop something pretty powerful with these cards, so I thought about raising. A raise to $30, $40 or $50 would probably get the three most dangerous players (the two small blinds and the big blind) out, meaning that I would be able to play this hand against the three weaker, more predictable opponents – and on top of that, while in position.

On the other hand, I had a stack of only $420. The most likely flop which would make me want to continue with the hand, would be something like a straight-and/or flush draw. If I raised before the flop I could very well be forced to go all-in on the flop or on the turn – that is, before I had hit my hand. In contrast, if I were to just call before the flop and then flopped a big draw, I could bet the flop if everybody checked to me, using my position (and then check the turn if I didn't hit or continue the semi-bluff if I thought it might win me the pot right away). Or if someone bet into me, I could decide whether to call, raise a little or raise a lot (depending on what I thought I would have to beat and what I would be trying to accomplish) without the burden of having invested a lot of money already. So I decided to just call.[13] The two small blinds also called, the big blind checked, and we took the flop seven-handed, pot size $70.

---

[13] This article was written in 2002, when my PLO experience was still fairly limited. Nowadays, I *would* have raised in this situation, probably a minimum raise to $20.

# The flop: K♥-9♦-8♥

Belinda bets out $70 (the pot). The three pre-flop callers fold and it's up to me. I have a pair of eights, the nut flush draw, an open-ended straight draw on the ignorant end as well as a backdoor flush draw. What do I have to beat? I have played with Belinda a lot, including quite a few times in pot-limit, and she isn't the kind of player to bet a hand like two pair (K-9, K-8) aggressively into a lot of players with so many draws possible, especially not into the players on her left who don't fold easily. She could have a two-pair hand *and* straight or flush draw though (something like K-J-10-9 for example) but since she's the big blind a quality hand like that isn't too likely. She could have flopped a set, but kings aren't very likely (her being big blind) and three nines or three eights would typically be check-raising hands for her (that is, considering her stack size and style of play).

About 10 minutes before this hand there had been this big pot I mentioned, the one Belinda had lost to Ed. Often, after losing a big pot, she loosens up a bit and starts betting her draws a little more aggressively than usual. Therefore in my opinion she could very well have a wraparound straight draw say, something like J-10-7-x or Q-J-10-x. The bare flush draw didn't seem too likely since I have the nut flush draw, but she could be betting a straight *and* flush draw obviously. Anyway, what are my options?

I have the option to pass, call, raise small (say to $140) to slow her down, or raise the pot to try to make her fold the hand and if not possibly still be a (money) favourite. I decided to call, reasoning that this might induce a call by one of the small blinds, which would give me better odds in trying to hit my flush. A three-way pot might also stop Belinda from trying to (semi-)bluff on the turn if a blank were to arrive. (People know me as someone who can lay down a hand and as someone who doesn't like to invest a lot of money in small pots.) So if we're heads-up and the turn is a blank, I think she will bet the pot nine times out of ten, especially if she suspects I'm drawing, but if other players are also still in, she probably cannot afford to be this aggressive, which would be to my benefit. Both blinds folded, however, so we're heads-up, pot size $210.

# The turn: 3♣

Belinda bets the pot ($210); she's now got $110 left. By the manner in which she makes her bet it seems to me like she wants me out: she bets quite forcefully, which is the opposite of the way she acts when she has a very good hand. I have a few options now: I can pass and just get on to the next hand, I can call or I can raise her all-in. If I raise all-in I'm sure she'll call. It doesn't matter if she has a draw or a made hand, she'll be getting the right odds to call no matter what she has. I can call, but since I think she might still be pushing her draw, I might even call her on the end with just my pair of eights if a blank were to come on the river. If on the other hand the river is a blank and she checks, I must suspect that she has at least some kind of made hand, and I don't have enough money to bluff her out – in fact, *neither* of us has enough money for a meaningful river bluff. On top of that, if I just call on the turn she *knows* I'm on a draw, because if I have some kind of made hand that I think could be good, she knows I'll just raise her all-in on the turn. So she would check-call any river bet of mine for sure then, even with just one pair. But since there's so much money in the pot I might be *forced* to make that bluff on the river in this situation – even though I'm almost sure she'll only call if she has me beat.

All in all, I don't see a lot of benefit in calling as opposed to raising all-in. If, for example, the river is an offsuit ten, I'm pretty sure she has hit her wraparound straight draw with the Q-J, but I'll pay her off anyway with my understraight. And if a flush card hits and I bet she might not even pay me off. The third option (folding the hand) might have been the best decision of all, but since I think she's weak and I might even be winning with my pair of eights (and if not I have a lot of outs), I decided to raise her all-in.

## The river

...is the ultimate blank: 2♠. Belinda waits for me to show my hand, but according to Dutch rules she has to show first. She shows a quality hand: she has the Q-J-10 (the drawing hand I suspected), but also a nine – so she wins an $800 pot with just a pair of nines.

## Analysis

Taking into account the cards she had, there were nine flush outs for me on the river (she had no hearts), three fives that would have made me a nut straight, three aces that would have given me aces up, and two sixes and two eights that would have made me three of a kind. I had 19 outs out of 40, a 47.5% chance to win the pot, even with just one card to come. After the flop I had put $370 more into the $800 pot (rake $20), so in this specific case my expectation was about break even, and thus it *seems* that all in all, I have not done that much wrong.

But simulations show that on the flop, i.e., with two cards to come, my hand was a 61-to-39% favourite over Belinda's, whereas on the turn (the time that I actually moved in) I had become a slight dog. So clearly, raising the pot on the flop would have been a +EV decision, instead of the neutral one I actually made. In fact, this was probably the best option by far, because that way I would clearly have had the odds in my favour. And not just that – a big raise on my part could very well have forced her to lay down the current best hand, meaning that I would have won the pot there and then on a semi-bluff. The fact that I didn't *automatically* choose this option, knowing that she was likely to be pushing a draw, is what I perceive to be an unforgivable mistake.

In general, I don't like to go all-in on a draw[14] in pot-limit games when I'm in position, and especially not on the turn, but in this case I suspected that she was making a play at me and by raising all-in I tried to protect my pair of eights, which might have been winning. The fact that she won the pot with just a pair of nines may have made my actions look like sucker play, and I'm sure some of the other players may have thought: what the hell is *he* doing? Looking back, not just a large raise but even a small raise on the flop would have been much better than my actual call. Because she probably would have called this small flop raise and then saved her last $240 had I bet the turn. (She would have reasoned that she had something like 10 or 11 winners out of the remaining 44 cards with just one card to come, which would make her call quite anti-percentage. As it happened, she would then have folded the current best hand.) But then again, if she chooses to reraise me all-in on the flop with her wraparound straight draw + pair, then I'll simply have to call and the end result will be the same.

Still, it is not the *results* I should be focusing on, it is the actual play. And in this case there can be no question that I had flat out butchered the hand – despite the fact that at the time I thought I was actually making the best possible decisions.

# Some tough decisions

In our regular pot-limit Omaha game in Amsterdam, a hand came up in which I had to make some tough decisions. I was in the hand with Thomas Wolf, a strong Norwegian player who reached the final table at a World Series of Poker event earlier this year.[15] (He finished fourth in the pot-limit hold'em event; in fact he was praised by Mike Paulle in his Internet WSOP report for the way he had played.) Since he had joined the table, he had been playing lots of hands, had been playing them aggressively, but hadn't been able to come up with any winners at the showdown.

A couple of hands previously, Thomas and I had been involved in a hand together. He had raised pre-flop from the button, and I had reraised pot from the big blind.[16] We took the flop heads-up. With aces single-suited I flopped the nut flush (three clubs were on the board) and bet half pot, which he immediately raised. I knew that he figured me for aces, perhaps he thought I was betting the

---

[14] Again, this is not true anymore. Nowadays, I try to play my draws *and* my made hands in a similar manner: very aggressively, both *in* and *out of* position. For instance, in this example, I would not have hesitated at all: I would have raised the maximum on this flop without a second thought.

[15] This year means this year *at the time of this writing* – 2001 if my memory serves me correctly.

[16] Based upon the recommendations in this book, not a play that I like very much – simply because I am giving away the content of my hand with a lot of money still in play.

bare ace of clubs (a play that I might very well make), so my play here was pretty easy. I called his raise, checked the turn and then he bet all-in, which of course I called, holding the nuts. I was a little scared when the board paired on the river, but he said he was bluffing so I won the pot. My opponent was obviously upset that he had lost this pot, and I was sure that he would try to get back at me if he could get the chance. Then, ten minutes later, the following hand developed:

# The hand

A nine-handed pot-limit Omaha game with $5-$5-$10 blinds, and a $500 minimum buy-in. I was in the $10 big blind; there was only one caller (the Norwegian, who was on the button), the two small blinds also called. I looked at my hand, saw K-K-8-8 single-suited and made a small raise to $30. I didn't want the other players out, but I wanted to make some money in case I flopped a good hand.

### Play on the flop

The flop came 8-7-3 rainbow (none of my suit), and both blinds checked to me. I was sure that Thomas figured me for a high pair and would want to put some pressure on me, so I checked the nuts to him, hoping that he would bet, put the blinds in the middle, and I could then blast them off their (drawing) hands with a pot-sized (check-)raise. However, both blinds folded against the bet they faced, and even though it was a dangerous play, I decided to just call and set him up for the turn.

### Play on the turn

The turn was an offsuit 4. I checked and, once again, he bet the pot ($360). What was the best play here? I had $1750 left, just like him, so the money was deep. My plan for the turn had been to make a pot-sized check-raise had a deuce, queen, king or ace come, or check and call had the board paired, but now I faced a tough decision. I had the option to just pass and get on with the next hand, because I knew this was going to be a monster pot and that Thomas might now have me beat. He could have made the straight (in fact, I feared he had), so I figured that if I were to a check-raise it would make things easy for him: to go all-in if he either had the nuts (the 6-5) or a premium draw and fold everything else – meaning that I would never be able to let him bluff for the pot one more time on the river. After two or three minutes thought, I decided to call.

### Play on the river

The river was a horrible card: a jack. There was now also the possibility of a straight on the upper end (he might very well have been semi-bluffing with an open-ended or wraparound straight draw, including 10-9, all the way). I checked, and he bet the pot ($1,080) instantly. My first reaction was: I'm going to pass. OK,

I've tried to win a big pot by checking the flop and the turn, but now he must have made a straight and have me beat. He showed no sign of weakness and was in fact talking to his neighbour about his final table result at the World Series.

I had to think for a long time, I mean a *really* long time. If he had made the straight on the turn with the 6-5, why would he bet the pot now with a new nuts possible? Remember, *I* might have the 10-9, why else would I call two pot-sized bets with no flush draw on the board? He doesn't think I have a set, that is, I raised pre-flop and – also because I've tried to make it look like that by the way I played – I'm sure he suspected a high pair (kings or aces), maybe even a hand like J-10-9-8 (in which case I would have made the nuts now), but no set. I asked the dealer for time once again and still Thomas gave me no clue about his hand whatsoever. He likes to bluff though, I knew that. Plus the fact that he's up against me (the guy who had won that big pot against him just a few minutes ago) *and* that he's in bluffing position (some guys always bet in late position after it's been checked to them) – all indications that my hand might be good. He seemed confident however… I picked up my cards, held them in the air for about ten seconds while looking at them (like players often do when they are about to fold their hands), said something like 'Yeah, you must have me beat now' and took the cards into my right hand as if preparing to muck them. During all these actions I had looked at him through my dark sunglasses, and he gave no reaction, as I was about to fold my hand, he did nothing to stop me, nothing… 'Call!' I shouted, quickly putting the $1,080 into the middle.

Thomas showed three fours (he had made a small set on the turn), so my three eights won. The dealer pushed the pot to me, saying: 'What a call!' as did some of the players from other tables who had come over to watch the action. It was a tough call, a very tough call, and I was surprised to see the hand he had. I don't see why he bet the river though. If he thinks I'm in there with just kings or aces, why make such a huge bet. Does he *really* think I can call a pot-sized river bet with bare aces against that board? And if he thinks his three fours *aren't* good, it's not very likely he can make me fold a better hand, is it? Besides:

- ♠ He doesn't think I have a higher set, and therefore he couldn't have made this big bet as a bluff to drive out a bigger set – because he doesn't give me credit for having one.
- ♠ I can't have the 6-5 (as I would almost certainly have check-raised him on the turn then).
- ♠ And if I have the 10-9, then he just hands me his money by making this massive bet.

But hey, that's not what this article is about. Suffice to say that he *did* make me sweat quite a bit.

## Some final words

The thing is, in limit poker all you have to do is call one more bet if you suspect your opponent is making a play at you. In pot-limit, you can't just grit your teeth and pay off. The difference between being right and being wrong might be your entire stack, which makes the game much more interesting, much more skilful than limit poker… and also much more dangerous.

# The amount of the bet in pot-limit Omaha

Some poker authors have stated that in pot-limit poker, you should not vary the size of your bets, but always bet the same amount (full pot). That way, your bet won't give your opponents information regarding the strength of your hand. There are for instance players who bet full pot on the flop when they have some kind of made hand (set, top two pair), but make a smaller bet when they are on a draw. A good player will always know where he stands when people play like this, and it will be only a matter of time before he gets the money. While it's true that always betting the size of the pot is better than betting according to the strength of your hand (great hand/pot, good hand/half pot, mediocre hand/small bet), it is not the optimal strategy. There are some situations where betting a smaller amount is sometimes better than betting full pot:

♠  When you are playing a small or medium stack,
♠  When there are no draws on the board, or
♠  When you have bet the pot on the flop and then on the turn the board pairs.

In fact, there are a few (great) players who bet a smaller amount in other situations as well. For instance, on www.twoplustwo.com Ray Zee's frequent underbetting in big-bet poker has been discussed extensively. But because playing like this requires advanced theoretical thought processes and the ability to read your opponents perfectly, I won't get into this here. I think that for quite a few players it *is* good to always bet the pot when they decide to bet at all[17], whether they've got some kind of made hand or a (premium) draw. This way, you:

---

[17] For those who *don't* play according to my system, that is. As should be clear by now, I come out betting for the size of the pot only on very rare occasions. And those of you who follow the guidelines from this book, will also find that – especially when the money is fairly deep – there are not all that many situations where coming out with a pot-sized bet would be the preferred play.

- ♠ Don't give away too much information about your hand
- ♠ Show your opponents that you are serious about trying to win the pot, which will make them less apt to play back at you
- ♠ Are giving your opponents the worst odds in case they try to draw out on you.

Still, if you always bet full pot regardless of the circumstances, you will sometimes face the situation where you'll only get called (or raised) when you're clearly beat, and your betting action will have cost you a lot of money. Sometimes making a smaller bet will send the same message to your opponents (that you probably have the goods) as a full pot bet, and you will save money in the event that your hand *isn't* good.

## Aspect 1: Varying the bet according to stack size

Your own stack size can be an important consideration in your decision to bet full pot or a lesser amount. In some of my articles on pot-limit poker I advocate having more chips on the table than any other player whom you figure to make money from, *if you know how to handle a big stack*. Pot-limit Omaha is a complicated game and playing a big stack makes it even more complicated; playing a large stack requires much more skill than playing a small or medium stack. Now if for some reason you are playing a small (or medium) stack, then always betting full pot is far from automatic. Let's say you're in a $1,000 buy-in game, and you are in early position (possibly one of the blinds) with a $520 stack. You hold J♠-10♣-7♦-7♠, there's $180 in the pot and six players see the flop J♥-10♦-6♣. You figure your top two pair is probably good now, but there are many draws possible, making your hand very vulnerable. In fact, the only good cards on the turn for you are the jacks and tens that are left, as well as any deuce, three, four and five. Betting the pot here would be very unwise, because if any other card comes on the turn than the ones mentioned, you might have to give up the hand. (After all, with just one card to come, you aren't getting the right odds to call a big bet in order to improve to a full house or quads if you think the turn must have made someone a straight. And in that case, you would have wasted $180 – more than a third of your total stack – without even getting to the river.)

So, if you decide to bet at all on this flop, then betting $80 would seem like the right amount here, much better than the $180 pot bet. Against this board you can expect two or three callers, assuming that in fact your hand is good at the moment. Now if the turn is a blank then your $80 flop bet has put you in perfect position to defend your hand as much as possible by betting full pot. But if you had chosen to bet the pot *on the flop* and got the same number of callers as you have now, then you could *not* have defended your hand anymore after this same, good, turn card. There would be $720 in the pot already, so the $420 you had left would not be enough to make a small wraparound straight (or even an open-ender or some kind of combination hand) fold.

Now, let's take another flop: K♠-7♥-2♠ and you're in there with K-K-x-x. There is $400 in the pot, four players and you are playing a $1200 stack. A common scenario would be this: you bet the pot, get one caller, the turn is the third spade and your opponent bets all-in (and you either fold, knowing you're beat right now, or call, trying to improve on the river). If the pre-flop betting suggests that someone else might be in there with aces, you have to consider the possibility of him having the nut flush draw as well, a hand that is not going to fold against this board no matter how much you bet. So, why not try to make some money with your set when your hand is still good, yet avoid getting broke with it? A $200 bet on the flop would seem reasonable here, especially taking into account the ill-coordinated nature of the flop. (In fact, betting one-third to half the pot with top set against this board will give you credibility for the many times when you make the same kinds of bets against these ill-coordinated boards as a bluff.) This $200 would be the perfect amount to induce even bare aces to come along for the ride. Perfect for you, that is, as he will probably be drawing to just two outs while getting only 3-to-1 on his money. Furthermore, you would not be giving a flush draw the proper price to call, knowing that the 7♠ is not even an out for your opponent(s). If the aces decide to play back at you (or if you think you might be able to check-raise the pre-flop raiser all-in), then by all means try to get all your money in on the flop with the nuts, top set. That would be the best possible situation of all, but you can't always expect that to happen – and you *definitely* can't expect that to happen if you come out with a bet that is too big for this ill-coordinated board.[18]

So, let's say that indeed you bet half pot, $200. If this $200 bet of yours gets called and the turn is a spade – or, even worse, an ace – you can fold against a big bet and you would then have 'saved' the extra $200.[19] If there's no danger on the turn,

---

[18] Quite frankly, in the situation where you have flopped three kings and you suspect that the pre-flop raiser is in there with aces, this would be the perfect situation to go for a check-raise on the flop. Especially if the pre-flop raiser is not up against *too* many opponents, he will almost certainly take at least one big stab at the pot now that the board is so uncoordinated. But if *you* made the last raise before the flop and thus a) it seems like no one has aces, and b) no one will do the betting for you, then it is best to simply come out betting 30-50% of the pot rather than full pot. In fact, this is the exact same bet that you would also make as a bluff to simply pick up the pot – so you also need to make these kinds of bets when you have flopped a really big hand. So if you choose to bet at all, it is clear that the half pot bet is quite superior to the full pot bet that many players would make with their top set here.

[19] Having said that, there *is* obviously some chance that your opponent has called you with his flush draw only because you gave him a good price by betting just half pot – meaning that he *would* have folded against a full pot bet. So this means you now *lose* a pot that you would have won with the 'normal' big bet. This 'giving your opponent the chance for a cheap outdraw' is one of the clear downsides

however, you can simply bet the pot if you think it's time to protect your hand as much as possible, or bet a lesser amount if you want your opponent to call you rather than fold. (If you *know* what your opponent holds, you don't have to fear a river bluff, meaning that you can afford to give your opponents a much better price than just the 2-to-1 they get after you make a pot-sized bet. So you can bet less than the pot and then if a spade or ace comes up, you can safely fold, having 'saved' some chips that you would not have saved by betting full pot. Also, if by chance you make a full house on the river after your 'small' turn bet, your opponent may even pay you off now that he has made aces up – so you still double up, despite having bet less than the pot on every street.) Remember, if you bet $400 on the flop and get called, you don't get the right odds in trying to make a full if you think the turn has made your opponent a flush. You will have to call $800 more for a total pot of $2800 and you would have only ten outs maximum.

All in all, I'm not suggesting that you should *always* bet less than the pot when you're playing a small stack. What I *am* suggesting is that you take a close look at the board and at your (and your opponent's) stack size, so that you will then try to find the best strategy to a) maximise your winnings on the hand and b) minimise your losses.

## Aspect 2: Varying the bet due to the texture of the board

### When you have bet the pot on the flop and then the board pairs on the turn

Flop: J-8-4 rainbow, you bet the pot and get called in two places; now the board pairs on the turn. What do you do? A lot of weak players do this: they bet when they are full but check when they only have a draw, fearing that someone else may be full now. Some other players do this: they check when they are full and bet when they have nothing. Both plays are horrible – although the second is not as horrible as the first. The thing to do is to bet small (a bit less than half the pot) *whether you have made your hand or not*. If you bet with nothing and your opponents are on a draw as well, they are not going to call you and you have (semi-)bluffed them out of the pot at a relatively cheap price. If you *do* get called, you know you're probably up against a full and you're not going to put any more money into the pot. By always betting like this your opponents will fear your relatively small bet as much as a full pot bet. You might be able to steal an occasional pot by playing like this and if your (semi-)bluff doesn't succeed because your opponent has filled up, well then it was relatively cheap. By betting full pot when the board has paired, the same hands as before are going to fold, but if you get called (and thus are beat) you've cost yourself a lot more money than necessary.

---

to this play I am suggesting. Therefore you should rarely make this type of bet against more coordinated boards, and/or against boards that have multiple drawing opportunities.

### Playing against an ill-coordinated board

When the flop comes something like J-9-6 with two of a suit, you know your opponents may have flopped some pretty powerful draws. But if the flop comes K-8-3, A-9-4 or Q-7-2 rainbow, there *are* no draws. If you bet a hand like top two pair or a small set (or maybe even a lesser hand) against this board, you'll usually get called only when someone has you beat *whether you have bet the pot or not*. A lot of good players always bet one-third to half the pot on flops like these, whether they have a set or not.[20] By playing like this they are able to steal quite a few pots without putting a lot of money at risk. And if they do get called (or raised) by an obviously big hand, they may be able to get away from their hand cheaply. So, the 'half pot' strategy against these types of boards gives them information at a cheap price, and helps them to steal small pots at a cheap price – a very good combination. Only once the opposition becomes more knowledgeable, and only once you start running into players who use this type of thinking too, will this strategy lose a lot of its value.

## Some final words

The things I've discussed here are in fact common situations where the average player can make (or save) a lot of money. Just make sure that when you decide to sometimes bet less than the pot, you are not giving away information about the strength of your hand. If your opponents can figure out what you hold because of the amount you've bet, they can save money against you when they know you've got the goods, and raise you off your hand when they know you're weak.

# Strong plays/weak plays (1)

For the past couple of months, I have been playing pot-limit Omaha exclusively in Vienna. Pot-limit poker has become very popular over there. Because a lot of players lack experience and therefore their skill level isn't up to the usual standard, most games are still pretty easy to beat. However, that doesn't mean that you don't see some expert moves or strong plays occasionally; it just means that if you're playing a solid game of poker, the money will very likely be yours in the end. In this article, I'm going to discuss a couple of hands that have been played here during my visit. Unless stated otherwise, the games are rather passive, the

---

[20] Don't even *think* about checking a small set here. You're not going to give free cards in this game; just bet small and pick up the pot – don't try to get fancy by letting your opponents catch up. The only hand you could afford to check here is top set, because then the free card could make one of your opponents a very good but costly second-best hand. Even then, I usually prefer betting with a big hand over checking, for the simple reason that you want your opponents to know that you also bet your monsters aggressively in situations where slowplaying would have some merit.

opponents somewhat predictable, and the minimum buy-in is relatively low (from $60 up to $300). Even though the games have a low ante structure (and playing tight is therefore recommended), at least five or six players see the flop every hand. In this first part of the article, I'm going to share with you a couple of weak plays I witnessed or was involved in. In the second part, I will then discuss a few strong plays that have been made.

## Weak play #1

The first weak play I'm going to discuss with you is one that I made myself. I'm in middle position and make my standard raise of three times the blind. In the games here, I make it a habit to always raise the same amount before the flop, regardless of position, to avoid giving away information about my hand – so this hand is no exception.[21] My cards: A♦-A♥-7♠-3♦. Three people behind me call, so we take the flop seven-handed.

The flop is favourable to me: K♦-5♦-4♥. That is: I have an overpair, the nut flush draw and a double belly buster (both non-nut) straight draw. Three people check to me and I decide to check also, trying to let someone behind me do the betting, get one or two callers in the middle and then blast them off their hands with a pot-sized check-raise. However, it gets checked around, so everybody sees the turn for free, turn 3♣.

Once again it gets checked to me, and now I have no choice but to check also. Why? Well, because if I bet and get check-raised, I'll have to pass – and I will have bet myself out of the pot with a hand that could either be best already, or else *improve* to the best hand on the river. The opponent to my left thinks for some time and then bets half pot. He gets called in three places when the action gets back to me. I don't think the nut straight is out there; I figure the bettor for 6-2 or A-2 maybe and one of the callers for 6-2 as well. However, I don't think I can make them all lay down their hands. They are just not good enough to lay down a hand that strong, which is precisely the reason why this game is so profitable in the long run. All in all: no semi-bluff check-raises here, and I decide to just call to see the river.

The river comes 7♦, making me the nut flush. There are three people behind me who will most likely not bet out themselves but who might pay me off with hands like the king- or queen-high flush (hands that they could very well have since there are so many players still in the pot). I decide not to 'sell' my hand but bet full pot instead, and everybody folds. I win a modest pot and while people compliment me on my play (I seem to be winning every pot here once I take my hand to the river), I'm not too pleased myself. My check on the flop was a huge mistake. I

---

[21] For more information on this, see some of the hands I discussed in my two-part article series 'A few Omaha simulations', available in the archives at www.cardplayer.com.

might very well have been able to build a monster pot by betting out but went for the fancy play instead, when the situation was not right (as the players behind me weren't the types to bet every time it's been checked to them; they weren't aggressive enough to bet any marginal hands solely on the basis of their good position). Also on the river I should have been able to make at least *some* money with my hand. After all, the 7♦ was the card that completed all the draws that people could possibly have been in there with, but I didn't get paid off even in the slightest.

Remember, poker is not about winning pots, it's about winning money. In this case I won a relatively small pot with a hand that had the potential to win a huge one – and I only had myself to blame.

## Weak play #2

This is a hand I witnessed and is a classic example of how pot-limit Omaha *shouldn't* be played. Seven players see the flop in an unraised pot. When the flop comes A-10-9 rainbow, it gets checked around to the button, who (holding A-10-9-3) bets the pot. The blind[22], a fairly solid player who isn't out of line often and who rarely bets his draws aggressively, makes a pot-sized check-raise. Everybody folds to the button, who thinks for a minute, acting a little disgusted (as if to say 'how can I get check-raised with such a big hand?') and then calls – getting more than half his stack in. When the turn comes an offsuit deuce, the blind checks and the button checks also. The river is a seven, the blind bets everything he has and the button calls all-in with his top two pair (which is good; the blind doesn't show his hand but folds).

Even though the button won this pot, he made almost every mistake he could possibly make in just a single hand. His flop bet is OK; after all, he has to charge people to draw out on him. (He knows that, if he gets called, any 6, 7, 8, J, Q or K could cripple his hand.) Once he gets check-raised, he's got to re-evaluate: Is his two pair good or not? In Omaha, you don't want to play two-pair hands heads-up against a set. The hands the blind most likely has (ruling out aces; even though they're possible, they're not very probable) are 10-10, 9-9 or A-10 also – maybe even A-9 or a semi-bluff with a draw, in which case the button's hand is good right now. The button's call here is debatable because he would be risking his entire stack on a nothing pot to begin with – meaning that a fold would probably have been in order, especially given the characteristics of his opponent. In fact, I would much rather have reraised than called here.

However, if I were to decide to call, I do so because I think my hand is best. So when the blind decides not to bet the turn, checking it back is horrible! By checking it back, the button basically said he *didn't* think his hand was good, but then

---

[22] In Vienna they usually play pot-limit Omaha poker with just one blind, instead of the two or even three blinds that are common elsewhere.

why on earth did he call the check-raise on the flop? On the river, when facing an all-in bet by his opponent (who could well have made the straight he might have been drawing for) he suddenly decided his two-pair hand might be good after all, when all he could beat at that moment was a bluff from a busted hand. However, if he thinks his opponent could be in there with a drawing hand, then either charge him on the flop or turn for drawing out – but *don't be a calling station!* Even though in playing like this he got the best possible result for this specific case (the button won all he could possibly win on the hand), this won't last. In limit poker, calling stations can't last very long; in pot-limit, they can't last at all.

## Weak play #3

This is a hand I played when the game *was* aggressive. There was one talented, highly aggressive Chinese player and also the well-known (tournament) player Jin Cai Lin, a very dangerous and aggressive player. Jin was raising eight pots out of ten before the flop, and if someone else had raised, he would most of the time pop it again. When I found A♠-K♦-Q♦-10♠, I was in early position with a medium stack. I decided to raise myself (my standard raise, three times the blind) rather than let Jin take the initiative. There were two callers and Jin (in late position) decided to raise again. However, rather than raise the pot he raised only a small amount. It seemed to me that he wanted some more information about what he was up against, as good pot-limit players like him often make small (re)raises early in the hand to be able to make more accurate judgments later on. I was certain that if I reraised again, he would figure me for almost 100% pure aces, knowing that he sees me as a not-very-creative rock and as a bit of a nit on top of that. His raise was called by the blind, and I decided to raise pot once again for almost 25% of my total stack, with both Jin and the blind calling. I figured that if an ace or king flopped, the pot would be mine nine times out of ten, and that if I hit any pair, straight draw or flush draw and the flop was unlikely to have helped others, I would just put my stack in and hope for the best.

Flop: 6♦-5♠-4♦. The blind came out betting into both me and Jin for about one-third of the pot. I thought he was unlikely to have made a straight – why not let me do the betting then – but hands like two pair or an open-ended straight draw + pair were likely (and favourite over my hand as well). I thought the pot was too big to let go and called. When I called, Jin said something like: 'Ooh! Aces + nut flush draw,' (which was exactly what I was representing, of course) and then quietly folded.

Turn: Q♠. By now I had top pair/kickers + *two* flush draws (nut draw in spades, second nut in diamonds), and when my opponent checked I could have bet everything I had since I had a powerful, multiway hand (with lots of outs, regardless of what my opponent held). Instead, I decided to bet only half of what I had left since I figured my opponent for two pair probably, a hand that he could never lay down at this stage even against a big bet, and I wanted to create some room to manoeuvre on the river. The river didn't help me and of course I should have checked and saved the money I had left. (The only better hand that my opponent might have and could possibly fold here was K-K, since he figured me for aces anyway. But quite frankly, he was not all that likely to have specifically kings in this situation.) But I didn't do that: I bet all-in and he called, showing 6-5 for two pair – the exact type of holding that I had figured him for.

It seemed like I was unlucky to lose the pot since my hand was a big favourite over his on the turn. However my call on the flop was debatable (remember, he might have been pushing an ace-high flush draw) and a fold or a reraise all-in would each have been more appropriate than my actual call. My bet on the turn was horrible. I should either have checked or bet all-in, knowing that I was a favourite for sure with so many outs. Additionally, my pair might even have been winning – my opponent might have had something like the bare nut flush draw or a straight draw + pair, for example. And finally, my bet on the river was nothing more than the act of a desperate man. In fact, I can't remember having played a pot-limit Omaha hand quite this badly in a very long time. The fact that I was able to keep my cool and even book a nice win for that particular session was a good thing, but it couldn't take away some of the major mistakes I had made on this hand.

## Some final words

In the second part of this article I'll discuss some *strong* plays I witnessed or was involved in during my time in Vienna.

# Strong plays/weak plays (2)

In the first part of this article, I discussed some of the weak plays I witnessed or was involved in when playing pot-limit Omaha in Vienna. Here I'll discuss some of the strong plays that have been made during my six-month stay.

## Strong play #1

I am in the big blind with a fairly strong hand (K♠-J♣-J♦-9♦). Six people have called the initial bet, there are no raises and I decide to build the pot a little by making a small raise (three times the blind), which they all call. The flop comes Q♦-J♠-2♣. Even though I like to check-raise with hands like middle set when there are some draws on the board, in this case I decide to bet the pot. I get two callers: a big stack on my left (I've got lots of chips myself) and one caller on the button, who by now is pretty close to all-in. The turn: A♦. I've now got a set, an inside straight draw and a (non-nut) flush draw. However, I know the big stack might very well have made the nuts with the K-10. (Since it's a rainbow flop, it's very likely that he's in there with some kind of straight draw – and quite frankly, K-10 would be the most logical one.) I decide to check, for two reasons mostly:

1.  If my three jacks are still good now and especially if the other big stack doesn't have a higher flush draw in diamonds, then there are not that many river cards that will cripple me. This is especially true because any ten on the river (a key card for those who are pursuing straight draws) would now also give *me* an ace-high straight.

2.  A check on my part might induce someone to either bluff at the pot, or bet with a relatively weak made hand like aces up – hands that are drawing thin to mine, and that would probably fold if I came out betting big. In particular, a hand like aces up would be one that my opponent could fold if I bet, yet bet with if I check. So I want to induce my opponent(s) to bet not just the nut straight (which obviously I cannot beat yet), but also a wide range of hands that I *can* beat, while at the same time I try to avoid going broke if it looks like the big stack indeed has the nut straight that I figure him for.

The big stack thinks for some time and checks as well. The button then decides to bet all-in – which is a rather small amount, compared to the current pot size. That is: even if I think he's got the straight, pot odds dictate that I cannot possibly fold. (However, this particular player can come up with *any* hand in this situation.) The question is: What does the other big stack have? A straight is out of the question: he wouldn't check the nuts after having thought this long – he isn't creative enough to make a play like that – but he might have top two pair or even a bigger flush draw. If the button *does* have the straight and I have to draw out, I don't want these hands in – that is, if improving my hand on the river might actually be more beneficial to my opponent than to me.

So I decide to check-raise and build a side pot with a hand that figures to be best even if I get called. I don't mind him calling with a higher flush draw or two-pair hand, since some of the cards he might need are in my hand. Besides, if he is lucky enough to improve on the river, then it should be pretty easy to fold my hand, because I *know* what kind of hand he's got whenever he calls my check-raise. And if he *doesn't* improve, I will have won a decent-sized side pot, meaning that I have actually made some money on this hand even if it turns out that the button *does* have the nut straight. Anyway, the big stack folds, the river is a blank and the button shows three deuces; my three jacks win. Now the button starts yelling: 'How can this be? This guy folds 29 hands in a row, then plays Hand #30 and wins. Is this magic or is this poker?'

He probably didn't notice the way I played this hand. Had the big stack bet the pot on the turn I might very well have folded even with my set, flush draw and gutshot straight draw. The problem is that I have just a few nut outs, I am out of position *and* I cannot be certain whether hitting my draw would also mean winning the pot. For instance, my opponent could also have a hand like three aces + gutshot straight draw, or something like a slowplayed three queens with a higher flush draw – hands that would have me in even worse shape than the simple nut straight. (In other words: I would not have much in the way implied odds – if any. In fact, up against one of the hands mentioned, I would have clear *reverse implied odds*.) But instead, I won a nice pot against a scary board for two reasons:

1. The predictability of the big stack.
2. The bad play (plus his being all-in) by the button.

By playing like I did I made sure that I would be playing my hand only against the small stack and avoided playing out of position against the other big stack – both of which are important considerations in pot-limit play.

## Strong play #2

When I decided to play this specific hand (A♠-K♦-9♣-9♦), I was under the gun and hadn't played a single hand in two hours. I knew that if I raised people would figure me for kings or aces. Since I didn't have to fear a reraise much – most people in Vienna only reraise with kings or aces and I had one of each in my hand – and might be able to represent a big hand in case an ace or king flopped (with no possible draws, of course; remember this is Vienna where people don't like to fold), I decided that I might become aggressive with this very marginal hand. I made my standard raise of three times the big blind and was called in six(!) places.

The flop came 9-5-5, giving me top full. Instead of checking and letting one of the trips do the betting, I decided to bet out, for three reasons:

1. I knew that because of my pre-flop raise, most players would figure me for kings or aces. Many players over here who raise pre-flop with aces automatically make one big bet after the flop hoping to win the pot there and then. Now, even though *I* would never make a bet without at least the third five in a seven-handed pot, my opponents would – and thus they would not automatically give *me* credit for more than aces up if I chose to bet out on this flop. So I knew that no one was going to fold a five here, and this was exactly what I wanted, of course.

2. I was playing fairly deep money, so I wanted to bet first, hoping that someone could raise and be committed there and then – or else simply have him call my bets on every street. If I went for the check-raise on the flop, I could have given someone with three fives the chance to get off his hand cheaply, i.e. having lost just one chunk instead of multiple ones.

3.  Most players over here prefer calling over betting or raising. Especially in a multiway pot like this, someone with three fives could be afraid of betting out, yet could quickly call any bet I might make.

I bet two-thirds of the pot and got one caller. Now obviously I would rather have had two callers than one, because then I could have them drawing dead in case they both held a five. But by the manner in which my opponent called, it was obvious that he held *one* five, not two – meaning that I had him exactly where I wanted him. The turn was a jack. I now bet half pot as I didn't want to scare him out now – betting full pot might have convinced him that I somehow had jacks in the hole. He quickly raised pot and I reraised him all-in, knowing that my nines full was good. He called, showing J-5 and having only three outs (two jacks, one five). He received no help, so I won a monster pot.

**Analysis**

When you flop a super hand like top full in PLO, always think about what your opponents think you might have. Most players would automatically check top full here – but why would you ever want to do that? Maybe the player with the five is timid and checks also, thus keeping the pot small. Even worse, an overcard may come on the turn, making someone else a bigger full and putting your entire stack in danger.

In pot-limit, I like to play for big pots. Especially when the money is deep, betting out and having somebody play back at you is the best way to create these big pots, rather than hoping that someone else will do the betting for you. Betting out with big hands also gives you credibility for the times that you will be trying to steal a pot when there's an open pair on the board. Now, *you* of course know that you would never try a steal against so many opponents, but not all of your opponents may be aware of this. They will just remember the fact that you have come out betting with top full against a paired board. And this means that the next time, when you just have one or two opponents, a flop with a small pair will present an excellent stealing opportunity for you – in part because of the way you have played your top full here.

# Strong play #3

There is a guy in Vienna who is obviously irritated by the way I play: always the same standard raises, hardly ever playing a hand but when involved showing a winner, never showing any real emotion (whether winning or losing), never commenting on anybody's play etc. Whenever I make my standard pre-flop raise he often makes a small reraise to show that 'he's not impressed'. Therefore I always choose to sit on his immediate right. Then, whenever I make my small raise and he makes his (also small) reraise, I've got all the other players in the middle.

And when the action gets back to me, I can decide to just close the betting by calling and see a flop cheaply, or go for a massive reraise in order to blast them all out.

The strategy he uses isn't a very good one, of course. He's basically got three options when facing a raise by me: folding, calling (if he thinks his hand is too good to pass) or re-raising pot (if he thinks his hand is better than mine). By re-raising only a small amount I can usually see the flop cheaply in case my hand is average, yet make it expensive for him when I've really got the goods. This is especially true since he cannot lay down his hand easily when he gets repopped.

In pot-limit poker, seat selection is very important. When playing deep money, you'd like to have not only aggressive opponents to your right, but also the weak ones and the very good ones. Basically the only players you want to your left are the rocks and the weak-tight players, but how many rocks or weak players like to play pot-limit Omaha anyway? It's hard to make money from someone who's sitting on your left in pot-limit when the money is deep – but that's just what I've been doing during my visit here.

# Strong play #4

In Vienna, some players seem to have a tendency to raise before the flop every time they've got aces – regardless of stack sizes, position, and whether their aces are in fact *quality* aces. I like to be aggressive with aces myself, but in the specific situation I'll describe here, I decided to just flat call an under-the-gun raiser who was seated to my immediate right. My hand: A♣-A♦-6♣-2♦. We both had large stacks and I didn't want to reveal my strength too early in the hand. After all, it's hard to make money after the flop when there's a lot of money left to bet and your opponent knows exactly what he's up against. If someone behind me had reraised, then I might have popped it again, but there were only callers – meaning that we took the flop six-handed, flop J♠-8♦-7♣. When someone bet, I just folded my aces and got ready for the next deal, having lost hardly any money on a hand that I could have lost a lot with.

## Analysis

A lot of people seem to think that every time you have aces, you've got to raise, 'because it's the best hand you can have'. In Omaha, no hand is by itself (that is, without substantial help from the board) good enough to win a decent pot. In this case I lost the minimum with my premium hand. Had I reraised and succeeded in getting everyone out except for the raiser to my right – which, as I've stated, is extremely doubtful – what would the best course of action have been *then*? My opponent *knows* I've probably got aces. So when he bets out on this flop there's no telling whether he is doing so because he has me beat, or because he knows that if I have unimproved aces it will simply be impossible to call. I might lose a lot if he *has* the goods if I decide to call or raise him, but more likely I will be (semi-)bluffed out of the pot because of the information I provided him with (too) early in the hand.

Aces can be very powerful in Omaha, but the conditions have to be right. There's no need to put your entire stack in danger every time you get a decent starting hand; there are also times when just calling to see the flop cheaply is best. So unless you are able to get enough of your chips in the middle to make all post-flop decisions a formality, you should *not* always raise or reraise the maximum before the flop with your aces. This for the simple reason that you would be giving away too much information to your opponents – information that they *can* and *will* use against you later in the hand, when the real money is at stake.

# A few flops in pot-limit Omaha

In pot-limit Omaha (just like in any other flop-type game), the flop is *the* decision point in whether or not – and how – to continue with the hand. It's important to have your cards fit in with the flop well; that is, it is usually unwise to continue with your hand if you haven't received substantial help from the board. Having said that, it is often just as important to know if the flop might have helped your opponents. If it seems rather unlikely that the flop has been beneficial to them, the pot may very well be up for grabs. Let's take a look at a few flops in Omaha and how they relate to your own starting hand, and to the hands your opponents most likely hold if they bet or call – with the ultimate goal of deducing your best course of action.

## Flop #1: Q-8-3 rainbow

This is one of my favourite flops and one I frequently bet into, whether it has in fact helped me or not. The beautiful thing about this flop is that you know exactly what you're up against. If you bet anywhere from half pot to pot against this board and get called, you know exactly what your opponent holds: J-10-9-x. The only turn cards that would slow you down here would be the jacks, tens and nines; with any other card you would most likely bet the pot again. (Or, if the board pairs, you might decide to bet a smaller amount – see also my article '*The amount of the bet in pot-limit Omaha*'.) You play like this:

- ♠ If you have some kind of made hand (maybe even as weak as a pair of queens with a good kicker), or
- ♠ If you don't have anything yet (maybe you hold the J-10-9 yourself), but think you may be able to make your opponent lay down his hand.

Always look at your and your opponent's stack sizes though. For instance, don't bluff if either one of you is about to go all-in. If you are bluffing at the pot, thinking that your opponent is drawing, then if your turn bet gets called there should be some money left for you to bet on the river. It's a shame if you have figured out your opponent's hand perfectly, only to see him win the pot in the showdown with a single pair or even ace-high, because there was no money left on the river to make him fold. Beware of someone who just calls your flop bet (rather than raises) with a made hand rather than a draw. There are people who will just call with hands like Q-8, 3-3 or even 8-8 or Q-Q on this flop, waiting for you to bet again on the turn so that they can raise you then. But you should know who those players are, and ascertain their tells, habits and tendencies when they call on the flop with a made hand rather than a draw. Because usually, people who go for a delayed raise have a whole bunch of tells and giveaways like facial expressions (thinking), sounds (sighs) and pace of betting (calling more slowly than usual, as if in a true predicament) that you can use to your advantage.

When you play your hand the way I described here, you play the way some of the truly great players do quite often: They play their *opponent's* cards, rather than their own.

## Flop #2: J♦-9♥-5♦

Flops like these are often referred to as 'action flops': there are so many draws possible that a multiway pot is likely. In fact, if there are highly aggressive players in the game, a *monster* pot could even be possible. If you have a fine draw, you might play your hand aggressively, even though you know you'll probably get called and will have to make your hand to win. My favourite hand here would be a combination of a good draw and some kind of made hand. If I have K♦-Q♦-10-x for example, I have a huge hand that I will probably play very aggressively. But if I hold the same hand plus a jack as well (say, K♦-Q♦-J♠-10♥) then there's no stopping me; all the money's going to be in the middle. The nice thing about having a made hand *and* a draw, is that if you get called by a draw but neither of you make it, your one- or two-pair hand might win you a huge pot. But if you have the same fine draw *without* the pair, then you will simply have to make your hand to win.

One of my favourite hands on flops like these is in fact one of my favourite starting hands: a pair of aces single- or double-suited; in this case aces with the diamond nut flush draw. Whereas most people would bet out with this hand or even check and call, a large check-raise is the proper play most of the time – especially if the money is not all that deep (like in most online games). If you are in early position, you should check. Someone will certainly bet this board for you. Because of all the draws that are possible one or two players may call this bet, and *then* you surprise them by raising the pot. You might win the pot uncontested, or if one player decides to call you, the others might follow suit and you could in fact win a monster pot. It is great to get all your money in on the flop with a hand like this (overpair + nut flush draw) when you're up against two-pair hands and/or straight draws, because you are almost always a huge money favourite with two cards to come. The only type of hand you really fear here is a set, but even then you are not in terrible shape.

## Flop #3: Q♥-J♦-10♠

Playing against this flop shouldn't be too hard. You are only going to play A-K here (or Q-Q, if it's not too expensive[23]). Don't be too eager to put any chips into the pot on the flop, thinking your K-9 or 9-8 might be good; someone will be in there with A-K waiting for you to do the betting for him. Especially beware of playing J-J or 10-10 here: if someone bets and there is a call, you are probably facing the nut straight and top set, leaving you almost drawing dead. Even if there is no bigger set than yours out there, your only winners might be a running pair and the remaining tens or jacks (a queen might make somebody else a higher full).

## Flop #4: 8-5-5

In full-ring PLO games, you don't draw for straights or flushes when there's a pair on the board, period. There are people who will call a bet on this board with one (or two) overpair(s) to make top full, but I hardly ever do that. I always fear that the nuts might be out there. If there's a bet and a call, this *might* mean both players hold a five (which is good, as I will most likely get action if I make my full and I'll have them drawing dead), but it could also mean that one of them has eights full or is bluffing – while the other one has quads.

If *you* are the one holding wired eights on this flop, you should bet the hell out of your hand. People usually won't give you credit for top full when you bet out aggressively[24] and might play back at you with just a five and a few good kickers; you should do all you can to get all the money in the middle as soon as possible. (Remember: If you are up against quads, you are probably going to lose a lot of money anyway.) Don't do what a lot of weak players do: check the hand once on

---

[23] There is another time when you could play your Q-Q for a profit here when in fact it *is* expensive. If you know for a fact that two players both have the nut straight and no one is blocking any of your full house/quads outs, then you would be gaining an edge if you could get both their entire stacks in the middle on the flop. You would be getting more than 2-to-1 on your money with a hand that (with two cards to come) does much better than that. However, this play suffers from quite a few drawbacks, meaning that especially for people who cannot read their opponents that well, it may not be worth it to push their edge here – because for them, there *may* not be an edge.

[24] Please note that 'betting aggressively' does not automatically mean betting the pot. Against a flop 8-5-5 and holding 8-8-x-x, a half-pot bet is usually big enough to get rid of the overpairs who could potentially pose a thread to you, yet small enough to convince someone with a five that his trips could still be good – and thus that he should call or even raise you.

the flop (because their hand is so strong), only to see that the turn has made someone else a higher full. It is always better to win a small pot than lose a big one – and this is especially true in big-bet games where the money is deep.

## Flop #5: 7-3-2/K-7-2 rainbow

Ill-coordinated flops like these are excellent candidates for steals. Of course, you shouldn't overdo it, but normally you should be able to steal two or three pots an evening away from your opponents on flops like these. Ill-coordinated boards are excellent to try to (semi-)bluff aggressive pre-flop raisers out of the pot, because they will often be unable to call you unless they have flopped specifically top set. But also if the pot is still small, then betting out on these flops (especially when you're one of the blinds) could easily win the pot for you. However, if you make a bet against the K-7-2 rainbow flop and get called, you should usually be prepared to give up your hand. If someone decides to call a decent-sized bet on the flop with this board, he will most likely go all the way to the river with his hand.

## Some final words

The flop is very important in pot-limit Omaha, and you'll often see that the best players make their decision whether or not to commit to the pot on the flop rather than on the turn or river. It's not unusual to see two big stacks putting all their money in on the flop, most often when one player has the temporary nuts (a straight or top set) and the other a very good draw that wants to see both cards. (Rather than calling on the flop and then having to give up on the turn when the hand hasn't improved. After all, in this game it is entirely possible for the draw to be even money or even a small favourite against the temporary nuts with two cards to come.)

The fact that the flop is so important in this game, doesn't mean that playing the turn and river is automatic or easy. In fact, playing those streets can be very complicated (especially when the money is deep), and it's almost impossible for someone to be a winner in this game if he *isn't* proficient at playing the later streets.

# Playing the blockers

I've been playing poker professionally for four years now.[25] Although I still regard myself as a limit hold'em player, I have been focusing almost entirely on pot-limit Omaha for the past 18 months. Basically, in every poker game you get to see the same kinds of player. There are the people who don't know much (the fishes), the

---

[25] This article was written in the spring of 2002.

people who *act* like they know much, and the people who *really* know much (the professionals). In Europe, we play limit or pot-limit poker, high only. It is a rare occurrence to find a good hi/lo game here; in fact, only a small percentage of the players actually know the rules, let alone know how to play well. Players over here who act like they know a lot, always try to impress the other players by referring to hi/lo, by saying they want to start a big hi/lo game (knowing that this won't happen anyway). In pot-limit Omaha high these same players want to impress you with their knowledge by telling you about 'playing the blockers', knowing that many players aren't aware of this strategy anyway. The fact is, blocker play *can* sometimes enable you to skilfully bluff your opponents out of the pot (some of the best English and Irish players don't *talk* about the play very often, yet they are able to steal some of the biggest pots away from you using it), but the situation is hardly ever perfect.

## What does 'playing the blockers' mean?

Let's say you're in the big blind, holding J-J-J-6, and since there was no pre-flop raise, you are still in the hand. When the flop comes 10-9-8 (or better, Q-10-9), you know that it is unlikely the nuts is out there because you've got three jacks in your hand – that is, it is unlikely somebody will have specifically the Q-J needed to make the nuts (or, in the second example, the K-J). If you bet out on the flop, you might get one or two calls by players trying to draw out on the hand you've represented (the nuts), but if the turn is a blank and you bet the pot again, your opponents will most likely give up the hand – and you will have 'stolen' a pot, very important in any big-bet poker game. There are a few problems with this strategy, however:

♠ In pot-limit Omaha, there are almost always players who are about to go all-in. If they have some kind of hand, they will call you, and you have just thrown away your money.

♠ Because in this game drawing hands can sometimes be so powerful, someone with a fine draw (or a combination of a draw and a made hand) may decide to commit himself to the pot by going all-in on the flop or turn, even if he doesn't have the nuts. Let's take the flop 10♥-9♣-8♦, you're in early position with A♣-10♣-10♦-6♠, and have checked and called the flop. Now the turn comes 3♣ (giving you the nut flush draw in addition to your set), you check, the flop bettor bets again and there is one caller. At this point, you think you might have 15 to maximum 18 outs against the bettor (the board might pair/a third club might come), *if in fact he's got the hand the hand he is representing.* Since you're in early position and you might not get paid off if you make your hand (or might get bluffed out of the pot if a blank comes if the bettor doesn't have the straight), you could decide to commit fully by check-raising all-in. You know that if you get called or reraised all-in by the bettor and the other guy folds, you might be a small underdog, but you will still be a money favourite in the hand – making this a very reasonable play. And if the other player calls as well, that's even better of course. Now if *you* are the one who gets check-raised here when you have just been playing the blockers, your hand will go into the muck after having made two pot-sized bets, and you've cost yourself a lot of money representing a hand you don't have.

♠ If the pot gets big (or if your opponents are simply bad players who are unable to fold their hands) you might get called by the second or third nuts (or even worse) and you've given away valuable chips. Let's get back to our first example. Why did I say the Q-10-9 flop was actually a better candidate for blocker play than the T98 flop? Well, with the 10-9-8 flop someone may stubbornly hold on to his understraight (the 7-6), whereas with the Q-10-9 flop there are no straights possible without the jack.

♠ Although it is *unlikely* that the nuts is out there, it is not *impossible*. You are betting your money that nobody will be able to call you, because the odds are against your opponents holding the hand you are representing, *but this doesn't mean they can't have it*. In my example I was in the big blind with three jacks, but in Omaha you don't play hands like that out of freewill (although there are players who do). You are not going to call before the flop with 9-9-9-x, hoping the board will show 10-8-7 so that you can bluff your opponents out of the pot. Most of the time, you will only have two blockers (therefore the term playing *the* blockers isn't actually very accurate), which means that two of the cards needed to make the nuts still remain out there. Because of this, the situation is hardly ever perfect for making this play. Although it's nice to be able to skilfully steal a pot once in a while, the golden rule for almost everything in poker also applies here: do it, but don't *overdo* it.

# The strategy in practice

For the past four months I've been in Vienna, playing pot-limit Omaha exclusively. Although I'm well aware of the principles of blocker play and the merits this strategy has, I've only been able to profit from it on one occasion. I was in seat #2, the $2 blind (they play pot-limit Omaha here with one blind only) with K♣-K♦-8♣-3♠, when seat #10 (the game is played ten-handed here) raised to $10. Since there were lots of callers already who were unlikely to reraise, I decided to call although I had a rather weak hand. (In fact, the only kind of flop I am going to like is when a king flops, and even when this does happen it's by no means certain that the pot is going to be mine.) The flop came A♣-Q♣-5♠, and even though I was mentally prepared to give the hand up (I am not going to call a pot-sized bet out of position with the nut flush draw against someone who might very well hold three queens or three aces), this is not what happened. Everybody checked to seat #10 who bet only $20 into the $70 pot; seat #1 called, as did I. It seemed like the bettor had made the classic mistake of flopping a set and trying to make money with it, rather than charging people to draw out.

The three of us saw the turn, J♦. Although a case could be made for trying to represent the nuts here (K-10, I had two kings in my hand), I decided to just check. Seat #10 was a rather weak player who at this point would never lay down his most probable hand (three aces) knowing that he would still have quite a few outs against this probable nut straight – and seat #1 might in fact have made the nut straight himself! (What else could he have been calling with on this flop, given that I had the nut flush draw?) Anyway, seat #10 bet small once again ($30), and again got called by seat #1. Even though I was now certain that the nut straight was not out there, I also thought I couldn't make them lay down their hands by check-raising. So I decided to simply call as well.

The river was an offsuit ten, 10♥. I waited for about half a minute to feel the reactions of my opponents, and then decided to represent the straight I didn't have. (But from their perspective, I was in there with the king-high flush draw together with a second picture card maybe, so it seemed unlikely that they would call me with anything but the nuts.) I bet $60, a bet that seemed to beg for a call – the kind of bet many players would make on the river when holding the nuts – and both players folded without much thought. No one even *thought* that I might have been bluffing in this spot, and although it was just a small pot I picked up, winning just one or two small pots an evening with nothing adds up to a lot.

## A few words of caution

After having successfully bluffed someone out of the pot, *never* show your hand, for the following reasons:

- ♠ You might upset your opponent, making him leave, or forcing him to play better against you.
- ♠ Showing you've bluffed someone out of the pot disrupts the friendly atmosphere at the table. (And as you should all know, friendly games are often the most profitable ones.)
- ♠ You show the other opponents the strategy you've been using, making it more difficult to use it again in the future. In addition, predictable opponents who previously didn't even know the strategy existed might also get tricky and start using it once in a while – thus costing you money.

## Some final words

In this article I've discussed one of the most advanced strategies in my favourite game, pot-limit Omaha. The best players in this game often don't play their own cards, *they play yours*. They try to figure out what kind of hand you most likely have, and more so what you *don't* have, and then try to find the best way to play against you. If you are a tight player and it's not likely that you're in there with the nuts, they'll put pressure on you until you finally fold. The blocker strategy is based upon exactly this: if the nuts is not out there, the pot might very well be up for grabs. The best players know when the time is right to use it; they also know when the time is *not* right.

# All-in in pot-limit Omaha

In some of my articles I've written about the importance of having a lot of chips on the table in pot-limit Omaha. If your (weaker) opponents are also playing a big stack, you might be able to take their entire stack in just a single hand. More often, however, you'll find that some of your opponents are playing a *small* stack. They buy in for the minimum, and will buy in for the minimum again and again until they are up (in which case they leave) or are broke (in which case they will have to leave). Playing against an all-in has some consequences in the way that you, the big stack, should play your hand. If the small stacks in fact are playing well (if they are waiting for premium hands and, when they get them, become aggressive) it's important for you not to give them any action; you shouldn't make it *too* easy for them to double or triple their stack. Having said that, if you figure the all-in player for a good hand but there is another opponent with a big stack who may be in there on lighter values, then you might decide to build a big pot (even though you know you'll be an underdog against the all-in player) to try to break the other player and take his entire stack. In this article I'll describe two pot-limit Omaha hands in which all-in players were important factors in how the hands were played.

## Hand #1

### The game
Pot-limit Omaha, one blind ($2), minimum buy-in $100, ten-handed.

### The place
Vienna, Austria.

### The players involved
Me (holding K♥-K♠-6♥-6♣, playing a $500 stack), Mutlu, a very nice Turkish

player/dealer with a loose/aggressive style (holding J♥-J♣-8♥-7♣, playing $310), and a colleague of his, playing tighter but also rather passive (holding A♠-A♣-K♣-K♦, and playing the minimum buy-in).

In the pot-limit games here I had made it a habit to raise three times the blind before the flop, whenever no one had yet raised and I wanted to play; that is, whenever I raised before the flop it would always be the same amount. I did this to build the pot a little with my good hands without giving away too much information. In this hand, I was in early position, holding K♥-K♠-6♥-6♣, raised to $6 and was reraised by the rather tight player, who made it $20. His colleague (holding J♥-J♣-8♥-7♣) called and there were two other callers when the action got back to me. Most of the time I might have just called here, but I wasn't sure if the guy to my left had in fact *wanted* to reraise: he isn't usually very aggressive before the flop (even with premium hands) and in this specific case he wanted to take ten dollars from his own bet out of the pot, for no reason I could think of, and acted a little strangely. I had made it a pattern to become very aggressive (coming over the top, re-raising pot when someone had reraised my first raise) before the flop with aces. Since I thought no one (besides possibly the reraiser) was in there with aces and I might therefore win the pot right away or, if someone called, my hand was pretty well-disguised (and thus I might be able to make some money after the flop), I reraised pot ($128). The tight player went all-in for $100, his colleague (Mutlu) called and everyone else folded.

The flop came 10♥-5♥-4♣. This flop was pretty good for my hand as I had an overpair, a king-high flush draw and I had possible straights covered with the sixes in my hand. And just as importantly, it was a flop that was unlikely to have helped my opponent – so I bet everything my opponent had left ($310). He called with a hand that looked good from his perspective (J♥-J♣-8♥-7♣ for an overpair, a jack-high flush draw, an inside straight draw and a backdoor flush draw), since he probably figured to be up against bare aces, but in this case his hand was a big dog to mine. (Calculations will follow later on.) Nevertheless, he managed to scoop the pot by making a straight (turn 9♠, river Q♣). I used Wilson's software to calculate my expectation at two stages in the hand: before and on the flop.

### Expectation before the flop

When the action came back to me, I could have folded for $6 since it was possible that I was either beat or my cards were somewhat dead. Instead, I reraised to build a big side pot. Was I right in doing this? (Figures found using Wilson's software for Omaha, simulation 100,000 hands.)

### Expectation for the main pot

K♥-K♠-6♥-6♣ (Rolf) 16.3% vs. A♠-A♣-K♣-K♦ (Mutlu's colleague) 50.3% vs. J♥-J♣-8♥-7♣ (Mutlu) 33.4% of total pot $342.

### Expectation for the side pot

Rolf 55.5% vs. Mutlu 44.5% of total pot $56.

### Total expectation before the flop

- ♠ **Rolf** (0.163 x 342 + 0.555 x 56) = $86.83. I had put $128 into the pot, so if we rule out implied odds here (I thought I would be able to make some money after the flop against this player, even though he had position on me) I lost $41.17 on the hand, and folding for $6 would therefore have saved me more than $35.

- ♠ **Mutlu** (0.334 x 342 + 0.445 x 56) = $139.15. His total expectation before the flop was +$11.15. Since he had called the $20 reraise by his colleague already, he was right in calling my reraise later on. In fact, folding here would have cost him $31.15.

- ♠ **Mutlu's colleague** (0.503 x 342) = $172.08. Since he had put only $100 into the pot, his expectation here was +$72.08.

### Expectation on the flop

The flop was pretty favourable to me and when I made my move on the flop, I was not only a huge favourite to win the side pot, I had also become money favourite for the main pot.

### Expectation for the main pot:

Rolf (0.348 x 342) = $119.02. Mutlu (0.182 x 342) = $62.24. Mutlu's colleague (0.470 x 342) = $160.74.

### Expectation for the side pot ($676):

Mutlu can only win by catching a jack (two left), a six (two left) or by backdooring a straight or flush. So, even though my kings are dead, my hand is a 77.48-to-22.52% favourite over his. Rolf (0.7748 x 676) = $523.76, Mutlu (0.2252 x 676) = $152.24. We had both put $338 into the side pot, so my expectation here was +$185.76, his –$185.76.

### Total Expectation:

On the flop, the total expectation for my hand had become +$204.78 ($185.76 + $19.02), for Mutlu –$223.52 (–$185.76 – $37.76) and for his colleague +$60.74; there was $42 dead money in the pot because of people folding.

### Analysis

It looks as if I was pretty unlucky to lose this pot. Although my expectation before the flop was rather poor, this was mostly because the all-in player not only had the aces I expected, but my kings as well. Before the flop I had expected to be a smaller underdog for the main pot and a bigger favourite for the side pot than I turned out to be. When the flop came this favourable to me, I was very unfortunate to lose the side pot, as it is very hard in Omaha for your hand to be a 2-to-1 favourite over your opponent's, let alone 3-to-1. My opponent with the jacks thought the flop was more favourable to his hand than it actually was, and quite frankly made a mistake in calling my flop bet (since it was such a big dog), but he was rewarded by not just winning the side pot, but the main pot as well.

Then again, the way I played my hand before the flop was not completely flawless either. In fact, I had gone a lot further with my hand than its quality warranted, and just calling the tight player's reraise or even folding may have been better options than the one I chose (popping it again).[26]

# Hand #2

### The game

Pot-limit Omaha, one blind ($2), minimum buy-in $100, ten-handed.

### The place

Vienna, Austria.

### The players involved

Me (holding A♥-K♣-J♥-3♣), Mario (holding K♠-J♠-8♦-4♠) and a third player (holding A♦-Q♦-9♥-2♠), on flop A♠-Q♠-10♥.

I was in early position and made my standard raise to $6 with a nice, double-suited hand, and was called in no less than five places. We took the flop six-handed, pot size $36. The flop was favourable to me (A♠-Q♠-10♥), giving me the nuts. I had raised before the flop quite a lot during this particular session, but not many flops had been good to me; most of the time I was forced to check and fold. I thought that this might be a good time to go for the check-raise, especially since second-best hands (Q-Q, 10-10, A-Q, A-10) would probably bet the pot, figuring their hands might be good. Someone in late position indeed bet the pot ($36) and was called by the button (Mario), a deceptive player who was a little bit on tilt after having lost a few pots in a row. I figured the button (who had the second-largest stack on the table, mine was the largest) for some kind of two-pair hand or perhaps a flush draw and wanted to play my hand against the bettor only or make the button pay to draw out. So I check-raised pot to $180 total. The bettor went all-

---

[26] An even more thorough analysis of this hand can be found in Chapter 7, under 'Hand Match-Up No. 4'.

in for exactly this amount, and then the button came over the top for all his money.

At first I thought Mario was making a play at me, but then I realised there was only one hand he could have: K-J of spades (that is, the same nut straight I had but with the nut flush redraw). I had the dealer count out his bet: $710 all-in. I decided that although I knew his hand had to be a clear favourite over mine (even with my own – distant – backdoor flush and runner/runner full house redraws), I had to call here. If it had been just him and me, I might have let it go, but with all this money in the pot already ($36 before the flop plus $180 by the all-in player *and* Mario's and my $180 bet as well) it seemed impossible for me to fold the current nuts. (For anyone who isn't too familiar with this game, in pot-limit Omaha it *can* sometimes be correct to fold the temporary nuts, rather than call or raise.) I ran a few simulations on Wilson's software and the results were as follows:

### Expectation on the flop (main pot: $576)

Rolf, Mario and the all-in player had each put $180 into the main pot on the flop. Including the $6 pre-flop bets by them and also by the three other players, the main pot amounted to $576 (180 + 180 + 180 + 36). Pot equity after the flop: Rolf 29.0%, Mario 55.0%, all-in player 16.0%. That is: my expectation here was (0.29 x 576) = $167.04, Mario's (0.55 x 576) = $316.80 and the all-in player's $92.16 (0.16 x 576).

### Expectation on the flop (side pot: $1,060)

For the side pot, Mario's hand was a big favourite over mine: 63.7% to 36.3%. The side pot was $1060 ($530 each) and my expectation was $384.78 of this (0.363 x 1060), as opposed to Mario $675.22 (0.637 x 1060). My wins: flush 5.3%, full 2.4%; wins for the button: flush 30.3%, royal 4.9%; split pots: 56.9% of the time (straight).

### Total expectation of combined main and side pot ($1,636 total):

♠ **The three players who had folded after the flop**
Expected return: $0
Investment: $6 each (pre-flop)
Average profit/loss: –$6 each, –$18 total

♠ **The all-in player**
Expected return: $92.16
Investment: $186 ($6 pre-flop, $180 post-flop)
Average profit/loss: –$93.84

♠ **Mario**

Expected return: $992.02 (316.80 + 675.22)

Investment: $716 ($6 pre-flop, $180 in main pot, $530 in side pot)

Average profit/loss: +$276.02

♠ **Rolf**

Expected return: $551.82 (167.04 + 384.78)

Investment: $716 ($6 pre-flop, $180 in main pot, $530 in side pot)

Average profit/loss: –$164.18

### Analysis

As you can see, my total expectation for this hand was –$164.18 – meaning that if we were to play this hand over and over again, I would figure to lose $164.18 on average. As negative as this figure seems to be, it clearly shows that I was right in calling Mario's all-in raise. After my check-raise I had $186 invested in the pot already ($180 on the flop plus $6 before the flop). But after having called my opponent's all-in raise, my expected loss had gone down to $164.18 – meaning that this call had 'saved' me almost $22 in the long run.

Of course, in just a single hand of poker there *is* no long run. You'll just win the pot or lose it (or, as happened here, split it, as blanks fell on the turn and river). Still, it's important to look at the long-term perspective in poker. If you try to always be the favourite in the hand or make mathematically sound decisions, then in time the money should be yours. And yes, these mathematically sound decisions include actively trying to get yourself in situations where you may actually *lose* money – provided that by entering these situations you lose *less* money on average than by *not* entering them.

# A pot-limit Omaha quiz

You are playing pot-limit Omaha in a fairly aggressive game, minimum buy-in $500, three blinds ($5-$5-$10). The game is nine-handed and the rake is 5%, maximum $5. You are playing in seat #9. There's a loose/passive player in seat #1, playing a small stack, a tight and predictable rock in seat #2, and two highly aggressive (and fairly competent) players in seats #5 and #6, all playing large stacks.

This quiz might be a little more difficult and more advanced than some of the other quizzes I have done over the years. In this quiz you don't just give the preferred course of action (fold/call/raise) for each situation, but also the preferred betting and raising amounts – so think very hard before you answer. You can rate all of these answers on a scale from 1 (horrible) to 10 (superb). So, don't just pick one answer as being the 'best', but rather try to analyse the pros and cons of every single option. Also remember that in pot-limit Omaha there isn't always a 'right' or 'wrong' way to play a hand, that there's more room for interpretation; that circumstantial factors are very important here; that two players can have quite different playing styles and still both be winners, and that the solutions I give for the problems in this quiz therefore don't necessarily have to correspond with your own ideas.

# The questions:

### Question 1

You're in the big blind with 8♥-7♥-7♦-6♣, are playing a $2,000 stack and have received a free flop. Seven players see the flop, no raises, pot size $70. Flop: A♥-7♣-2♠. Usually, you would bet out here, but in this case you think going for the check-raise might be a better option. Seat #2 bets the pot ($70) and everybody else folds. What do you do?

a) fold
b) call
c) raise to $140
d) raise pot to $280

### Question 2

You're in the first small blind with A♥-A♣-8♥-3♠ and have a $2,000 stack. Seat #5 has raised to $50, there are two callers and it's up to you. What do you do?

a) fold
b) call
c) reraise to $100
d) reraise pot to $280

### Question 3

You're in the big blind with 7♠-7♥-6♥-5♠ and, once again, are playing a $2,000 stack. Seat #2 has raised to $40 before the flop, there are three callers, the two small blinds have folded and you decide to call the raise. The flop comes K♥-J♠-7♣. Even though you have flopped a set, you're in danger of set over set here. All in all, you simply want to see how the hand develops before putting a lot of money in the pot – even though you do recognise that this could very well be an excellent check-raise opportunity. Seat #2 also checks, as do all others. Turn: 2♣. What do you do?

a) check/if there's a bet, fold
b) check/if there's a bet, call
c) check/if there's a bet, raise small
d) check/if there's a bet, raise pot
e) mini-bet $20
f) bet half pot
g) bet pot

## Question 4

You're on the button, holding K♥-K♦-Q♥-J♦ with, once again, a $2,000 stack. There has been one caller, seat #5 has raised to $40 and has been called by seats #6 and 7. Then seat #8 reraises pot ($230). What do you do?

a) fold
b) call
c) reraise to $460
d) reraise pot to $840

## Question 5

You're under the gun with A♥-Q♣-J♣-J♦, playing a $3,000 stack, and make your standard raise to $30 (you always raise the same amount before the flop, to avoid giving away too much information about your hand). Three people call your raise. The flop comes J♥-10♣-8♥ and you bet $80. Seat #2 raises you $160 more for a total sum of $240, the two others fold and you call. The turn comes 3♥. What do you do?

a) check/if there's a bet, fold
b) check/if there's a bet, call
c) check/if there's a bet, raise small
d) check/if there's a bet, raise pot
e) bet half pot
f) bet pot

## Question 6

You're in late position, holding J♠-10♠-10♣-8♥ and playing a $3,000 stack. There has been a small raise before the flop, which you have called. The flop comes to your liking: 10♥-9♥-3♠. It's been checked to you, you bet the pot and are called in two places; the pot is now $760. The turn comes 8♦. The first player (with $1,800 left) checks, the second player bets all-in ($200) and it's up to you. What do you do?

a) fold
b) call
c) raise to $400
d) raise to $700
e) raise pot to $1,360

## Question 7

You're second to act, holding A♥-A♣-8♥-7♠, and are playing a $2,000 stack. The under-the-gun player has called the initial bet. What do you do?

a) fold
b) call/if there's a raise, call again
c) call/if there's a raise, reraise small
d) call/if there's a raise, reraise pot
e) raise to $30/if there's a reraise, call the raise
f) raise to $30/if there's a reraise, reraise small
g) raise to $30/if there's a reraise, reraise pot
h) raise pot ($50)

# The answers/points per answer:

### Question 1: a) 8 b) 6 c) 5 d) 3

In Omaha, one of the most expensive hands to hold is middle set against top set. What other hand but aces can the rock be playing under the gun? Don't be misled into thinking he can't have aces (since there was no raise), because rocks like to limp/reraise or even limp/call with aces. Even if the rock has decided to bet a rather weak hand here (for example, an ace with three picture cards), the pot is simply too small to be worth fighting for. Remember, if you check-raise him here and he doesn't have top set, he will almost certainly fold and you are going to win just a fairly small pot. But if by chance he *does* have bullets, you are going to lose a very big one – heck, you could even get busted.

This is one of those situations where it could be better to simply forfeit a small pot with the possible best hand, rather than get involved in a situation with reverse implied odds – where you will either win a fairly small pot, or else might lose a very big one. There is no shame in choosing the 'weak-tight' option of folding a good, but possibly second-best hand when facing a very tight player who is unlikely to be messing around.

### Question 2: a) 3 b) 6 c) 7 d) 5

Even though your side cards are junky, aces single-suited are a strong hand in pot-limit Omaha. Still, raising pot isn't good strategy: your opponents will know you have aces so you're giving them implied odds on the hand. If your image is right, the old trick of reraising small might work: if the aggressive player makes the mistake of raising you back again, you might be able to go all-in before the flop. Just make sure you would also make this play of reraising small occasionally with speculative (double-suited rundown) hands like J♠-10♥-9♥-7♠ and even 7♣-6♣-5♦-4♦.

### Question 3: a) 4 b) 3 c) 4 d) 8 e) 8 f) 4 g) 5

There's no question whether your hand is good right now: it is. The rock would have certainly bet if he held kings or jacks and since no one behind him bet even after the weakness he had shown, your set is good now. Since many river cards could cripple your hand, you've got to defend it. Still, betting out is not the best option. Straight and flush draws may call you and you might be bluffed out of the pot if a scare card comes on the river. Just check the hand down a second time: this being pot-limit Omaha, someone (maybe even the rock) will almost certainly bet to pick up the pot, maybe one player will call or even raise, and then you can check-raise the maximum to make them all lay down their (drawing) hands.

Or, as an alternative, you can choose to make a strange-looking mini-bet. If you know that your opponents may not respect this bet anyway, and could still make big raises even with little, then this mini-bet could have three advantages over going for the check-raise. First, if indeed you get raised the pot, you will now get a slightly larger percentage of your stack in than you would by check-raising some-one's pot bet. Second, it could help you get some more dead money in the pot from players who first call this $20 bet of yours, but who then fold when it gets raised and reraised behind them. And third, if people see you make this mini-bet as an attempt to induce action with the best hand so you can come over the top of any raisers, this may lead to your mini-bets getting more respect in the future – meaning that you could start to use this bet while holding just marginal hands, in order to see the turn or river cards cheaply.

Still, despite these three advantages, going for the check-raise seems like the 'natural' choice here – considering that you hold such a strong hand, without your opponents having any way of knowing this.

### Question 4: a) 7 b) 6 c) 3 d) 4

You might very well be up against aces, so even though you've got a premium hand, folding here might not be such a bad idea. Even though calling is an option (there's still a lot of betting leverage: you are in position, plus it looks like this is going to be a multiway pot giving you good odds on your money), there's the danger of someone popping it again – since your call doesn't close the betting. Reraising small is probably the worst option of all, because if the aces are indeed out there, you'll make it very easy for them to raise you out of the pot. If you think your hand might be good right now, then it could be better to commit fully. Still, I would say that against all but the very wildest and loosest reraises, a fold would probably be your best option here.

### Question 5: a) 3 b) 3 c) 3 d) 4 e) 8 f) 7

The rock is not going to bet this hand for you! He is in there with Q-9, has flopped a straight and maybe he has some kind of flush as well. Still, you've got the ace of hearts. You raised before the flop and called his raise on the flop; from his point of view you're in there with aces + nut flush draw, which has now been completed. You can bet either pot or half pot, both will get the same result: he'll fold his hand. If he does call, you still have outs, as the board may pair.

### Question 6: a) 3 b) 4 c) 6 d) 8 e) 6

The all-in player almost certainly has a straight, but you're getting the right odds on your call, trying to make a full house, so folding is not an option here. Even though this straight would have you beat, your set figures to beat the other player – who probably holds the nut flush draw, maybe with some kind of straight draw as well. The thing to do is to build a side pot: You don't want to make the other player fold, but you want to make him pay for his draw, and $700 seems like the right amount here. (Then, if the flush card comes on the river without the board pairing and he bets out, you can safely fold.) If you raise pot on the turn, this third player might very well fold – but you don't mind him in, since you've got to improve yourself to win the pot. In fact, you actually *want* to keep him in, as he will be giving you better odds on your money. Additionally, if you can create a side pot for the two of you where you have the best of it, then you may even be able to come out ahead for this hand even if the river does *not* offer you any help.

An additional benefit of this raise to $700, is that if by chance the third player *does* have a (non-nut) straight with no flush extras, your raise will almost certainly make him fold. So the option you have chosen could lead to you getting the best of two worlds: He may fold when he has you beat, yet call when he is trailing. And finally: If by chance the first player has been trapping and *is* in there with the nut straight, well then he could simply be winning a very large pot. His check-reraise all-in would be only $1,100 more for you, with a potential $3,560 to be won. (Total pot after your call: $4,560.) And with this kind of money in the middle, folding would not be an option now that any pair would almost certainly give you a winner, and any queen could lead to a split pot. So, in this case one could claim that player #1 has simply made a very clever play.

### Question 7: a) 2 b) 5 c) 4 d) 5 e) 4 f) 4 g) 8 h) 5

In pot-limit poker, you don't want to give away your hand when you've got a lot of money (betting leverage) left. If your opponents know you've got aces, they are getting implied odds on the hand: they are more likely to make money from you after the flop than the other way around. A way to avoid giving away your hand is to always raise the same amount. If someone then makes the mistake of reraising you, you could reraise the maximum with your aces. A lot of players raise a little when they have a good but not great hand and raise the maximum when they have aces, therefore option h) isn't one of my favourites. The limp/reraise strategy would have been excellent when playing a short stack (say, less than $1,000), but in this case this reraise wouldn't get even close to half your stack in before the flop. Thus you would be giving your opponents implied odds – and when playing deep money, this is something you should always try to avoid.

## Analysis

Minimum points: 20
Maximum points: 54

### 20-36 points

This quiz was in fact a little more complicated than most other quizzes. Still, in all but the weakest PLO games you are going to be faced with some of the tough decisions I just described. You obviously aren't ready to get into the games yet.

### 37-42 points

You seem to have some knowledge about the game, but probably not enough yet to be a truly dangerous competitor. It is also possible that you are in fact a rather experienced player who just happens to disagree with me in some situations; like I've said, there is often more than one 'right' way to play a hand in this game. In this quiz I have given reasons why I prefer certain decisions over others – but this doesn't mean that all the other options are flat out wrong.

### 43-48 points:

Very good. You are definitely a force to be reckoned with at the pot-limit tables.

### 49-54 points:

Excellent. If your play at the table is in fact as good as your score suggests, then pot-limit Omaha might be the perfect game for you.

# Chapter Six

# Practice hands

After all the information you have received, it is now time for you to actively participate and put all of these strategies into practice. All in all, here are lots of situations where you can test your own views by rating all options on a scale from 1 (horrible) to 10 (superb). Keep in mind that the ratings are important, but not nearly as important as the *reasoning* behind these ratings. And focusing on just coming up with the correct scores, while not really knowing *why* this would or would not be the proper play, is not the way to tackle these problems.

Note that not all of the example situations in this chapter are easy or straightforward. Quite the contrary, some of them are quite hard. So, I hope they will help you get some real insight into the thought processes and mathematics of PLO, and in the way *I* think this game should be played. But again, these are *my* views, they are how *I* view the game – they are by no means the *only* correct way to become successful.

## Practice hand 1

### The situation/question

Pot-limit Omaha live game, minimum buy-in $500, blinds $10-$10. You hold A♠-A♣-5♠-4♦ in early position (under the gun). You bought in for the minimum $500 but have not been able to win any pots, so that your stack is now down to $360. You tried to go for a limp/reraise before the flop, but since there was no raise, six players saw the flop for $10 each, including the two blinds. The flop comes Q♠-9♠-5♥. It is checked to you. Not knowing anything about the other players, what would be your best course of action?

a) Check with the intention of folding if there is a lot of action
b) Check with the intention of calling any reasonable-sized bets
c) Check with the intention of raising small
d) Check with the intention of raising the maximum
e) Bet small, say $20 or even $10
f) Bet pot, $60

# Answers/Reasoning behind these answers:

### a) 3½

An awful choice. You have a powerful holding with your overpair/nut flush draw/bottom pair. Even in the worst case scenario, of you running into a set, you would still be getting almost the proper odds if by chance all the money went in on the flop – even more so if there were callers in between the set and you (assuming, of course, that you were to go for the check-raise which, as you will see, is my preferred choice).

An example of you running into top set, A♠-A♣-5♠-4♦ versus Q♥-Q♣-7♣-7♦ on a flop Q♠-9♠-5♥, shows that you are trailing 38.41-to-61.59%. This means that you would be a clear dog. From the flop onwards, you would have to invest $350 into a total pot of $760, assuming no dead money from callers in the middle, and assuming that your check-raise gets called. To break even here, you would need 350/760 = 46.05% pot equity, and you clearly don't have that. You've got just 38.41%, meaning that in this situation you would lose (46.05 – 38.41) x 760 = $58.08 on average.

Please note though that many hands that would call you are actually a clear underdog to yours, hands like pair + weaker flush draw, or a wraparound straight draw. Additionally, there are also many times when your check-raise will help you to win the pot uncontested. So all in all, check/folding with a hand that could very well be best, in a situation where even if you *are* wrong you are not *that* wrong, seems like a very bad choice to me. And finally, in most cases where you go for a check-raise, there would be at least one caller in the middle. This could have the benefits of: a) making the pot bigger, b) improving your odds, c) getting almost all of your stack into the pot instead of just a large percentage, and d) creating dead money if they first call and then fold to your check-raise.

### b) 3½

Another weak choice. You automatically assume that you will have to hit your draw to win the pot. But a bet from someone behind you, especially from someone in middle or late position, doesn't necessarily mean a quality made hand at all. It could just as well be from a hand like a straight draw or something like pair + weaker flush draw – meaning that you would actually have the best hand *and* the best draw. Also, you are out of position. Not knowing what you are up against, it is easy to make mistakes on the turn if you just call on the flop. Or, better: It is possible that your opponents could *induce* you to make mistakes on the turn, either by making you fold the current best hand or by making you pay off with a losing one.

### c) 4

A strange play that I would not recommend. Let's say that on this flop, you check, someone behind you bets $50 or $60, and then you double the bet by check-raising to $100 or $120 or so. Assuming that your opponent now calls you, you have not accomplished much, because you still don't know what you are up against. The amount of money you have left now accounts to just about one pot-sized bet or a little less than that, and the situation looks like this. If the turn card is good and gives you a lock (say, a third spade comes up when your opponent was drawing to complete a straight), you are not going to make any more money, unless maybe if you are up against a habitual bluffer. Yet if a card comes that doesn't help you but that in fact could have helped your opponent, your flop play may now have committed you to the pot. You may feel forced to put the remainder of your stack into the middle, when with just one card to come you may be drawing thin or even very thin. (Or, perhaps even worse, if you don't put the money in yourself but check after this seemingly bad turn card and then make a 'prudent' fold, you could get bluffed or semi-bluffed out of the pot when in fact your aces *were* still good.)

### d) 8½

The clear best choice by far. What you want with your aces + nut flush draw is to get all the money in on the flop. You have three pre-flop callers behind you who are still to act and who may very well like this flop. Unless they are extremely passive, they could be tempted to bet here with a wide range of hands, including two pair, pair + wrap, pair + flush draw etc. If you can then check-raise the maximum against their bet, you will have put a very large percentage of your stack in. By doing this, you will have maximised your expectation, and you will have taken away any implied odds that your opponents could be getting based upon their hand and/or their good position. You will probably get called by people with big straight draws, but you don't mind that. Even against a decent wrap like 10-8-7-6 (any 6,7,8 or J would complete your opponent's straight here) you are still a clear favourite. Simulations show that you will win the pot no less than 68.17% of the time. So, from your opponent's point of view, he may think he could have 13 outs twice – but in reality, you have both the best hand *and* the best draw. By check-raising the maximum now, you will get all of your opponent's money into the pot (at least the amount of money that you are playing), and this has some clear advantages. If by chance the turn card is the third spade, you now have most of his money in the middle already – money that he would not have wasted if the money had been deeper and if you had played the hand in a more passive manner. Also, if by chance the turn is bad and your opponent *has* completed his straight, then there is so little money left to be bet on the turn that you are now committed – but you could still have up to nine outs to redraw against your opponent, and win the pot after all. This scenario would *never* have happened if you had taken a less aggressive approach on the flop. Because then you would have seen the probably bad turn card, had looked at your chips thinking 'Hmm, the money is too deep and I'm not getting the proper odds with my maybe nine outs or so,' and you would have folded what may have been the eventual winner.

Remember: When you hold a combination of a made hand + nut flush draw, you usually *want* your opponents to call you with a straight draw, provided that you can get at least 55-60% of your stack in on the flop. In fact, you don't automatically need to be in a heads-up situation to make going all-in with your aces + nut flush draw profitable. If you are in a three- or four-way pot with this hand and no one has a set, then you could very well win the pot close to 50% of the time, while in order to have a positive expectation you would need to have a pot equity of just 33.33% or 25% (in fact, even less that that, taking into account any dead money in the middle). Aces + nut flush draw against a semi-coordinated board is *the* best check-raising hand of all, especially if the money is not too deep and/or if the players behind you are at least fairly aggressive. Playing the hand in this manner is an excellent way to take advantage of overaggressive players on or near the button who like to bet their draws. It is also *the* hand and *the* opportunity to show your opponents: 'Hey guys, just because I check doesn't *automatically* mean I have nothing.' Even if you know for a fact that the bettor has two pair with nothing else, then you should *still* make this check-raise the maximum play, because with two cards to come your hand is almost never a dog, let alone a serious one. In addition, there is almost always at least *some* chance that your opponent will fold his two pair, knowing that you could either be pushing a big draw, or else have a better made hand. This means that he will either be about even money or a massive dog – and especially fairly tight or weak-tight players could tend to take the easy way out and fold.

Just to show this exact situation, I have simulated our A♠-A♣-5♠-4♦ on this same Q♠-9♠-5♥ flop against Q♦-9♦-7♣-4♣ for top two pair with nothing else. In this case, our aces + nut flush draw are actually a 51.83% *favourite* to win the pot, meaning that one could argue that even against a currently better hand, we would be check-raising for value. Remember, there is also $60 dead money in the pot, meaning that we would need pot equity of just 46.05% to make this a profitable play – and clearly we do much better than that. This is even more true when we take into account this possibility of our opponent first *betting* $50 or $60 with this hand, and then *folding* it against our check-raise. Don't forget that if *you* are the one who has first bet with two pair/no extras and then face a pot-sized check-raise by a very tight player like me, you will probably start liking your hand a lot less than before the check-raise. Any decent player will recognise that top two will almost *never* be a significant favourite in this situation, but it *could* be a massive dog (against a set, or against the same top two + good redraw). Whereas most players will reason 'Well, it's only $350 total to see how bad a shape I am actually in' and then make that call, some players *will* make the 'prudent' move of laying their top two down – and this will be to *your* advantage.

Finally, one additional reason why I prefer this check-raise over betting out is that it limits your opponents' opportunities to outplay you. Let's say that the person who is sitting on the button with this Q♦-9♦-7♣-4♣ is in fact a very good player. If he sees you betting the pot from under the gun, he will immediately recognise the possibility that you had been going for the limp/reraise before the flop, and that you are now betting with aces + nut flush draw. In response, he will probably *not* raise you, but simply flat call. He will wait for a safe turn card to commit fully, knowing that by this time, with just one card to come, his two pair is a significant favourite over your hand. By waiting until the turn to raise, he will be manipulating the odds in his favour in a very smart manner. But by check-raising him all-in on the flop, you are depriving him of this possibility.

### e) 6

Not a bad option at all. By making this strange bet, you hope that one of your opponents will read it as a sign of weakness, and try to raise you off your hand. Obviously, when the action gets back to you, you will simply come over the top for all your money, again with a hand that could very well be the best hand and the best draw. This play would be even better if between you and the raiser there are quite a few players who have called this $10/$20 and who now fold to your reraise – creating some extra dead money for the eventual winner of the hand. Please note that this last reason (creating dead money from players in between the bettor and the eventual raiser) means that I actually prefer this 'mini-bet with a strong holding' as the first one in a long line of people, not as the third in a line of six – as we are here. For this reason, I give this option only 6 points. Had we been in the small blind in a similar situation, I would probably have rated it a 7 or even 7½.

Now, if this little bet of yours does *not* get raised, you can then let the turn card, in combination with your read on your opponents, decide whether or not it is worth it to commit fully. You wouldn't like to see any K, J, T, 8, 7 or 6 pop up, as they would almost certainly force you to give up. But with any other card, you could decide to take your hand to the river – especially if you figure that your opponents were calling you on the flop with weak hands, rather than slowplaying a good made hand.

It should be clear that both this option as well as option d) try to accomplish similar goals: finding a successful combination of maximising your wins and minimising your losses. What you don't like with your aces + nut flush draw is making one big bet on the flop and then being forced to give up on the turn because a dangerous card has arrived, one that suddenly has you drawing to just the flush, probably. So you are trying to find the best way to get all the money in on the flop. And while I like this option quite a bit less than option d), it is still not bad. And also, if you are someone who regularly makes these types of mini-bets (as I do), then there is nothing wrong with occasionally doing this with fairly big hands as well, for instance like the one we have here. This will also help you for those times in the future when again you come out betting unusually small. It could then protect you from getting raised because your opponents know that you are capable of making this play with a big hand. Anytime your opponents fear the betting combo 'mini-bet/if raised, come over top for maximum reraise', they may be reluctant to raise you – and you will get to see many cheap turn cards when in fact you were mini-betting with some marginal or even longshot hands.

### f) 5

Has the disadvantages described above. The problem with making this play is that a) many straight draws and other hands that rely on implied odds will call you, all of them while having position on you, and b) there are very few safe cards for you on the turn – assuming that your aces are actually good right now. With a stack of less than $200, I think betting out *would* have been the best option. But here, the money is just a little too deep to make this play. With your combination of a made hand and a big draw, you want to be either entirely committed, or not committed at all. What you don't want is to bet a large enough percentage of your stack to make you *almost* committed – when in fact there are a whole bunch of turn cards that can suddenly leave you drawing very thin.

# Practice hand 2a

## The situation/question

You are playing in the 'Vienna game'. You have built your stack from the initial $100 to $200, in a game with one $2 blind. You hold 9♥-8♠-7♥-6♠ on the button. Three limpers to you, including a tight under-the-gun player who usually only enters the pot with high-quality hands. He is someone who raises with a large percentages of the hands he would play in this position, yet he almost always goes for the limp/reraise when holding aces. The two other callers are both relatively weak players, a bit too loose and not overly tricky. For the sake of this practice hand, we'll assume that everyone is playing a $200 stack. How would you rate the following:

a) fold
b) call
c) mini-raise to $4
d) raise pot to $12

## Answers/Reasoning behind these answers

### a) 3

If you fold a hand this good and coordinated while on the button, then you have no business playing this game.

### b) 6

Not bad in itself. Many players would auto-call here, knowing that they have a speculative hand, and simply hoping to catch a good flop while having all the action in front of them.

### c) 7½

The 'book play' – at least according to the book that you are currently reading. This is almost the exact same situation that I described in the 'Vienna Way' chapter. Mini-raising here has three clear advantages:

♠ You take the initiative.

♠ Because of your raise, your opponents may figure you for big cards rather than the medium rundown that you actually have, and this could give you clear playing advantages later in the hand. People may think that you could be mini-raising here with aces in order to reopen the betting, hoping that someone will reraise and you can then come over the top – and in fact, this is a play I would indeed make with aces in this position. If indeed your opponents read you for a different type of holding than you actually have, and your raise will be called but not reraised, then you may be able to pull off a successful (semi-)bluff if the board shows one or two big cards and no one holds the temporary nuts. Or you could get excessive action when in fact you *have* flopped well, if your opponents figure that because of your pre-flop raise 'you cannot hold these cards'.

♠ You will expose the tight under-the-gun limper. If indeed he's got aces, he will almost certainly come out of the bushes now – either by making a minimum reraise or (more likely, given his description) a pot-sized one. While *he* may think he is doing the right thing here, he doesn't know that hot and cold, your holding is usually close to even money against any hand containing two aces, and that you have mini-raised with a great counter-hand to his bullets. (For instance, against a hand like A♣-A♥-9♣-4♠ you are just a 44.41-to-55.59% dog, and this is actually far from the best possible situation for your 9-8-7-6 double-suited. Against a A-A-K-2 rainbow hand, you would even be a 50.62-49.38% *favourite*.) Add to this the fact that you are in position, with fairly deep money *and* a good grasp of what you are up against, and it should be clear that even against his $20 total reraise, you have a very easy call. This is even more true because your opponent has no clue as to what *you* are holding. This is a great situation for you with very good implied odds, meaning that it is very worthwhile to make this pre-flop mini-raise in order to *get* yourself into this favourable position.

### d) 5

Even though you are almost even money hot and cold against aces, there is no need for you to escalate the pot at this point. Remember that when the pot grows bigger, and thus the money becomes shallower, your positional advantage becomes less important and less pronounced. Additionally, if the tight UTG habitually plays – or better: *mis*plays – his aces this way (as, from my description, he seems to be doing), you should *create* this situation for him as described in c). You want to give him the opportunity to make this mistake, while keeping your own investment as low as possible. Note that if you raise the pot now instead of the mini-raise that I recommend, the UTG could now make it $42 (if the big blind folds) or even $52 if the blind actually calls your raise. This would mean that with about one quarter of the stacks already in before the flop, there's only enough room for not much more than one pot-sized bet once the flop arrives. Thus you have taken away a large part of your own implied odds that you *had* created in option c). And not just that, you have entered a very high-risk situation now, where you have invested such a substantial part of your stack that you cannot fold very liberally after the flop – even if you suspect that you are beaten. This means that compared to option c), *you* are not a whole lot more likely to take your opponent's entire stack now – but he *is* much more likely to take yours.

# Practice hand 2b

## The situation/question

We'll assume that the expected (and recommended) situation has actually taken place. You mini-raise to $4, the big blind calls, the UTG reraises to $20, both other limpers fold and you call. The big blind gets out of the way, so that you and the limp/reraiser are now heads-up. The flop now comes K-6-4 rainbow. Your opponent bets the pot, $48, and still has $132 left. What do you do?

a) fold
b) call
c) mini-raise to $96
d) raise pot to $192

# Answers/Reasoning behind these answers

### a) 5½

This is not the best of flops for you. It is quite clear that your pair of sixes is not the best hand right now, and you only have four nut outs. Using the old 'never draw to an inside straight' adage, you would have a clear fold.

However, for those who look a little more carefully, this is a situation with quite a bit of value. After all, you have position, you know what you are probably up against, and there *is* still quite a lot of money left. You know that any 7, 8 or 9 on the turn could give you the best hand, any 6 will almost certainly leave your opponent playing for a two-outer (unless he has specifically A-A-6-x, or the K-K for top set that you don't figure him for), and any 5 will give you an almost certain lock. All in all, this seems like a rather too many outs/rather too profitable situation to fold here.

Having said that, if you are *not* entirely confident that your opponent has just aces here, for instance because your pre-flop read could have been wrong, or because your opponent's body language suggests that he could have actually received some help from the board in other ways than through his aces, then this slightly profitable call will have turned into a clear fold. Remember that many of your two pair outs will still put you in front by only a small margin, even if you are 'just' up against aces. So before making that call on the flop with your marginal holding, you should be at least *fairly* certain that you are not up against someone who has actually received a good or very good flop.

### b) 7

The 'natural' choice. You know that your opponent almost certainly still just has one pair. You are behind, and you know that you will need to improve to win. If you think that you could semi-bluff your opponent off his hand here, then option d) is best. But most tight players are simply *incapable* of releasing their aces in this situation, especially after having made a pot-sized reraise before the flop, and even more so against just one opponent. If your opponent fits this characteristic, then you do not want to give him the chance to simply stick in his money when there is a much better and much more obvious choice available for you: calling. With a maximum of 15 good turn cards out of the remaining 43 in the deck (assuming A-A-x-x for your opponent), it is worth it to call that $48 if you know that your opponent is now committed and will not fold his hand – even when the turn card is obviously bad for him and may have favoured you. So I would recommend calling despite the fact that many of these 'outs' are not clear winners by any means. And I would give even more points than 7 for calling if by chance you are up against someone who would *not* automatically bet pot on the turn, but who could possibly give you a free card if you have not yet improved. Against a 'Labelled with Aces' player who suddenly gets scared on the turn and then often goes into a check-call mode, calling on the flop is not even a *possibility* anymore – it is the only correct option.

### c) 3½

A very bad choice. You will both get yourself committed when you are actually trailing, and you will give your (weak! exploitable!) opponent the chance to re-raise all-in. This means that not only will your read on this player have become worthless, you have also given up your positional advantage and the implied odds that you could have received.

### d) 5½

A good option if you know that there is a good chance you could make your opponent lay down his aces. For instance if (because of your pre-flop mini-raise, and your calling of the pot-sized reraise) you judge it likely that your opponent figures you for kings. If you know that he could give you credit for three kings when you raise him against his 'obvious' strong holding on this rainbow board, then raising the pot would be a very good choice. It would be a very *bad* choice though if your opponent is too stubborn or too committed to even *consider* laying down his aces. And based upon the characteristics of this player as described in the example (tight but predictable/overplaying aces regardless of the stack sizes), and also based upon my own experience with people who give away their aces too early in the hand, it seems that this semi-bluff pot raise usually does not have a very large chance of success.

# Practice hand 2c

## The situation/question

We will now change this scenario slightly. All hands and pre-flop actions remain the same, but this time the flop comes 7-6-4 rainbow instead of the previous K-6-4 rainbow – giving you top two pair + open-ended straight draw. How would you rate these same options now?

a) fold
b) call
c) mini-raise to $96
d) raise pot to $192

## Answers/Reasoning behind these answers

### a) 2

No way you can fold here, now that you have flopped what you wanted.

## b) 4½

Quite a few 'good' players would just call here. They figure: 'I know my opponent almost certainly has two aces, a hand that he might not be able to release against this board with just small cards. So, even though I *know* that I am in front now, I will simply wait for a safe turn card to commit fully. That way, I might save myself a bit of money if either a four or an ace pops up.' Now, while I understand this reasoning, and as I said it is often the good rather than the weak players who would choose this option, I still disagree with the logic. In my view, you are simply in a highly profitable situation, where you know that you are almost certainly going to get called by a weaker hand. What's more, even if by chance the turn is bad, you could still have up to eight outs (in case of an ace on the turn, which would give your opponents trip aces, and thus any five or ten would still give you a winner) or even twelve (if a four comes on the turn and thus you would also redraw with any seven or six on the river).

So, in my view you should simply push your edge now, and get the money in while it is clear that you have this edge. This is especially true if there is at least some chance that you could make a mistake on the turn. For instance, if an ace comes on the turn and you fold against your opponent's 'obvious' three aces when in fact he's got K-K-x-x or even J-10-9-8 or so, then you would have made a horrible play – and on top of that, one that could easily have been avoided. In order to avoid costly mistakes like this, I always recommend keeping things simple, especially when the pot grows big, and even more so when you are probably in good shape with a good-but-not-monster hand. So simply stick the money in right now, and if your opponent happens to outdraw you either on the turn or river, well then good luck to him. But don't get frisky in a big pot, or go for an advanced fancy play when the most obvious choice is almost guaranteed to get you into a profitable or even highly profitable situation. (In the situation here, with your 9♥-8♠-7♥-6♠ on a 7-6-4 rainbow flop, your opponent's A♣-A♥-9♣-4♠ would win a measly 21.22% of the time. In fact, if the 7-6-4 rainbow flop were to contain a heart and a spade but no club, the fact that you also have two backdoor flushes now puts your opponent in even worse shape – his pot equity dropping to 16.83%.)

## c) 7

You know that you have flopped a monster against your opponent's most probable hand, and thus you don't necessarily want to blast him out of the pot. But because your opponent is not likely to fold against a big raise either, I would simply choose *that* option – option 'd'. Still, giving him a 'discount' and keeping him in the pot has some merits too – especially if you think he may be a bit weaker than you initially thought and/or if he is the type of person who *would* fold unimproved aces against a big raise. Just make sure that you know that even this small raise would leave you committed. No matter how scary (ace or four) the turn may look, you are *not* going to fold anymore – for all the reasons we discussed under option 'b'. So if your plan was to reraise small now, but then fold on the turn in case of an ace or four, subtract two points. That is *not* the way that I would recommend playing this hand.

### d) 8

The best choice of all. Even though both options 'b' and 'c' have clear merits, there are also two overriding factors to simply choose option 'd'. For one, you quite likely have the best hand by far, but just as importantly, you are almost certainly going to get called by a worse hand even if you raise big. And as I said: When the pot gets big and you are almost certainly in a very profitable situation, then you should not make things more difficult than they really are. The only reason why I would prefer option 'c' over 'a' is that by making a pot-sized raise I could possibly raise my opponent off a hand that is a clear dog – but in my experience almost every player would auto-call even the big raise with aces in this situation.

By the way, keep in mind that raising big here, in a situation where you almost certainly have the best hand *and* the best draw, gives you credibility for the times when you try to semi-bluff raise someone off his unimproved big pair. For instance, if you had a hand like 10-9-8-7 instead of our 9-8-7-6, then you *would* almost certainly have raised the pot on the flop to make the probable aces lay down, wouldn't you? Now, in order to give you the necessary credibility for those times, your opponents will have to know that you will *also* raise big in a situation where you could afford to make a smaller raise. And the perfect situation to get this into your opponents' heads is by raising them big with the current best hand in a situation where you know you are going to get called. In later hands, you can then use this new-found 'knowledge' of theirs to your advantage, by semi-bluffing them off their hands in situations where in fact you are only drawing.

# Practice hand 3a

## The situation/question

The $10-$10 blinds live game in Amsterdam. You have chosen your favourite seat to the immediate right of an absolute maniac, entirely in line with my recommendations throughout this book. You have bought in for the minimum $500, and having won one small pot, you are now playing a $700 stack. For simplicity's sake, we'll assume that your opponents are all playing exactly $700 as well.

You find K♠-K♦-9♠-8♦ in early position and, again according to my recommendations, you come in for a mini-raise to $20. The overly aggressive player to your immediate left now reraises the maximum to $80, just as you had expected. The button, a decent but little bit too loose player who likes to see many flops, calls this $80, and everyone else folds. It is up to you – What do you do?

a) fold
b) call
c) reraise the minimum to $140[1]
d) reraise the maximum to $340

# Answers/Reasoning behind these answers

### a) 3½

You almost certainly have the best hand. Even though you are facing a pot-sized reraise and are out of position, folding is not a real option here.

### b) 6½

Not bad at all. The nice thing about sitting to the immediate right of a maniac is the fact that you will often be able to close the betting. In this case, you could simply call this reraise and then check every flop to the maniac, who will almost certainly bet the pot, whether or not he has actually flopped something good or not. This flop bet of his will put the button in the middle. Depending upon this person's actions, the texture of the board, what you read your opponent(s) for, and not in the last place the strength of your own hand, you can then decide to check-raise all-in to $620 or check-fold. (Check-calling not being a serious option, for rather obvious reasons.)

### c) 5

Not the best of choices. Even though the player to your left may be rather overaggressive, he is probably no fool either. By reraising small you put a sign on your head: 'I have a big hand, quite likely a very big pair or four double-suited high cards that I want to get all-in with before the flop.' This means that, assuming both players just call your mini-reraise, it will be very easy for them to make the correct decisions against you after the flop – even more so because they both have position on you. What's more, by reraising small you are opening yourself up for a big reraise in case the maniac by chance *has* been lucky enough to pick up two aces.

---

[1] In the Amsterdam game that I describe here, a minimum raise equals the amount of the previous raise. In this case, the last raise was $60 more to $80, meaning that a minimum re-reraise would now be another $60 more to $140. A lot of casinos have different rules; rules that say any reraise should be at least double the amount that the previous raiser has bet. Thus the minimum reraise would then be $80 more to $160, and if another player were then again to reraise the minimum, this would be $160 more to $320. Frankly, I think this 'double the bet' practice is the better rule. The reason for this is simple: Because in big-bet poker there is no cap on the number of raises as in limit, two players could put a third one in the middle by making a whole bunch of 'limit-like' raises. Frankly, for the style of play that I used, this Amsterdam rule was excellent, and I have used it to my advantage on many occasions – but that does not mean I think it is a good rule, because it isn't.

So, if indeed your kings are good, then you don't push enough with this small reraise, and you give your opponents implied odds by revealing the content of your hand at least to *some* degree. At the same time, if by chance the maniac or even the button *are* in there with aces, you are simply reopening the betting for them, so that they can do what they want: move all-in before the flop with the current best hand. So, it should be clear that unless the maniac is crazy enough to make a *fourth* raise with crummy cards, your minimum reraise doesn't do you all that much good.

### d) 7½

The best choice. You simply commit fully with your premium hand, and basically get the hand over with. You know that if you reraise the pot here, all other decisions in the hand have become a formality, as you will simply stick in the remainder of your stack at the first opportunity – regardless of what your opponents do or don't do. One could argue: 'Well Rolf, if we reraise here and are up against aces, we will lose our entire stack just as in c), won't we. So what is the difference – why do you rate this option a 7½ and the previous one just a 5?' My answer is simple. With the quality hand that you have here, you are probably going to lose your entire stack anyway, regardless of whether you just call, reraise the minimum or reraise the maximum. You have chosen this exact seat because you know that the person to your left often raises on very light values, and seated to his immediate right you are hoping to capitalise on this. If you decide to just flat call the reraise (as I said before, not a bad choice by any means) and then the flop comes something non-threatening like 2-2-7 rainbow, you will almost certainly go for the check-raise all-in, taking advantage of the fact that the maniac will probably do the betting for you. So if by chance you *are* up against aces, you are very likely to lose your entire stack anyway. But at least if you decide to reraise the maximum, you will push your edge and maximise your wins in the much more likely situation that you actually hold by far the best hand. Additionally, this aggressive play of yours will for a large part negate your positional disadvantage, because you will get a very significant percentage of your stack in – almost 50%. Since you are not going to give any of your opponents credit for aces anyway, it is correct to simply raise the maximum now and avoid any headaches.

In pot-limit Omaha, you should not try to outthink yourself, especially not when the money is relatively shallow. You have a great hand, and are up against a maniac and a very liberal caller. What's more, even if in fact you *are* up against aces, it is not like you are dead. You would be a big dog yes, but especially your suits and the 9/8 combo could prove very useful here. For instance, despite the fact that kings versus aces is one of the worst match-ups in PLO, against a hand like A♠-A♣-5♣-4♥, your K♠-K♦-9♠-8♦ will still win the pot no less than 41.52% of the time. So yes, being in a heads-up situation with very deep stacks you would lose quite a bit of money on average. But in this case the dead money in the pot from the button, in particular, and also the $20 that you have already put into the pot, means that you don't lose much money at all. After all, assuming the total pot is $700 + $700 + $80 + $10 + $10 = $1,500, then you would have an overall expectation of $622.80. This means that once the action came back to you, with $680 left, and you decided to put in the maximum reraise, you all in all wound up losing just $57.20 on average – despite being in this extremely bad match-up with kings against aces.

Well yes, you say, but in this case your cards were very live, right? The person with the aces could just as well have had a hand that also contained one of your kings, that had higher spades or diamonds than you, or even something like A-A-9-8 – correct? Well yes, again that is true. But in situations where I know there is almost no way back for me anyway, I usually don't think in terms of a worst-case scenario: I think of what is realistically possible. And in this case my conclusion would be that the maniac is very likely to be reraising me with just random garbage. Even if by chance he *is* in there with aces, even then my cards will have some or even quite a lot of potential. Also there is quite a lot of dead money. And if the button does not fold but comes along for the ride then I will get even better odds on my money – knowing that in a three-way pot my double-suited quality kings will usually win close to 30% of the time even when one of my opponents has bullets.

So had I been in good position, one could have given many correct reasons why flat calling would be better than moving in here. But since I am out of position with my quality kings that are likely to be good, and taking into account the possibility of getting in almost half my stack before the flop, I would say: Just put the money in and hope that if good, my hand will stay good and if not good, I will draw out. That is how *I* would play the hand – and my guess is, so should you.

# Practice hand 3b

## The situation/question

We have changed the situation somewhat. You have the exact same holding as before, only this time you and the other players all have a $1,200 stack. You are again in early position. Just as before, your plan is to raise, hoping that the maniac will reraise, put other players in the middle, so that you can come over the top for a pot-sized reraise. (Assuming you judge it likely that no one is in fact in there with aces, of course. If you fear that you could be up against aces, then you would change your initial plan of reraising the pot to just calling or even folding – depending upon the exact situation.) Because the money is quite a bit deeper for you than in the previous example, you now make it $40 to go instead of your usual $20, hoping that if the maniac makes a pot reraise to $140, you can come then over the top to $440, $580 or even $720 (assuming no callers, one caller and two callers respectively) for a significant enough percentage of your stack.

However, the maniac disappoints you, reraising to just $80 – the same amount as in the previous example. The same caller as last time now calls again, and as before both blinds fold. What should you do now?

a) fold
b) call
c) reraise the minimum to $120
d) reraise the maximum to $340

## Answers/Reasoning behind these answers

### a) 2½

This is even worse than in the previous example, because here you are getting an even better price on your money than before.

### b) 7½

The best choice now. You have a good hand, but the money is quite deep. Whereas with shallow money, it is not that horrible to occasionally run into aces while holding quality kings (because especially if the pot is multiway and/or there is quite a bit of dead money, you usually don't lose that much money on average even in this bad situation), with deep money this is not the case. Here it is clear that you want to avoid the chance of reopening the betting for someone with aces. And it is not just the maniac who could have aces here. Now that the money is somewhat deeper than before, the button could very well be playing 'second hand low': first flat calling with aces, hoping that someone will reraise so that he can come over the top for all his money. Note that in the previous example it was quite unlikely that the button had aces, because he *could* have made it $280 by reraising the maximum, for no less than 40% of his total stack – a chance that he would undoubtedly have taken. But in this situation, he *can* make it a bigger amount than before ($300 instead of $280), but this $300 accounts to just 25% of his stack instead of the 40% from before. This means that with aces, he *might* have come over the top in situation 3a, but not in 3b. So we have to take into account at least the *possibility* of the too loose caller being in there with aces this time. And coupled with the fact that even maniacs tend to become a little more conservative with their reraises (and also their *calls* of raises) once their stacks get bigger, it should be clear that the opportunistic approach of just moving in is not automatically correct anymore. This is especially true now that the money is deeper, and your $340 total reraise would account to a significantly smaller percentage of your stack than before.

There is one simple rule in pot-limit Omaha: When the money is deep, you don't want to build a huge pot before the flop with kings if you think there's a decent chance that someone is lying in the bushes with aces in order to trap you. So calling is quite clearly the best play here. This is even more true because after the flop you will be in a perfect position to check-raise the maniac if you catch a good or even just a decent flop, thereby putting the button in the middle. It should be clear that I judged reraising the maximum in situation 3a as the best from a 'maximising wins' perspective, whereas here just calling is the best from a 'minimising losses' point of view. This last point may not be so glamorous as the first – but in big-bet poker with deep stacks, it *is* a concept that is of paramount importance.

Please note that had the maniac reraised to $140 instead of to just $80, and again the button had called, then you probably *should* have reraised the pot, for the following reasons:

- ♠ It is now somewhat less likely that the button is playing second hand low with aces. Because he would have been able to reraise to $480 now instead of just $300, he could again have got 40% of his stack into the middle instead of just 25%. And unless this person is an absolutely awful player, he *would* have made the correct play of committing fully with his aces here rather than flat call and invite other players into the pot.[2]

- ♠ You can now make a reraise to $580 total instead of the $340 from before. This means that as in situation 3a, you will have almost half your stack in before the flop with the probable best hand. This will make you entirely committed, whereas in the reraise to $340 situation, you were on the *verge* of being committed or not. Also, if you flat call, it will now cost you $140 instead of just $80, for more than 10% of your total stack. This is a lot of money to invest before the flop if you are not that confident really that your double-suited kings are the current best hand.

### c) 4½

This has the good aspect of making it seem like a 'gambling' type of reraise, now that the money is a little deeper than before. This *could* lead to the maniac responding by making yet another (small, or even big) reraise with a hand that is not that good actually. Still, I don't like this option much, because with relatively deep money you usually should not reopen the betting with kings, plus this little

---

[2] This argument *for* reraising is slightly offset by the fact that in this situation the maniac may actually be *more* likely to have aces – now that with fairly deep money he has decided to make it the maximum $140 reraise, instead of the more 'goofy' $80 from before.

reraise of yours may be making your post-flop play much harder. For one, if the maniac decides to call your mini-reraise, he is less likely to do the betting for you if you check to him on the flop – meaning that you will have lost an excellent check-raising station. And in addition to that, your opponents will know, after you have made the third raise, that there is at least the *possibility* of you holding a big pair, making it easier for them to make the correct decisions after the flop. And with fairly deep money, this would be a pretty bad situation for you, especially now that you are out of position. All in all, this means that your option c) will increase your initial investment, while not adding much (if any) potential reward – quite clearly, not the best of decisions if you ask me.

### d) 5

With a stack of $800 or less, reraising the pot would have been my number one choice with this K♠-K♦-9♠-8♦. But here your pot-sized reraise is to just $340 total, meaning that you would still have $860 left after the flop while being out of position. Let's say that one of your opponents – or even both of them – calls your reraise, and then the flop comes A-7-2 rainbow. What do you do then? Are you committed or not, and will you stick in the remaining $860 knowing that if you are called, you will almost certainly be playing for just a two-outer?

In pot-limit Omaha, you want flop play to be as automatic as possible, and you want to avoid predicaments like this whenever you can. What is needed for this is a balanced overall strategy, where the required post-flop decisions follow logically from the pre-flop actions. What this means is that you either invest a relatively *small* percentage of your stack before the flop and then let the flop/your opponents' actions decide whether to continue or not. Or you will invest a very *large* percentage of your stack to be entirely committed while holding the probable best hand – and to turn post-flop play into not much more than a formality.

With regards to this example hand, the current stack sizes make a pot-sized reraise one of these in-between situations. In borderline cases like this, it may be better to take an aggressive posture in shallow-money situations, and a slightly more conservative approach with deeper stacks. So for this reason, I would wait until *after* the flop to make a move here, when I could be getting an even bigger edge that I have now – while experiencing significantly less fluctuation.

# Practice hand 3c

## The situation/question

We now change the situation one final time. Again you have made it $40 to go with these double-suited kings of yours, and again the maniac has made it $80 to go. Instead of calling, the button now reraises the pot to $300. As before, you all have $1,200 stacks. What do you do?

a) fold
b) call
c) reraise the minimum to $250
d) reraise the maximum to $1,000

# Answers/Reasoning behind these answers

### a) 6½

Against not one but two reraises, you can usually fold even quality kings without the slightest hesitation – because you will almost always be up against bullets. However, in this case things are not as clear as they usually are. Because the maniac might have anything, this means the button *could* very well be making a move to isolate him, say with a hand like Q-Q-10-8 or A-J-10-9 or so. It *seems* likely that he has aces, but he is also on the button and some players seem to think they can *automatically* play a hand strongly when they have last action. Also, because you already have $40 invested, you will have to call 'only' $260 more. If by calling I could close the betting, I might actually have called. But because I not only have to contend with the button, who could very well have aces, but also the unpredictable maniac behind me, who could raise again, I think a fold is in order.

### b) 5

If you call now, you do so because you think your kings are actually the current best hand. But if this is your read or your analysis, then you should not meekly call – you should commit fully. So, being out of position with fairly deep money in a situation where you do *not* close the betting, this looks like a clear 'reraise or fold' situation to me. One of the few advantages of calling over reraising would be that if indeed the button turns out to have aces, by just calling you may invite the maniac to come along for the ride. By reraising you would probably have blasted him out, and you would have ended up in the (for you, extremely bad) situation of kings versus aces with relatively little dead money. But despite the fact that you would have avoided this bad scenario by simply calling, calling here is not much more than the act of someone who doesn't know where he stands in a hand. Furthermore, that would *also* get you in a –EV situation when facing aces. So, if reraising is wrong, then *calling* would not become the best option for you – no, *folding* would.

### c) 4

A silly choice that serves no real purpose. There *are* times for small bets and minimum raises and if you have read this book carefully, you will know that I think there are actually many times when these plays can be very useful. But this is clearly not one of them. Here you simply have to decide: Is my hand good or not? If you think it is, you commit fully, and if you think it isn't, you fold. Simple as that – even though it *does* require excellent reading abilities on your part to figure that out.

## d) 6

Again it is the quality of your reads that will be the deciding factor here. You will have to weigh the chances of the button having aces as opposed to some other hands that he could be holding. My estimate at the table would have to be 65-70% pure aces for me to lay down my kings here. In other words: If I thought there was a 35% or more chance that the button does *not* hold aces, then I would simply re-raise the pot with my quality kings here. (Frankly, I would use my 'feel' here, and try to analyse my opponent's body language to see whether he would actually *welcome* me into the pot or not.) As so often, my decision here would depend on the strength that I feel from my opponents, mostly from the button but to a lesser degree also from the maniac.

Note that against maniacs and loose players I am much more likely to give action with a less than lock hand, not in the last place because I don't mind that much if they win a big pot against me.[3] I know that if I *give* these players action with other hands than just aces, I may *get* even more action from them than they would give the typical 'I wait for aces or other nut hands' type of player. I also know that for the overall long-term health of the game it is good if weak, loose or overaggressive players win big every once in a while – and if this goes at the expense of me sometimes, well so be it. (This is especially true when facing the same opponents time and again in some sort of 'regular' game.) So I *would* give the loose gooses and the Action Men some action in return even if in fact I was not all that certain about my kings here, while I would simply *fold* them against the good players, the tight players and the professionals.

# Practice hand 4a

## The situation/question

The big $2,000 maximum online game, blinds $10-$20. You are using the minimum buy-in approach described in this book, and still have $340 left out of your initial $400. You are in the $10 small blind with A♥-9♣-8♦-6♥. One early position (EP) limper, one middle position (MP) limper, and the button also calls. The first limper is very loose/aggressive, especially post-flop, whereas the other two limp-

---

[3] This is especially true in a live game, where you can simply take as much money out of your pockets as you want in order to cover the live ones and the weak players. After all, if you lose two big pots against them, but then take their entire stacks in a truly *massive* third pot, you still have reached your goal, despite having lost two pots out of three. In online games where there is a cap on the buy-in, you don't have the luxury that you can always cover everyone. In these cases it may be wrong to gamble with the other fairly big stacks – knowing that if they happen to beat you, they could suddenly have *you* covered by a wide margin.

ers are a little weak-tight. All of these players have stacks of more than $1,500. The big blind is unknown to you. He has just come to the table with $2,000 and is now playing his first hand. What do you do?

a) fold
b) call
c) mini-raise to $40
d) raise pot to $120

# Answers/Reasoning behind these answers

### a) 4½

Even though when playing a short stack, you would in general employ the system 'play for all my money or don't play at all', in this case there's nothing wrong with simply calling the $10 extra to see a flop. After all, you do have a hand that has the potential to flop something good, and folding a hand this decent while getting such a good price on a call would simply be too tight.

### b) 7½

The 'logical' choice. Even if the big blind were to turn out to be extremely aggressive (say, with a PFR of 18% or even more), then you should still call. That is because if the big blind does indeed decide to raise, a profitable situation may present itself to you. If the big blind raises pot to $120 and all three limpers now call this raise (a not uncommon situation), you would now have the option to reraise all-in. If the big blind turns out to be a locksmith, then he will probably be in there with a big hand, most likely aces, and he will reraise the pot. While this *seems* bad for you, it should be clear that his reraise will almost certainly make all the initial limpers fold, meaning you that will be all-in for $340, against one player, with no less than $360 dead money in the middle! (Remember that the three limpers will now have to *call* for their entire stacks, with hands that they did not initially raise with themselves. So unless they have been limping with aces in order to limp/reraise, they will probably surrender now.) What's more, if it turns out that the big blind is an absolute maniac, it is actually very likely that he will come over the top of your all-in raise with a very wide range of hands. Hands as weak as Q-J-9-7 double-suited maybe, in order to make everyone fold and play heads-up with four live cards against your 'obvious' aces. So in both of these scenarios, you will have to beat just one player, while getting more than 2-to-1 on your money. I have simulated both these scenarios, and the results are as follows:

> **Scenario 1: You are up against aces – In this case, A♠-A♣-5♠-4♦.**
> You will win the pot 36.18% of the time, meaning that you are a very

big dog to win – that is the bad news. But the good news is that even in this bad situation of being up against aces, you are still a money favourite in the hand! Your total expectation of the $1,040 pot is $376.16. Knowing that you started the hand with $340, you would show an average profit of $36.16 here. What's more, calculated from the decision point onwards (when the action came back to you for $120 total, being in there for $20 already), your decision to move all-in rather than fold has actually made you $56.16 – and this in a situation where you were actually faced with a hand that you did not want to see (aces).

**Scenario 2: You are up against a much weaker hand than aces – In this case, Q♠-J♥-9♥-7♠.**

Despite the fact that you *seem* to be in the pot with clearly the best hand, your A♥-9♣-8♦-6♥ is not much more than just even money here. You will win 50.17% of the time and the pot will be split 0.48%, meaning that your total pot equity is 50.41% here. All in all, you expect to get back $524.26 for a net profit of $184.26, or even $204.26 from the decision point onwards.

So here we see the impact of dead money in turning a not-much-more-than-average hand into a real money-maker. Because if in this same pre-flop situation the big blind had again raised pot to $120 and there had been no callers, then an all-in reraise would have had much less value. In fact, your hand would probably not even have been good enough to call here!

Anyway, this very long story is all a little hypothetical, as most likely the big blind will simply check. And you will then be in a fairly profitable situation as well, holding a decent hand with quite a lot of nut potential in a five-way pot – where you have called the extra $10 getting no less than 9-to-1 on your money.

## c) 4

Even though I like to use the mini-raise frequently, in this case it wouldn't be too smart. One of the limpers could very well hold aces and if you raise small now, you are opening yourself up for a big reraise that you probably cannot call – because there may not be enough dead money in the middle. And with a hand that contains an ace you usually don't want to be involved heads-up against aces in an all-in coup before the flop. You *wouldn't* mind being up even against a quality hand like K♠-K♥-Q♥-J♠ though. In that case you *would* have the proper odds to commit fully with your hand, holding 41.72% pot equity in a situation where there is anywhere from $60 to $120 dead money in the pot (depending on who is reraising you), and where you have already invested $40 yourself. This would be one of those situations where because of your mini-raise, you would have 'created your own odds'.

### d) 5½

A pressure play that I may in fact have used had my hand been double-suited. By making big raises with nice double-suited hands with relatively shallow money, you would negate your bad position, and create a big volume pot in which the big stacks may bet each other off their hands after the flop when you are already all-in. But as I have said, your hand is probably a little too weak to make this play, and also your stack may be just a bit too large. With a stack of $220 or so, I *would* have opted for this 'no headache' pressure play.

# Practice hand 4b

## The situation/question

The same situation as before: same hand, same opponents. You have indeed called the $10 extra with your A♥-9♣-8♦-6♥, and as expected the big blind has simply checked his option. The flop now comes 8♠-7♥-3♣. You are first to speak. What do you do?

    a) check intending to fold against any big bets
    b) check intending to call any reasonably-sized bets
    c) check intending to raise, especially if the bet comes from late position
    d) bet the minimum $20
    e) bet $60
    f) bet pot $100

## Answers/Reasoning behind these answers

### a) 6

There is nothing wrong with this. All you have is top pair/top kicker (TPTK), an open-ended straight draw where just a five gives you the nuts, and a backdoor flush draw. Not a premium hand by any means – so there is nothing wrong with the somewhat 'weak-tight' option of check-folding.

### b) 4½

This is an option I don't like. If you decide to call a $60 or $70 bet on the flop, you would have just $250 or so left on the turn, when you don't know where you stand, and what you are up against. Whatever card comes on the turn, you won't have enough money left to pressure your opponents out of the pot, meaning that you would have very few bluffing or semi-bluffing opportunities. The only cards that would give you an easy play would be the four fives in the deck, because then you would have the nuts and can charge other people for drawing out. With *any* other turn card you simply don't know where you are, and you may make many bad decisions because of this.

One of the worst things about check-calling with this hand on the flop is the possibility that your call may invite other players to come along for the ride. Now if you had a premium draw with many nut outs this would not be so bad, but here you don't have a premium draw at all. Marginal hands like J-10-10-x or J-J-9-x (overpair + inside straight draw) may now decide to call as well, figuring that they are getting a good price on their call. Now obviously this would be very bad for you because they could be taking away some of your outs – for instance, against a J-J-9-x any ten would now suddenly be a *bad* card for you. You could end up in a three-way pot with one bettor who could be holding anything, and one caller who is holding a better hand *and* a better draw than you. It would be disastrous for your hand to pick up this caller, as you absolutely don't want to face more than one opponent with your holding, and you especially don't want the hand combo 'higher pair + better draw' to come along for the ride because of your weak flop play. You know that heads-up your hand *would* have quite a bit of value, most of all if the bettor is someone who is known to push his draws, or to be betting aggressively with just an overpair against what he considers to be raggedy boards. If the bettor fits this description, then you should not have check-*called* on the flop; you should have check-*raised*.

### c) 4½

This would have been my preferred choice if in fact the late-position players had been overly aggressive. But as you can read from my initial description, they are not aggressive at all – quite the contrary, the last two players in the betting are both somewhat weak-tight. This means that if they *do* bet, your hand has become a clear muck, because you are extremely unlikely to be any kind of favourite over those hands that they could be betting with.

### d) 6½

As you should know by now, I am one of the few players who uses the mini-bet as a weapon, and with a clear strategic reason. I especially like to use the mini-bet in the following three situations:

- ♠ When being in the blinds, especially the small blind.
- ♠ When up against fairly weak opposition, preferably weak-tight players.

♠ When I am playing a small to medium stack – meaning that if I get raised now, any pot-sized reraise by me would put me all-in or close to it.

In order to use this strategy in a profitable manner, you have to make these mini-bets somewhat indiscriminately, with the following types of holdings:

♠ The one you have here: A combination of a fairly weak made hand and a draw with quite a bit of non-nut potential. Especially if you also have some backdoor (nut) outs, this is a hand where you would like to reach the turn at relatively little cost. In other words, you would be mini-betting with a hand that may not be good enough to call a pot-sized bet. All in all, your mini-bets with these types of holdings have three clear goals. They a) would give you the initiative, b) could work as a stop bet, preventing people from raising you off your hand, and c) could provide you with quite a bit of information as to your opponents' holdings, while not giving away much about yours.

♠ A total bluff. Sometimes in three- or four-way pots with either/or flops like K-K-6 rainbow, 3-3-9 rainbow and K-7-2, a simple $20 bet will win the pot for you. Betting this $20 from first position will often result in you winning a $77 pot (assuming $3 rake) while holding absolutely nothing – simply because your opponents don't hold much either.

♠ A really big hand. In order to balance your play, you should also mini-bet into the field occasionally with a big hand like a set or top two pair on a nondescript board. Yes, you should also mini-bet occasionally when you flop super hands like the nut straight on flops like 6-3-2 or A-5-4, or top full on a flop J♠-J♥-8♥. The best time to make these mini-bets when holding a super hand, is if in previous hours you have been using these mini-bets very frequently. If your timing is good, this will be the exact moment when your opponents are 'fed up' with these mini-bets of yours. They will then raise you with some fairly marginal hands, 'knowing' that you will fold. Now, if you have a stack of anywhere from $300 to $500, this may be an excellent way to commit your opponents to a pot that they initially had no intention of playing at all.

Anyhow, in the specific situation that we have here, the mini-bet might work very well. As is often the case when employing this strategy, you will let subsequent actions from your opponents decide *your* best play once the action gets back to you. Your initial plan after having mini-bet on this flop, would be to immediately give it up against significant action by more than one opponent. And you would also give up if the weak-tight players happen to take an aggressive posture. At the same time, your plan would be to reraise all-in if the loose-aggressive player (LAP) were to raise you, and the weak-tight players have got out of the way. This is because the LAP could be raising with just a draw, just one big pair with nothing else, or even with an entirely random hand. After all, he could simply become aggressive because he thinks that your mini-bets mean nothing, or because he thinks you can be raised off your hand. Since against this player you would hardly ever be a big dog, reraising all-in with your marginal TPTK/non-nut openender/backdoor flush draw would almost certainly be a good decision.

One reason why I have rated this mini-bet at just a 6½ instead of a 7 or even 7½, is that the $20 minimum bet actually accounts to a relatively large percentage of your total stack. Had this exact same situation occurred in the $5-$5-$10/$10-$10 blinds live game in Amsterdam, then the minimum bet would have been just $10. In that case, with the exact same stack sizes as here, I would have rated the mini-bet even higher than the current 6½.

## e) 4

The worst choice of all. By making this 60% of the pot bet, you help create the exact situation that you don't want. You induce people with relatively marginal hands to get involved, thereby creating the multiway action that your hand cannot stand. At the same time, this $60 bet may not be a very significant investment for the others – as they are playing much larger stacks than you – but it *is* a significant investment for you. This is the exact type of bet that will get you *almost committed*, and as I have said before this is a situation that you want to avoid. And it should especially be avoided in this case, where if you bet now and get called or raised, you just don't know where you are. But the problem is not only the play on the flop. Just as importantly, you will face lots of problems on the turn, where you have just enough room for about one pot-sized bet, when just four cards in the deck (the four fives) will make turn play easy for you. With *any* other turn card, with the possible exception of the two remaining eights, you are likely to be making very big mistakes. For this reason, you should focus on two things when playing this hand in the situation described:

♠ Keep the betting amounts on the flop small enough to avoid being committed yet, or:

♠ Make the betting amounts on the flop big enough to be entirely committed.

It should be clear that this option 'e' does not do *any* of these things. It is one of those 'a little bit of both' decisions that in poker, as in life, just don't work very often. The reason why this strategy does not work here is because you are playing a *short* stack, and thus these bets amount to a fairly large percentage of your stack. When playing deep money, this 'half pot' type of betting is actually one of the most powerful plays – in fact, probably even more powerful than the mini-bet with short money. But when playing short money, it is usually one of the *worst* betting strategies for you.

### f) 6

Much better, because at least you are committing fully now, instead of just half. Still, your hand seems to be just a little too weak to make this play. And especially the 8/7 combo on the flop may mean that more than one opponent could be interested in this pot – even after this pot bet of yours. (And as we have said before, in this situation this is something that you don't want.) Had your stack been $240 or less after the flop instead of the $320 that you have now, then betting the pot *would* have been my no. 1 option.

# Practice hand 5

## The situation/question

Again, the big $2,000 maximum online game with $10-$20 blinds. This time, you actually have the biggest stack at the table, $4,400. You are very eager to bust the two big stacks to your immediate right, both rather weak players with over $2,000 in front of them. Unfortunately, there is also a good player to your immediate left who has just won a big pot, and who now has over $4,000 as well. All in all, we have a very big game, with lots of potential for monster pots.

You are in the cutoff with the 9♥-8♥-7♣-6♦. The two weak players have limped, and you raise to $80. Your goal: Hoping to isolate the two weak players while having both position and a well-disguised holding, and at the same time trying to 'buy the button'. Alas, your plan backfires. The button mini-raises to $140[4] and this makes the two weak players fold. It is up to you. It is clear that you don't like playing out of position against a good player while holding a mere nine-high, but at the same time you don't want to play according to *his* rules either. In other words: You don't want to meekly call his raise and then be forced to check-fold on the majority of the flops, because this would be giving your opponent *too* much of an edge: He would start reraising you on every possible occasion from now on if he knows that you will play this meekly against him. Knowing that you are up against a fairly good and thinking player here, you decide to play your hand in a creative manner, reraising him another $60 to $200. You know that even if the button has aces here and make a pot-sized reraise to $670, your medium rundown

---

[4] As you can see, the 'Amsterdam Rules' apply on this site. For more on this, see practice hand 3a.

would be a perfect hand to snap him off, especially with the money this deep. You also know that the button is aware that your reraising small to $200 is a play that you might very well make while holding aces, hoping that *he* will fall into the trap of raising you once more, so that *you* can then respond by coming over the top with another, this time massive, reraise.

As it happens, the button does not reraise but just calls. You know that this *could* possibly indicate that your opponent does have aces but has decided to play them in a deceptive manner. But more likely, this call of his that closed the betting indicates that he does not hold aces, while he fears that you *could* be holding them. (In PLO the person who has made the last pre-flop raise is *much* more likely to be holding aces than the person who has just closed the betting by calling, when he *could* have reopened the betting by making another raise.)

With a total pot of $470, the two of you see the flop K♥-10♠-6♠. You decide to bet out for an unusually small amount, $100, and the button raises you another $100 to $200 total. It is clear that the two of you are playing mind games here. You call, knowing that there is indeed a slight possibility that your opponent could be messing around here – but frankly, you expect him to have a big hand. You actually read him for top set, three kings. Your analysis is that by just doubling your bet, he is trying to lure you into making a mistake by giving you the chance to make a play at him, when *he* is actually loaded for bear.

The turn is the 5♦. Now, here is when things get really interesting. You again come out betting $100, and now your opponent raises the pot to $1,170 total. It looks for all the world like your opponent has finally come out of the closet with his three kings (probably). In fact, that is what you read him for: Three kings with not much back-up, a hand that he would very much like to win right now with all these draws on the board. Taking all this into account, what would be your best course of action?

a) Fold, because you only have the fours, sevens, eights and nines as winners. And even some of these cards are not clean outs by any means, because of higher straight draws (in the case of a nine) and/or a possible spade flush (in the case of the 4♠, 7♠, 8♠ and 9♠).

b) Call, because your real outs are very well-disguised (meaning that you might get paid off handsomely in case you hit them), while at the same time there are many scare cards on the river that could help you pull off a successful bluff.

c) Reraise pot to $3,980, because this way you can put your opponent to the test right now. Yes, he *may* indeed have three kings and be thrilled to get his chips in, but even then you could still have up to 13 outs. And if he *doesn't* have top set, then there is a very good chance that you can make him fold, and thus will be able to raise him off the current best hand.

# Answers/Reasoning behind these answers

### a) 6

There is nothing wrong with this. Your opponent has shown that he has a big hand, while you don't. Playing out of position with a marginal (drawing) hand, up against a good player who has shown strength and who has enough chips to break you, is usually not a great situation to be in. So there is nothing wrong with just taking your loss and preparing for the next hand.

### b) 7½

A – possibly – surprisingly high rating for this one. After all, it *is* bad strategy to call a pot-sized raise from a good player out of position with just a marginal hand – right? Well yes, that is true. But again, we have to look carefully at the psychology of the situation. (This is something you should always do when playing against good players in deep-money situations.) Before the flop, you have made the final raise. Possibly because of this, you know that if you decide to call this large raise now, your opponent will almost certainly read you for aces + nut flush draw in spades, possibly with a gutshot to go with it. First and foremost, he will read you for this hand, with as another possible candidate four big cards, for top pair + wrap. This means that if either an ace or a spade comes on the river, he will almost certainly think that his three kings just cannot be good anymore. And he will definitely view any queens, jacks and nines as scare cards as well.

Because there is enough room for one (massive!) pot-sized bet on the river, you know that you can put a *lot* of pressure on your opponent if any one of these spades, aces, queens, jacks or nines comes up. (Note that only the nines have in fact helped you.) In fact, because your play throughout the hand has been consistent with aces + nut flush draw, I am positive that with any of the non-pairing spades on the river, and with any of the remaining three aces (not counting the ace of spades), he will fold to any big bet by you well over 80% of the time. And if you decide to go for the flat-out bluff when one of the three remaining queens or jacks comes up, my guess is that this bluff should succeed close to 60% of the time – assuming that in fact you have a solid image. Yes, sometimes he may decide to make a stand, and you will lose. Other times the river may actually have completed his straight because of his two side cards, or because your read that he had three kings was wrong and he was in fact semi-bluffing on the turn with a wrap hand that he has now completed. But all in all, no less than 15 out of the remaining 42 cards (52 minus the four board cards, your four hole cards and the 'known' two kings in your opponent's hand) provide you with a bluffing opportunity that should have an excellent chance of success.

But that's not all there is to it. Just as importantly, there are quite a few cards in the deck that could look quite harmless in the eyes of your opponent, when in fact they would give you an almost certain winner. For instance, any non-spade four on the river will almost certainly not look like a scare card to your opponent. And your opponent will probably not fear any sevens or eights much either, for the simple reason that your play throughout the hand has been consistent with *big* cards, not with a medium rundown. The cards that he *could* fear a lot would be the nines, because he might give you credit for something like A-A-Q-J, so that this nine could have given you a king-high straight. So my guess is that if you bet big when a nine comes up, he will fold at least half the time, while calling you with the losing hand about 40% of the time. (The other 5-10% of the time, he may have made the same straight as you, or even a higher one.) So I think that if you bet the pot with any of the remaining eights, sevens and fours, for seven cards total, he will pay you off at least 4 times out of 5. The only times when he would fold against your bet would be in one of the following situations:

♠ He did not have a quality made hand at all, but was simply semi-bluffing on the turn with a draw that has not been completed now, or:

♠ He has a very good read or even a tell on you, and knows that you have hit.

All of this means that more than one-third of the time, you are *very* likely to successfully steal a $2,810 ($1,170 + $1,170 + $470) pot away from your opponents on a total bluff. And just as importantly: There are seven river cards that will almost certainly secure you of a monster $8,430 total pot, where there is a *very* high probability of getting your opponent to pay you off for $2,810 with a losing hand. The combination of these two scenarios makes this situation just too profitable to pass up – and that's why I think calling the $1,070 more on the turn with your seemingly weak hand is the proper play.

### c) 4

While I am a big fan of large semi-bluff raises on the turn if you think there is a good chance of making your opponent lay down the current best hand, in this case this does not look like the proper situation to go for it. This is mostly for two reasons:

♠ If your read is correct, then your opponent almost certainly has a very big hand, and will call you easily with a hand that is clearly favoured over yours.

♠ Your opponent knows that it is extremely unlikely that you have a hand that contains specifically K-K, simply because of your pre-flop actions. Just about the only hand that you *could* not have made this $200 minimum reraise with is kings. Why? Well, because you

would be opening yourself up for a massive reraise if your opponent indeed had aces – a reraise that you probably would have
been unable to call. In other words: By reraising to $200, you could
have been raising yourself out of the pot, and your opponent
knows that a good player like you would never have brought himself into that situation. So even though you *could* of course have a
big hand when you come over the top of your opponent's reraise
against this K♥-10♠-6♠-5♦ board, it is clear that your opponent is
*more* likely to read you for a big semi-bluff attempt rather than specifically top set. In fact, he will probably read you for specifically
aces + nut flush draw, or else a pair + wrap straight draw. And even
though you have a different kind of straight draw than he may read
you for, he *is* correct in his read that you would be semi-bluffing.
This means that your opponent may now call you even with hands
as weak as just two pair, knowing that almost certainly this would
be the current best hand. Coupled with the fact that he probably
has a much *better* hand than just two pair, the conclusion should be
that this would be something of an ill-timed semi-bluff attempt on
your part.

# River play

As to the river play, things are simple. You decide in advance what you will do
when either a blank, a scare card or a possible winner for you comes up on the
river. In the table below, I will show you what *I* would probably do in these situations, and explain the thought processes and the goals behind these plays.

| River card: | Action: | Desired result: | Chances of success: |
|---|---|---|---|
| Any non-pairing spade | Bet the pot | Win the pot as a pure bluff | Extremely good (possibly 80% or more) |
| Any pairing spade | Check/fold | None. You simply give up the pot now that your opponent is probably full. Downside: You may get bluffed out if in fact your read on the turn had been wrong, and your opponent was semi-bluffing with a wrap for instance | None. (You will have lost the additional $1,070 that you've called on the turn) |
| Any non-spade ace, queen or jack | Bet the pot | Win the pot as a pure bluff | Very good (close to 60% or so, possibly even more in the case of an ace on the river) |

| Any non-spade 4, 7 or 8 | Bet the pot | Hope to get paid off while holding the nuts | Extremely good (possibly 80% or more) |
|---|---|---|---|
| Any non-spade 9 | Bet half pot, say $1,000 to $1,200 or so | Hope to get paid off by a losing hand with your near-lock. Bet only half pot here because your opponent may fear the Q/J combo rather than the 8/7 combo that you actually hold. Problem: If you get *raised* here, you may in fact be up against a Q-J, and you could decide to pay off and lose a bundle. Or, if you *don't* pay off, he could force you into folding a possible winner – for instance, if your opponent is on a flat-out bluff or is overplaying his three kings | Good, but with quite a bit of risk involved |
| 3♠, 7♠, 8♠, 9♠ | Bet less than half the pot, say $600 or so | Hope to get paid off from a set or even two pair, but acknowledging the fact that your opponent could read you for a flush and thus may not be all that eager to pay off. By betting this small, he may be tempted to pay off after all, and you will have made a good value bet in a very marginal situation. Danger: If your opponent raises you here, you cannot be certain whether he is doing so because he actually has the flush himself, or because he has chosen to *represent* the nut flush, possibly because of this 'scared' little river bet of yours | Fairly decent. (I think you would get called by a losing hand about 30% of the time here.) Danger of making mistakes when facing a big raise though |
| Any of the remaining kings, tens, sixes, fives, treys and deuces | Check/fold | None. You will simply give up to any bet your opponent may make. Downside: If in fact your opponent has been semi-bluffing on the turn, for instance with a wrap like Q-J-9-8, you will have folded a winner on the end with your mere two sixes – thereby giving away a $2,810 pot | None. (You will have lost the additional $1,070 that you've called on the turn) |

It should be quite clear that you should know all these actions way in advance, i.e. before the river card is actually dealt. This is of paramount importance in the online games we are talking about, because unlike brick and mortar games you usually just have a very limited time to act here. So you should not decide to first call the turn raise and only *then* start thinking about your best possible course of action on the river – you should have figured that out already. Thus you should know in advance: 'With the following cards I will go for the big bluff; with these cards I will try to make a pot bet for value; and with these rivers I will try and sell my hand with my probable winner, knowing that the scare card may lead to my opponent being unable to call a full pot bet.'

What we have discussed here are the exact thought processes that are required to beat the biggest and toughest PLO games, and that are required to outplay good players in a deep-money situation. You will need to both think and act fast in situations like this, and both your calculations as well as your reads on your opponent(s) will have to be very accurate. And no, not just the read on what your opponent actually *holds* – but just as importantly, how he will respond to any bets that you may make on the river.

# Chapter Seven

# Hand match-ups and analysis

In the practice hands from last chapter, you were able to dig into some Omaha hands, to see if the choices you would make were also my preferred choices. In this chapter, I shall analyse some more PLO hands and situations, where for a most part I will be using percentages and mathematics as a guideline. Please note that not everything in this analysis will be straightforward. But in order to play at the highest level, you *will* need to understand these concepts. In fact, you should know all of these percentages by heart, so that if a situation like this occurs at the table, you will know immediately the best course of action, under the assumption that your opponent indeed has the type of holding that you have read him for. It is not that you will simply have to *remember* all the hands I will be discussing here. No, you will have to dig into these situations so deeply that you will automatically start to *see* the percentages, at least within a fairly small margin of error.

Anyhow, Omaha being such a drawing game, I will start with situations where we analyse a few drawing hands and their potential power – both heads-up, as well as in three-way pots. After that, I will focus on the best way to play kings in a multiway pot when an all-in player could have aces, and some other interesting hand match-ups.

## Hand match-up 1

We will start with one of the most common mistakes that people make: Overestimating their draw, while underestimating the made hand or even the better draw that the opponent could be holding. To be more concrete, I have simulated the following situations. On the flop Q♥-9♥-3♠, we hold K-J-10-8 rainbow (possibly because we are in one of the blinds), meaning that we have a pretty decent wrap.

Any king, jack, ten or eight would give us a straight, as would the combo 7/6 on the turn and river. All in all, a pretty powerful holding – especially at first glance. But we need to realise that making our hand does not always equal winning the pot.

# Situation 1

On this flop, up against Q-Q-7-2 rainbow for top set with nothing else, we are in the good situation of a) all of our outs being winners now that we are not up against a flush draw, and b) our opponent does not hold any blocker cards or card combos that could give him the same straight, and that would lead to a possible split pot. Many people would therefore reason like this: 'Well, we have three kings for the nuts, three jacks, three tens and three eights – for twelve outs twice. That's 24 cards out of the 41 left in the deck, making us at least even money.' That's their reasoning – but they are wrong. Yes, you are more than even money to *complete* your draw, but we should not forget that our opponent can improve too – even if we do. And since he is drawing to a bigger hand than we are, any time that he improves on the turn (for a lockout) or on the river (for a redraw, if in fact we have completed our straight on the turn), it has become completely irrelevant whether we actually complete the hand that we are drawing to. So with two cards to come our wrap is *not* even money. No, it is our opponent's bad and uncoordinated holding that is a clear favourite here: 59.76-to-40.24%.

# Situation 2

OK, so what about if we are up against a flush draw? Let's say that we are in the (not unrealistic) situation where we decide to go for a big semi-bluff raise on the flop with our wrap. (Maybe we bet out, get raised and then we reraise the pot, hoping to win the pot there and then but still having outs if called.) What happens if we get called by a flush draw? I have simulated our K-J-10-8 against the A♥-J♥-8♠-4♠ for ace high + nut flush draw + backdoor flush draw. Although many people might imagine that this would be not such a terrible match-up for us, it turns out that we are no less than a 26.34-to-73.66% dog! One should realise this golden rule, that I have never seen in print before, but is one of my real PLO mantras: *In Omaha, the straight draw is the flush draw's best friend – and conversely, the flush draw is the straight draw's worst enemy.* Although straight draws and especially big wraps *can* be very powerful in some situations, at the times when there is also a flush draw around this straight draw is almost always an underdog. Note that this is a clear reason why you should sometimes play your – even big – straight draws with caution on a two-suited flop. Because if one of your opponents actually has a flush draw that *he* decides to play aggressively as well, he is usually making money at *your* expense.

One final note about this hand match-up. Even though both we *and* our opponent are drawing to a bunch of nut outs, our opponent's hand has gained quite a lot of strength for the simple reason that his ace high is the current best hand. For instance, had his hand been J♥-8♠-4♠-2♥ instead of A♥-J♥-8♠-4♠, a seemingly insignificant difference, his win percentage would have dropped from 73.66% to 54.63% – meaning that *our* win percentage would have staggered from a mere 26.34% to no less than 45.37%, for almost even money. The difference here, of course, is all the times that the turn and river are brick/brick, for instance two small cards or cards that pair the board and thus seem to help neither one. So yes, this is indeed one of those Omaha situations where if both players go to war and put all their money in on the flop, a massive pot could be won in the end with a mere unimproved ace-high (in the case of our hand up against the A-J-8-4) or even king-high (up against the J-8-4-2).

## Situation 3

How do things change when we are *not* heads-up with our K-J-T-8 against either this top set or the nut flush draw, but we are in fact in a three-way pot. Well, up against both the Q-Q-7-2 and the A♣-J♥-8♠-4♠ from before, the percentages with two cards to come look like this:

- ♠ Our hand 21.47%
- ♠ Top set 51.95%
- ♠ Nut flush draw 26.58%

As you can see, this is another example of an important pot-limit Omaha concept. People often say that if you hold top set, your hand is not always all that strong because of the many draws that could be available. While it is true that draws can indeed be powerful, we see that the top set's win rate in this three-way match-up is still over 50%, despite the fact that he is up against a decent wrap, the nut flush draw *and* a backdoor flush draw. It should be clear that in this situation, the top set would actually *welcome* as many drawing hands as possible, knowing that if *his* top set improves, it doesn't matter anymore what happens to all these draws. So, for him this 51.95% three-way would actually give him a much better expectation than the (also good) 59.76% that he had heads-up against our hand. When adding more and more drawing hands, the win percentage of this top set will not go *down* that much, actually. But his expected win and the total pot size will both go *up* a lot, benefiting the top set while harming all those draws that battle against each other for just a relatively small slice of the pie. These draws may all *think* they have great odds because so many cards could improve their hands, but in reality it is only the top set that makes money here.

## Analysis

All in all, we can draw the following conclusions from all this:

- ♠ Straight draws perform badly when flush draws are also present.

- ♠ For this reason, flush draws can often be played aggressively on the flop if you know or suspect that you are up against a straight draw – even if it's a *premium* straight draw.

- ♠ The straight draw's best course of action if he fears that he is up against a flush draw may *not* be to raise big on the flop and try to make the flush draw fold. Because especially the nut flush draw often has extra outs like (possible) big pairs, a backdoor flush or some straight potential, these hands are often excellent candidates themselves for making a big semi-bluff all-in coup on the flop. And as we have seen, this would be a terrible situation for our straight draw. So a good way for our wrap to counter this semi-bluff danger of the flush draw, may be to wait until the turn to make a big semi-bluff bet of our own, with what seems like a delayed protecting of a made hand. (Note that many times, hands like top two pair or small sets would simply flat call or even check-call a bet on the flop from a possible big draw. They would then try to protect this made hand on the turn by betting big into the flop bettor, after this turn card has appeared 'safe', knowing that with just one card to come the odds for most types of draws will have been cut in half. What I recommend you should do with your straight draw is to mimic this exact play.) With just one card to come, an unimproved nut flush draw with some extras may *not* be so eager to get involved any longer against your 'obvious' good hand. So what you do with your straight draw[1] is to play slowly on the flop in order to a) wait for a safe turn card and then take the semi-bluff away from your opponent; b) hope to improve on the turn so that you can now charge the flush draw for drawing out; or c) simply check/fold once the turn has completed the flush – saving money that you would have lost if you had played the flop in the 'better', more aggressive manner.

- ♠ The top set on the flop may be one of the most underrated hands in

---

[1] Please don't think you should *always* play your straight draws this way. What I describe here is just *one* of the ways to play here, a very risky but good and creative way to misrepresent your hand – and then take advantage of that. This play should be used with caution, yes. But it *needs* to be one of your weapons, one of your potential strategies if you happen to hold a big straight draw on the flop, and think you may be up against a flush draw.

Omaha. Even up against two more than decent draws, the top set is not just *money* favourite (meaning in a three-way pot it would win more than 33.33% of the time), but as in our example could even be an *absolute* favourite (>50%).

# Hand match-up 2

We will now dig into this top set situation a little deeper.

## Situation 1

This time *we* are the ones with the Q-Q-7-2 no suits from before, and now it is our *opponent* with the K-J-10-8 rainbow. The flop is Q♥-9♥-8♦. Simulations show that our top set is a 32.44-67.56% dog against the nut straight + redraw from our opponent. This means that if by chance all the chips went in on the flop, and the money was quite deep, we would be making a clear mistake.

## Situation 2

If we just change our opponent's hand from K-J-10-8 to K-J-10-7, a seemingly insignificant difference, we would now suddenly have one out extra, with two cards to come. This means that our win percentage would rise to 36.83%. Still a clear dog, but this is mostly because we don't have any extras in our hand with regards to backdoor flushes, runner/runner (higher) straight draws, etc. With just one backdoor flush draw (Q-Q-7-2 with two diamonds instead of no suits), we would have over 40% equity – 40.27%, to be exact. Still not enough if by chance the money was very deep, but provided that there is at least some dead money in the pot, we would not be losing that much either. This despite the fact that your opponent with the nut straight + redraw will probably just call you very lucky or even stupid if you put all the money in on the flop and then happen to outdraw him.

## Situation 3

We again change the situation slightly. With our Q-Q-7-2 rainbow, we are still in the hand against the K-J-10-7 from before. But this time, there is also a third player in the pot: someone with the A♥-J♥-5♦-4♦ for the nut flush draw with a few distant extras – including a five-high backdoor flush draw and a runner/runner higher straight. Remember, in the situation before, heads-up with our top set against the current nuts, we just had 36.83% chances of winning, making this a situation with a clear negative expectation. Now, we are in a three-way pot with also the nut flush draw in – yet our win percentage has actually improved!

- ♠ Q-Q-7-2: 39.49%
- ♠ K-J-10-7: 37.84%
- ♠ A♥-J♥-5♦-4♦: 22.67%

The fact that (barring unusual circumstances) improving our hand equals winning the pot simply means that we won't mind a third player in. In fact, we would very much *welcome* him! The fact that the third player has no blocker cards means that four more 'bad' cards for us have gone out of the deck, meaning that our chances of improving to a full or quads have in fact gone up compared to the heads-up situation. In other words: Because we will need to improve to win anyway, we would love to be up against as many opponents as possible – especially if they don't hold any cards in their hands that affect our chances of improving in a negative manner (i.e., the queens, nines and eights). This means that from being a clear underdog heads-up where we would *lose* a lot of money on average, this exact same hand has now become a clear money favourite three-way.

## Situation 4

Having said all that, the third hand that I brought into the equation in situation 3 (the A♥-J♥-5♦-4♦) is not a very likely one. After all, this is not the type of hand that one would want to stick around with against any type of action. All decent players would fold a bare nut flush draw against a board this coordinated once the betting gets heavy. So I will change this hand into the A♥-J♥-10♠-4♦ for the nut straight + nut flush redraw, no backdoor flush. This is the more 'normal' situation where against this board, there are two nut straights who are both pushing, because they both feel that if some other player has the same nut straight, *they* could be freerolling. (Remember, the K-J-10-7 would have a redraw to a higher straight with any of the remaining jacks and tens, whereas the A-J-10-4 hand obviously has the nut flush draw to go with his current nut straight.) If you are in this situation with your top set Q-Q-7-2, would you want to get involved? Well, many players would say no, but in this exact match-up it is a clear yes. Our top set would win 39.64% of the time, much better than the 33.33% that we would need to be a money favourite at this point.[2] (In fact, the dead money in the pot could mean that this break-even point would be lower, say 32% or so – meaning that even if we were to just win the pot just a little over three times out of ten, we would still not

---

[2] Pay attention to the stack sizes here though. If you are up against two nut straights but one has a very short stack, whereas both you and the second nut straight have very deep money, you are not really in a three-way pot. You would be playing three-way for a relatively small main pot where you have a clear positive expectation, yes, but you would also be involved in a very large side pot where you would be a clear dog. Depending upon your exact win percentage and the depth of the money, this could turn a clearly positive expectation into a slightly negative one – meaning that you should *fold* on the flop rather than get involved.

lose that much money on average, if anything.) The two nut straights tie 28.83% of the time, while the straight redraw is successful in 8.41% of all cases, against 23.12% for the flush redraw. As you can see, this is another example of the fact that the flush draw is the straight draw's worst enemy. And, that top set usually fares pretty well in multiway pots – even when it is not in fact the current best hand. Total win percentages:

- ♠ Q-Q-7-2: 39.64%
- ♠ K-J-10-7: 22.82%
- ♠ A♥-J♥-10♠-4♦: 37.53%

## Situation 5

Now a situation when *not* all our full house/quad outs are still left in the deck. This time, the second nut straight does not have the flush redraw, but rather he has the 9-9 redraw for second set. His hand: J♥-10♠-9♦-9♣. Now, while for him this obviously does not do his chances much good (even though he is drawing to a bigger hand than previously, he only has one redraw out – the case nine – instead of all the flush redraws from before), it also significantly hurts *our* chances of winning. Because not only are two outs no longer in the deck for us (the 9♦ and the 9♣), but also the 9♠ that *would* have given us a clear winner with top full, will now give our opponent quads.

- ♠ Q-Q-7-2: 26.13%
- ♠ K-J-10-7: 42.12% (15.62% scoop, 53.0% split pot)
- ♠ J-10-9-9: 31.76% (5.26% scoop, 53.0% split pot)

So, now that the flush redraw is out, the pot is suddenly split between the two nut straights more than half the time, and just as importantly the same K-J-10-7 as before is now suddenly the 'best' redraw. Whereas in the previous situation, it was a clear loser with just 22.82% pot equity, now it has a whopping 42.12%, making it a clear money favourite. The presence of the second set has clearly come at our expense, as our top set has gone down from 39.64% to just 26.13%.

## Analysis

In the last situation, our top set would actually lose money on average. So when facing the decision we are in here, it is important to analyse the likelihood that other players could be holding the cards that we need in *their* hands. This is especially important in three-way situations like the one described here. With just one opponent, we would be trailing by quite a long way with our bare top set against the nut straight – meaning that, if indeed we would give our opponent credit for holding the nuts, we would have a clear fold. And against more than three opponents, we would not have much to think about either, as we would almost always be in a +EV situation with our top set, almost regardless of our opponents' holdings. So, the tough decisions for the top set would usually be in three-way pots, especially in three-way pots with deep money.

All in all, under any of the following conditions our top set would usually be in a +EV situation, even when the current nuts could be out there:

♠ We have a fairly short stack. (With a short stack, you can almost always go to war with top set on flops like this, even when you suspect the hand could turn out to be played heads-up between you and the possible nut straight. Don't listen to the people who tell you that even with short money, your top set should usually be folded if it seems you could be up against the current nuts. They are flat out wrong.)

♠ There is quite a lot of dead money in the pot. (This is the first reason why these people would be wrong, as short money means that the dead money in the pot becomes increasingly important. It accounts to a much higher percentage of your stack, and gives you much better odds, so that you would not need to win the pot even *close* to 50% of the time to still show an overall profit. The second reason why these people are wrong is that even if you *suspect* that someone has the nut straight, you can never be certain. Just a 10% chance of your opponent not having the nut straight but for instance a lower set, two pair + nut flush draw or even a total bluff, may turn a slightly –EV situation into a very good proposition. And it should be clear that usually someone would be betting without the nuts much more than 10% of the time. In fact, in my games people would just be betting the blockers – hands like J-J-x-x or 10-10-x-x for a total bluff on the Q-9-8 flop from before – much more than 10% of the time in this situation, and then we have not even mentioned the other *legitimate* hands apart from than the nut straight that they could be betting with. So, 'assuming' that your opponent has the nut straight, and as a result folding your 'clearly beaten' top set, would almost always be a horrible decision when the money is shallow – even if there are some people who will tell you otherwise.)

♠ You are up against many opponents, i.e. in a multiway pot.

## Some final words

There is one more factor that should not remain unmentioned, something that is very important when it comes to top set facing some possibly better holdings on the flop. In some cases, your top set may be an excellent pressure hand to try and blast a currently better hand out of the pot, while still not losing that much on average if we get called. An example would be when we have top set on a flop with three diamonds, and we suspect that based on the betting one of our opponents is in there with the queen- or king-high flush. If there is at least *some* chance that you could make your opponent lay down his flush out of fear of a bigger one, this may make a very aggressive move on the flop worthwhile. Now obviously, having the bare A♦ in addition to your top set would be of major importance here, because in that case you would *know* that no one is in there with the nut flush – giving your power play an even better chance of success.

# Hand match-up 3

## Situation 1

A marginal hand this time, in a marginal situation. The Amsterdam game, $10-$10 blinds, with a minimum $500 buy-in. I am the only one at this table who is employing the minimum buy-in strategy, and unfortunately have been unable to get my preferred seat to the immediate right of a maniac. The game has been under way for just five or six hands, as the table has just opened, and having just posted my big blind in the previous hand I am now down to $490.

In the $10 small blind, I look down to find a rather weak holding, the J♠-9♦-8♣-6♠. There has been an early-position minimum raise to $20 from a relatively weak player. Two players that I don't fear all that much cold call the raise, and I decide to put in an additional $10 with my pretty weak holding. The big blind also calls the $10 more. He is someone I have played with for many years, someone who I have a very good read on – more than anything because his table talk and mannerisms tend to give away the strength of his hand. For the sake of this story, we will call this player Carl.[3] Now, despite the fact that Carl is easy to read for *me*, he

---

[3] Nowadays, Carl and I are often in the same game online – the $2,000 maximum PLO game I have described throughout this book. While he used to be one of my favourite opponents in our regular brick and mortar game, I have to admit that online he is causing me *much* more problems. This is because I cannot judge his strength anymore based upon the way he bets, his facial expressions, the way he talks when he has a big hand as opposed to just a moderate one, etc. It is much harder for me now to correctly analyse what he has and what he wants me to do – so that I can disappoint him by doing the opposite, obviously. Nowadays I simply have to rely on his betting patterns to get a good read on him, and unfortunately this actual playing of hands and making the correct bets are two of his main strengths.

is a good and winning player, who is tight when it comes to starting hands and who usually plays his hands very well. All in all, five players see the flop for $20 each, including me, Carl, the pre-flop raiser and the two cold callers.

The flop comes 9♠-4♠-3♦, giving me top pair/weak kickers, a jack-high flush draw and some runner/runner straight potential. As I often do, especially from first position, I decide to bet into the entire field with a $10 minimum bet. A few reasons for using the mini-bet in this specific situation include:

♠ It often helps to clear the field, and shows who is playing what (gives information) for a rather insignificant investment. This will help me to make the correct decisions at the later stages and/or when the *real* money goes in.

♠ It may expose potential check-raisers. Check-raisers usually like to wait for the pre-flop raiser/an aggressive late-position player to do the betting for them, but when a third player bets into them, they usually don't have the courage to just flat call, hoping that it will get raised behind them: they tend to come out of the bushes immediately. This even when the bet they face is just a mini-bet that basically means nothing.

♠ It will give me the initiative, and tells the other players that I probably like my hand, while giving away not much more info than that. If I feel weakness or fear in my opponents when they call or even raise my mini-bet, I will often be able to come over the top and win the pot there and then – despite the fact that my hand was weak too.

♠ It may help me to see the turn card cheaply with marginal hands. This is especially true if people respect and fear both me and my mini-bets and thus are afraid to raise, whereas they *would* have bet the pot had I checked.

Anyway, I bet this $10 into the field, and Carl immediately raises the pot to $130. And by immediately I mean instantly, within less than a second – now, something that is very scary when you have a relatively weak hand like the one I am holding. Having played with Carl so often, I immediately know what he is trying to accomplish. He knows that my mini-bets don't necessarily mean a big hand, but he also knows that the other players at the table fear me for my tightness, for my results and for my 'being lucky'. So, in the eyes of the others there is a bet by Rolf and a big raise from another solid player, Carl – now, they would need a hell of a hand to get involved in a situation like that. What this means is that Carl is using his fast bet to represent more strength than he actually has. Yes, it *is* in a situation where he thinks he almost certainly has the current best hand, but also a hand that is vulnerable and easily overtaken. In other words: He simply wants to win the pot there and then.

When everybody folds and the action gets back to me, I take my time to think about the meaning of Carl's bet, and to analyse his table demeanour in order to come up with a good read. In this case, this read is quite easy. Being in the big blind, he is not likely to be holding a real quality hand, so he is unlikely to have something like aces + nut flush draw. With a real quality hand like a set, he would have acted a little more slowly and would have displayed at least *some* signs of doubts or weakness, because he always does that when he has a big hand. This is a tell 'as pure as the driven snow', as T.J. Cloutier would call it. With a big draw or with a combination hand, he would have needed a little more time to correctly assess his outs and whether it would have been better for him to just call and let the pre-flop raiser behind him get involved first or not. So, only one hand remains: Two pair with a few, but possibly not a lot of extras. It is a hand consistent with his being in the big blind, with his feigning strength, and with his unusually fast raise against my mini-bet. And probably most importantly: That is exactly the type of holding where he *thinks* he has the best hand, but simply doesn't want a fight – the exact type of holding where he would be happy to win the pot there and then.

All in all, it is now up to me and all I have is top pair/weak kickers, a weak flush draw and some remote backdoor possibilities, up against a solid player who has raised the maximum and who almost certainly thinks he has a better hand than the one I have been mini-betting with. Now while usually in situations like this my hand would have been a clear muck, in this case I decide to reraise all-in to $490 simply because I think that with two cards to come my hand will be a slight favourite over Carl's. And frankly, I expect that once I come over the top of his pot-sized raise, he will lay down many of these two-pair hands, because he would know that an over the top raise by me against a solid player like him would indicate a *lot* of strength.

Carl calls very quickly though, in a manner that seems to suggest something like 'I've got you, my friend'. I begin to fear that my read may not have been good after all, but I immediately show my hand anyway – something that I always do in an all-in situation, having made the last raise. Carl then instantly displays his hand as well, even though he doesn't need to. He shows 9♥-8♠-7♠-4♥ for top two pair + eight-high flush draw, and his entire body language says that *he* thinks this is a better hand than mine. And indeed, when I manage to win the pot by making a higher two pair he shows genuine disappointment and mutters something like 'Hmmm – lucky again'. But simulations show that my bad holding is actually a 53.35% favourite over his. So it should be clear that when up against this hand, the logical choice that most people would have made in this situation (folding those rags against the obviously better hand) would actually have been a *bad* one.

So in this situation, it turns out that I was right to move in, even when I knew or at the very least suspected that I was up against a currently better hand. But what if we now enter a range of other possible hands that a big blind could hold when deciding to pot-raise me on this flop?

## Situation 2

One of these possible raising hands for a big blind in the exact situation described here is something like Q-Q-4-3 no suits, for bottom two pair + overpair. On this 9♠-4♠-3♦ flop, my raggedy J♠-9♦-8♣-6♠ is again the favourite: 58.54-to-41.46%.

## Situation 3

In situation 1, I was pretty certain that I was up against a decent made hand like two pair with some, though almost certainly not a lot of extras. A crucial aspect here was the fact that I was almost 100% certain I was *not* up against a higher flush draw. But what if I were in a situation where my jack-high flush draw would not be good – what if my opponent had two higher spades?

For this third situation, I gave my opponent the A♠-J♣-10♦-5♠ for the nut flush draw + gutshot straight draw. (A deuce would give my opponent a wheel.) In this match-up, my hand suddenly does not look so hot anymore, with a win percentage of just 42.44%.

## Situation 4

But things can get much worse. At least in situation 3, I had the current best hand when the money went in – my pair of nines. And as we still remember from hand match-up no. 2, this seemingly unimportant factor can be of major importance in this game, especially in heads-up situations when up against a (big) draw. But if I *don't* have the best hand with my nines but my opponent actually has both the best hand *and* the best draw, my hand is truly in dire straits. Up against the A♠-Q♠-9♥-6♦ for top pair/higher kickers and a bigger flush draw, my hand is suddenly no less than a 21.52-78.48% dog. What this obviously means for my decision in situation 1, is that if my read on Carl is *not* reliable and he *could* have had a combination of a higher flush draw and a better made hand, that my decision to move in for all my money would have been a terrible one. This because I would now have been in danger of being either a slight favourite, or a very big dog.

## Situation 5

For completion's sake, I have also simulated my hand against the 7♠-6♥-5♥-2♣. This is the type of holding one could come up with from the big blind, having closed the betting for $10 extra against an early position's minimum raise. This good wrap (any A, 2, 5, 6 or 7 would complete a straight) would also be a hand that some players would decide to play aggressively in this situation. Even though I was fairly certain that this could *not* be one of Carl's possible holdings, I thought the analysis of this situation would not be complete without including this wrap hand.

As we have seen before, again my relatively weak holding performs very well against the opponent's big straight draw, for the simple reason that I am drawing to a flush whereas my opponent is drawing to a straight. My bad holding wins 62.93% of the time here, showing that it can also be a fairly *large* favourite even against some of the legitimate raising hands that the opposition could hold.

## Analysis

Marginal situations are very hard to play well. In this situation (situation 1), most players would have folded my hand thinking that if they get raised, this pair + weak kickers + marginal flush draw just could not be any good. And even if by chance the hand *were* a favourite, it would almost never be by much.

But these players are wrong. Unless I am up against a set or a higher flush draw + extras, my hand is usually in more than decent shape. Even against the top two pair + smaller flush draw that my opponent had (for a better made hand plus two blocker cards to my hand), it was *me* who was the favourite here. Against a bare two pair with no blocker cards, I would have been even more of a favourite. And if by chance I would have been up against just a (wraparound) straight draw, I would even have been a *very* large favourite. So, if based upon your read and the strength/weakness that you feel it is clear that your flush draw is good *and* you are not up against a set, well then it is almost never very wrong to simply come over the top and push your (yes, sometimes small) edge. This is especially true if your stack is not that large. If by chance you *do* play a very large stack, then it may be better to not come over the top but rather to throw away your hand there and then. In that particular situation you would be risking a whole lot of money in order to win relatively little, while holding just a marginal hand. And on top of that, provided that your raise gets called, you would be out of position for the rest of the hand not knowing where you stand and with lots of money still to be played. Not an enviable position to be in, to put it mildly.

# Hand match-up 4

## Situation 1

For this fourth hand match-up, I'd like to go back to the article *'All-in in pot-limit Omaha'* which has been reprinted and re-edited especially for this book. Whereas in many articles, I discuss the proper way to play with a short stack and exploit those who are playing with deep money, in this piece I analysed a situation where I actually covered everyone at the table. It was at a $2 blind PLO game in Vienna, many years ago, when I had worked up my minimum $100 buy-in to five times that amount.

Then a hand came up where I had K♠-K♥-6♥-6♣, had made my standard raise to $6 and then had been reraised the pot to $20 by a relatively tight player, with a few callers in the middle. Now obviously, when you have raised with kings you don't like to be reraised the maximum, because if you are up against aces your kings are usually not worth that much. This is especially true in a heads-up situation, i.e. when there's not much dead money and/or any other players in the hand that could improve your expectation and the price you are getting on a call.

In this actual hand, I had reason to believe that despite this pot-sized reraise by my (yes, tight) opponent I was *not* facing aces. Knowing that with his $100 stack he would be all-in soon anyway, I decided to raise the pot to $128[4], reasoning that even if I was facing aces, I would still be a clear favourite for any side pot that I would be trying to build. Anyway, my read on this specific player turned out to be pretty wrong. Not just did the tight player have aces – he had my kings as well! Hot and cold, in a heads-up pot, this would have led to the following win percentages:

♠   K♠-K♥-6♥-6♣ 24.09%

♠   A♠-A♣-K♣-K♦ 75.91%

As it happened, we were in a three-way pot for $100 each and $42 dead money, for a total main pot of $342. In addition to the two hands mentioned, there was also a third player in the pot, holding the J♥-J♣-8♥-7♣. For this three-way main pot, I had an absolutely horrific win percentage of just 16.3%. All in all, with an expectation of just $55.75 of this main pot for an average loss of $44.25, this was obviously not the best of situations for me to be in. Still, knowing that I had already put in the initial $6 raise, one could claim that my average loss from the decision point onwards was 'just' $38.25.

Also, I *did* have a reason for being in this pot for this much money. After all, I *could* simply have flat called the tight player's reraise to $20 in a risk-free manner, just to take a flop and decide the best course of action *then*. Instead, I decided to go for a much riskier option and put in a maximum reraise, in order to accomplish one of the following:

---

[4] Astute readers may notice that the actual pot-sized reraise would be to $122, not to $128 – because then I would be raising my own bet. This would indeed have been the correct amount. But in the actual situation (that, as I said, is taken from live play), the dealer said $128 and no one – not even me – objected to this.

♠ To make everyone else fold and fight the all-in player heads-up, in a pot that would contain quite a bit of dead money from people folding having initially called the $20 reraise. Even if the tight player *did* turn out to have aces, then the situation would still be not as bad for me as a normal kings vs. aces match-up would suggest.

♠ To try and create at least the *start* of a side pot. And being absolutely certain that no other player but the (short-stacked) initial reraiser could be in there with aces, I decided that it could be worth it going after the stacks of the three callers – who were all playing fairly big money. Even though my hand was pretty uncoordinated, it still seemed good enough to take an aggressive posture – knowing that people with small or medium rundowns would have to pay dearly to see a flop, with fairly limited implied odds.

## Situation 2

For the side pot, against my second opponent's hand, the J-J-8-7 double-suited, my K-K-6-6 was a clear favourite hot and cold. Even when taking into account the A-A-K-K as dead cards, my hand was still a 55.47-to-44.53% favourite, despite the fact that my kings were dead and my opponent's hand seemed rather live. (Not taking into account this A-A-K-K, and simulating just the K-K-6-6 vs. J-J-8-7 match-up, my hand would even win 63.43% of the time.)

## Situation 3

But obviously, my pre-flop over the top raise had led to a side pot of just $56. Even though I *expected* my opponent for the side pot, having invested this much money, to call me very liberally after the flop for the remainder of his stack (even on flops like 6-3-3 or 7-4-2 rainbow that would not offer him any direct help), there was no knowing for sure. In fact, as I wrote in the article, it certainly looked like I had been overplaying my kings quite a bit, and had taken a lot more chances with them that would seem reasonable.

Anyway, the flop came 10♥-5♥-4♣, giving me a pair of kings with a king-high flush draw. My opponent had jacks, the jack-high flush draw + gutshot straight draw. (Note that this gutshot would also give *me* a set, meaning that I would then have some redraw potential.) Taking into account the dead cards from the all-in player, our expectation now looked as follows:

♠ K♠-K♥-6♥-6♣ 77.48%

♠ J♥-J♣-8♥-7♣ 22.52%

## Analysis

As it turned out, my good expectation for the side pot more than made up for the short odds I had for the main pot. Having said that, this was quite clearly not the best of situations to go and create a side pot. The tight player's reraise was just to $20 and with him having a $100 stack, this meant that I would thus invest no less than $80 'bad money' (the main pot) to finally get into that stage where I could *possibly* be a decent favourite (the side pot).

Now, even though this was not the best of situations to pull this off, it *does* show that there are some cases where you can actively go after building a big side pot – even when you suspect that you could be beat for the main pot. Let's say that you hold kings double-suited against a reraiser who is almost all-in and who probably, though not definitely, has aces. Now, whereas with not much dead money and no other players in the pot you might simply let go, not wanting to double up a tight/aggressive player who has been waiting for this scenario for so long, things could be different when there is also a third player in. Good players know that if there is a weak player who has cold-called the tight player's reraise, it may now be worth it to go and try to break this weak player for a massive side pot, while possibly taking a bit the worst of it for the much smaller main pot. In fact, this could be one of those situations where the all-in player will more than triple his stack with unimproved aces, while *you* will take a massive pot with unimproved kings. And the third player? He will probably wonder how on earth it is possible that such nits, such ABC-players like you and the all-in player manage to win such huge pots with unimproved big pairs – hands that are always said to be such 'sucker hands' in PLO. While he will wonder about this, *you* will know the reason: It is because you had the courage to push your edge in a very high-risk situation, in a situation where many people would not even have *recognised* this edge. A situation where the majority of the players would just have called or even folded the kings against the 'obvious' aces, but where almost certainly they would not have had the courage to make that fourth or even fifth raise with just kings in order to break someone.

# Hand match-up 5

For the final hand match-up, I will simply focus on the expectation of one of my favourite types of holdings: aces + nut flush draw against a semi-coordinated flop. I will do six simulations against some of the most likely holdings that could give us action against this board. To be concrete, our hand is A♠-A♥-8♠-7♥ on the flop Q♠-10♠-5♣. This means that in addition to our overpair and the flush draw, we also have some remote runner/runner straight potential with the turn and river combos 6/4 (for the nuts) plus 9/6 and J/9 (both non-nut). All simulations below are done with respect to this Q♠-10♠-5♣ flop.

## Situation 1

Our hand versus TT22 rainbow (middle set):

- ♠ A♠-A♥-8♠-7♥: 35.51%
- ♠ 10-10-2-2: 64.49%

Against a set, our aces + nut flush draw are slightly better than 2-to-1 against.

## Situation 2

Our hand versus Q-10-6-4 rainbow (top two pair with some runner/runner straight potential):

- ♠ A♠-A♥-8♠-7♥: 50.61%
- ♠ Q-10-6-4: 49.39%

Up against top two with not many extras, an overpair + flush draw is usually about even money – sometimes a small favourite, sometimes a slight dog.

## Situation 3

Our hand versus K-J-9-8 rainbow (wrap):

- ♠ A♠-A♥-8♠-7♥: 65.12%
- ♠ K-J-9-8: 34.88%

No surprises here. As we have analysed before, the nut flush draw on its own is already a decent holding against a wrap, and here we have an overpair to go with it. We are favoured by almost 2-to-1 here.

## Situation 4

Our hand versus J-10-5-4 rainbow (bottom two with some runner/runner straight potential):

- ♠ A♠-A♥-8♠-7♥: 52.20%
- ♠ J-10-5-4: 47.80%

Again, no surprises. Against bottom two, we are a slight favourite with two cards to come. But just a backdoor flush draw or one or two blocker cards against our flush could shift the situation to even money again.

## Situation 5

Our hand versus K♣-J♠-8♥-5♠ (open-ended straight draw + pair + smaller flush draw):

- ♠ A♠-A♥-8♣-7♥: 61.95%
- ♠ K♣-J♠-8♥-5♠: 38.05%

When we are *not* up against a set, our aces + nut flush draw is almost always in decent or even excellent shape. In this situation, our opponent has some blocker cards to our hand, but still we are a clear favourite. Note that our opponent's draw is hampered by the fact that we hold two of his straight outs (the aces) and that even if he catches an ace, this would give us top set for some redraw potential.

## Situation 6

Our hand versus K♠-K♥-8♥-7♠ (kings double-suited for a smaller overpair/smaller flush draw/same side cards as we have):

- ♠ A♠-A♥-8♣-7♥: 90.43%
- ♠ K♠-K♥-8♥-7♠: 9.57%

No need to say more: Playing kings + the king-high flush draw is a horrible proposition if you are up against aces + ace-high flush draw. I bet very few people would have figured the situation for the quality kings to be *this* awful.

## Analysis

So, what does all this mean for the way you should play your aces + nut flush draw after the flop? Assuming a $200 pot in the $10-$20 blinds online game. With five players in the pot for $40 each, what is the proper way for you to play this holding? I will analyse this for three different situations: When playing a small stack ($400), when playing a medium stack ($1,000) stack and when playing a big stack ($2,500).

### Small stack ($400)

Not much advanced thought here. When it's your time to act, you bet the pot. When someone in front of you bets, you raise all-in. Simple as that.

### Medium stack ($1,000)

Now things get a little more complicated. Because if you play the same way here as with your $400 stack and simply bet the pot when it gets checked to you, you will then have $800 left on the turn. Assuming that one or two players call your flop bet, there will be just enough room left for about one pot-sized bet. Let's say that the turn is an offsuit eight, meaning that a straight draw *could* now be completed, and one of the flop callers now bets into you. You will almost certainly have to fold, while holding a hand that a) has a slight chance of actually still being the current best hand, and b) has potential to redraw on the river if it's not.

But that is not the only problem with betting the pot on the flop, because, if you bet the pot on the flop and then the turn actually completes your flush, you are probably not going to get much action from the people who have called on the flop with straight draws. So if the turn is bad you may be bet off a hand that could still improve to a winner. And if the turn is good, you may not make any more money. Two clear downsides of this simple 'always bet the pot' system.

Now, for both these reasons, you should usually try to get the hand all-in on the flop, so that you will reach the river regardless of potentially bad turn cards, and also so that you will get the money from the straight draws into the middle while they are still drawing live. The best way to accomplish all this is to simply check if by chance you are in early position, hoping that someone behind you will make a big bet, maybe get one caller in the middle, and then when the action gets back to you, you can check-raise all-in. If you are in late position, you will simply raise any bets that your opponents may make, especially if they are the types of players who like to push their draws. And finally, if it gets checked to you in late position, you could do the obvious of simply betting the pot. This will usually result in you winning the pot there and then, but if you get called you may face the exact unpleasant situation from before of possibly being bet off your hand on the turn when the river could have given you a winner. So, as an alternative you could do something frisky like betting an unusually small amount just to reopen the betting, possibly a mere $20 bet. If someone then decided to check-raise you because of this seemingly weak bet, you can reraise all-in and be in that exact situation you wanted: having all the money in the middle, possibly even with the best hand *and* the best draw. Frankly, this is how *I* would play the hand – but it *has* to suit your personality. So for some players the obvious choice (bet pot when checked to) would probably be the best one – despite these obvious drawbacks that I mentioned.

### Big stack ($2,500)

Because the money is quite deep here, we suffer from another problem: Our hand, while good, is not automatically the same through ticket anymore as with the small and the medium stacks. If we run into lots of resistance, we may actually be up against a set – and as we have seen, in that case we are probably about a 35%-65% dog. With the stacks this deep, this means that we could lose quite a bit of money if we take our hand to the river. (Say that four players are in the pot for $50 each, and you have been the pre-flop raiser, for a $200 total pot. This means that if after the flop you and one of these players go to war, in a situation where you have 35% equity, your expectation of the $5,100 total pot would be just $1,785. This means a net loss of no less than $715 – or, taking into account the $50 we had already invested, $665.)

Because the money is deep here, we will often simply make our standard half pot bet when checked to, and then decide what to do if by chance someone comes back at us with a big raise or even check-raise. Most of the time, we would then simply move all-in because there are just too many ways for our opponent to be messing around (i.e. semi-bluffing). This could be because he thinks we may simply be making a simple continuation bet with a mediocre holding that can't stand the heat – and then we surprise him by coming over the top. However, if we are up against a *really* tight player who rarely makes any kinds of moves, then we may decide it is best to simply lay down our aces + nut flush draw, if we decide that this player would not make such a move without a set. (Note: If we know for a fact that we are getting raised by two pair, then we are obviously *not* going to fold. Quite the contrary: We are going to come over the top for all our money, putting our opponent to the test there and then in order to try and make him fold. Of course, we do all this in the knowledge that even *if* we are called, we are still about even money – meaning we can consider it a 'risk-free power play'.)

When someone bets into us – the pre-flop raiser – and the money is this deep, it is hard to come up with an automatic best way to play the hand. A lot depends on what you read your opponent for: Do you think he is making a feeler bet, or do you think that he has some real strength and would happily come over the top if you decide to raise here? But it is also important to realise what he will read *you* for when you decide to call or raise, because this will determine how much leeway you will have for the rest of the hand. This factor could influence your chances of running a successful semi-bluff, for instance. Let's say that you are up against someone who either plays his hands in a very tricky manner and expects that of other players too, or who simply respects you a lot. If by just calling on the flop you can successfully convince your opponent that you may be slowplaying a big hand here, you could then semi-bluff a hand like two pair out of the pot on the turn. But against other players who see your flop call as an 'obvious' draw, you cannot suddenly become very active if the turn is a blank – because they will call or even raise you with their two pair.

In general, when you have been the pre-flop raiser and then someone bets into you against this Q♠-10♠-5♣ flop, you will usually either call or raise with your aces + nut flush draw – as folding for just one bet would usually be giving a little too much credit. Also take into account your opponents' stack sizes here. Just because *you* have a big stack, it doesn't mean your opponents should have one. So, if someone bets into you who you have labelled as a somewhat liberal bettor and he is playing a fairly short stack, well then you should probably just raise the maximum, in order to set him all-in there and then, and get the hand over with.

Either way, you look at many more factors than just the quality of your own hand, in order to make the best possible decisions. By taking advantage of your opponents' tendencies and their respective stack sizes, you try to get the money into the middle in the – for you – most favourable situation, in order to play with the biggest possible edge. Best of luck!

# Glossary

Not everyone will be familiar with all the terms that I use in this book. Especially some specific Omaha or big-bet terms may not be automatically clear to everyone. For them, I have completed this list of terms *as they are used in this book by me*. This does not mean that they are the official definitions, or even that they are always 100% accurate. Because this glossary is intended to help and to keep things simple, *not* to create some new questions, I will occasionally – for simplicity's sake – say something that technically may not be 100% correct. Also, because some terms have other meanings in addition to just the one that is used, I will only describe the meaning that is applicable in this book – not all of the other meanings that a term may have.

### Aggressive/Overaggressive

When players bet or raise a rather large, or even extremely large, percentage of the time. As opposed to: Passive/weak-tight.

### All-in

When you have put all of your chips in the pot, you are said to be 'all-in'. You will play for a 'main pot' that carries your bets and the bets by other players – of course, only up to that bet amount of yours. If other players in the pot have more chips than you, any additional money that they put in will go into a 'side pot' that you have no part of. Being all-in, you will always reach the showdown, regardless of any bets the other players may make, and of the amounts that they may put at risk for this.

## Backdoor

When you need to catch good cards both on the turn and river to complete your hand/to possibly win the pot. Say, you've got two hearts in your hand and there is only one heart on the flop, then you are said to have a 'backdoor flush draw'. Also known as runner/runner.

## Bare ace play

When you bet or raise as a bluff, pretending to have the nut flush when you just hold the lone ace of the suit – not the second card that is required to actually have that nut flush. Example: The flop is 8♠-5♠-2♠ and you hold A♠-K♥-Q♥-T♦. By betting or raising here, you are *representing* the nut flush, and you hope to make better hands (for instance, non-nut flushes) fold because of the strength you have shown. Also known as naked ace.

## Betting leverage

The amount of money left to be played in relation to the size of the pot. Example: If you call a $300 bet on the turn, and both you and your opponent have more than $2,000 left, there is lots of betting leverage. But if either one of you has just $100 left, there is very *little* betting leverage. Related to: Depth of the money (deep money/shallow money).

## Blank

Turn and/or river cards that don't change anything, meaning the drawing hands have almost certainly not been helped, and thus the current best hand will most likely *stay* the best hand. Also known as 'brick'.

## Blind pressure

The sum of the blinds (and possibly even antes, even though they are rarely used in PLO) that you will have to put in per round, and how much they account for in relation to the stack/amount of chips that you have. Example: With a $2,000 stack, blinds of $20 and $40 would account to much higher blind pressure than blinds of $5 and $10. With these lower blinds, there is 'more room for play', and games with lots of room for play are said to be more skilful than games where you can be all-in in just one or two betting increments. On the other hand, a higher blind pressure tends to promote action, simply because players cannot afford to wait for very long.

## Blockers/Blocker cards/Playing the blockers

1. If you hold a few specific cards in your hand that make it unlikely for an opponent to have the nuts or at least a very strong holding. Example: You hold J-J-J-3 and the flop is Q♠-10♥-9♣. Your opponent

is unlikely to have a completed straight because you hold three out of the four jacks in the deck that are needed to make this straight. If you now choose to bet or raise on the premise that your opponent probably doesn't have a straight, and thus will be unable to stand the heat, you are said to make a 'blocker play'.

2.  Cards in your hand that make it harder for your opponent to complete his hand/draw, and that give him fewer actual outs than he may actually *think* he has. Example: Your opponent is drawing to an ace-high heart flush draw, but you hold a couple of hearts yourself – meaning his drawing odds have become worse, now that there are fewer good cards left for him in the deck.

### Bonus deals

Deals where online poker sites give you free/extra money if you choose to deposit money and/or play in their real money games.

### Brick

See 'blank'.

### Brick and mortar (B&M)

'Regular' casinos or cardrooms. As opposed to: Online/Internet play.

### Bully

An overaggressive player who often bets and raises on light values, and who likes to run over the table. Related to 'maniac', the even more aggressive/reckless version of the bully.

### Buy-in

The amount of money you put on the table. In the past, the only requirement for entering a game was almost always a *minimum* buy-in, a minimum amount you needed to bring in order to participate in a game. Ever since the popularity of online poker, most big-bet games also have a *maximum* buy-in, meaning you cannot just put as much money on the table as you want. This maximum buy-in is more than anything to protect the weaker players, and to not let the size of the game escalate because of players who decide to buy in for massive amounts.

### Buy the button

When you bet or raise early in the hand, either before or on the flop, in the hopes of making the players behind you fold. This way, you would have secured yourself the best position throughout the hand, and you are said to have 'bought the button'. Usually, a play made from middle or late position.

## Calling station

See 'loose-passive'.

## Cap

A maximum. As in: 'cap on the buy-in' (when there is a maximum amount you can buy in for), 'cap on the number of bets and raises' (does not apply in big-bet play), or when the rake is said to be 'capped' at $3 or so (say, a 5% rake with a $3 maximum).

## Checks

Chips in play/money in front of you.

## Cold-call

When you call a raise without having invested any money already. As opposed to: Calling a raise from the blinds, or after having limped.

## Combination hand

A relatively weak hand that gains strength because it has multiple ways of winning. Every way of winning by itself is not that powerful, but when combined it can lead to a decent, or even fairly strong, holding. Example: A hand like middle pair + kickers + a gutshot straight draw + non-nut flush draw.

## Come over the top

When you make the third or even fourth raise before the flop, by re-reraising the reraiser.

## Committed

When you have invested so much money in the pot already that folding is no longer an option.

## Coordinated hand

A starting hand where all four cards work together. A hand like J♠-10♣-9♥-8♥ is said to be coordinated, whereas a hand like K♠-K♥-8♦-3♣ is not: It has just the kings and not much else.

## Covering the table

When you've got more chips in front of you than any other player in the game – meaning that you can break any one of them on a single hand.

## Customers

Those players in the hand that, based upon the strength of your holding in relation to theirs, you figure to make money from – and that therefore you want to keep *in* the hand, so that they can pay you off. As in: 'I didn't raise, because I did not want to lose my customers'.

## Dead money

Money in the pot from players who have folded already, but who *have* contributed to the pot. These contributions are good for the remaining players in the hand, because they would give them better (drawing) odds, and they would lead to a bigger pot for the eventual winner. Also counted as dead money are any blinds that you have put in, or any bets you have already made now that you are facing a big raise. In this case, your previous investment either from posting the blind or making a bet is not part of your stack anymore, but is part of the pot – and therefore considered 'dead'.

## Deep money

When people are playing with lots of money in relation to the size of the blinds, the size of the bets or the size of the pot. See also: 'Betting leverage'.

## Demeanour (table demeanour)

The overall way someone acts and behaves in a hand, and that *could* be an indication of one's strength.

## Delayed bluff

When you wait to go for the bluff until a later street. Example: On the flop, you call a bet (rather than raise or fold) with absolutely nothing, to try and take the pot away from your opponent either on the turn or river. Usually a rather advanced move, used only *by* good or experienced players, and *against* players who have at least some level of thinking to their play – meaning that they could see this call as a sign of strength, rather than as weakness.

## Double-suited

For example: When your starting hand consists of two hearts and two spades, say A♠-8♥-7♥-6♠. As opposed to: rainbow (all four cards are of different suits, meaning that you can never make a flush – say, A♠-8♥-7♦-6♣) or single-suited (when you have two, three or four cards of one suit in your hand and then zero, one or two non-suited cards to go with it – say, A♠-8♠-7♦-6♣ or A♠-8♠-7♠-6♠).

## Early in the hand

Before or on the flop. As opposed to: On the turn or river.

## Equity (Pot equity)

The winning percentage of your hand based upon the current hand distribution, calculated at the current stage that the hand is in. Example: In a three-way pot, you and two other players go all-in on the flop with the exact same stack sizes. If, based upon the flop and your opponent's holdings, you would win 35% of the time, you are said to have 35% pot equity here. Note that this would be a situation where you have 'positive expectation', as anything more than 33.33% pot equity would be a good or even very good situation for you – meaning that if you would play the hand over and over again, regardless of short-term fluctuation, you would figure to make money.

## Expected value/expectation/EV

The figure that is used to analyse whether you have made a decision that in the long run would either *cost* you money, or *make* you money. Comparison of cost versus reward. As in: 'I called a $100 turn bet in a $500 pot while I had 12 clean outs – making this a +EV decision', or: 'Calling a pot-sized bet with just a gutshot is a play with a clear negative expectation'. Related to 'equity'.

## Feeler bet

A bet designed to test strength that may or may not be out there. Usually a bet of much less than the pot, where you will immediately back down or give up if you get called or raised by strong/tight players.

## Fire a second barrel

Bet another time. Usually designed to describe someone who has made a flop bet with a rather marginal hand, and has been called. If he then decides to come out betting his marginal hand yet another time on the turn, despite the threat of this caller, he is said to have 'fired another barrel'. As opposed to: People who fire only once, and who give up immediately on their (semi-)bluff attempts by checking the turn if someone happens to call them on the flop.

## Fluctuation

Also known as 'swings'. The amount of (short-term) upswings and downswings you may experience because of simple chance. A game with relatively little fluctuation would be one where a good player is unlikely to suffer any big losses, and where in general his wins would also not be exceptionally large. As opposed to: Games with very large fluctuation, and very high *volatility*.

## Free card play

When you bet on the flop in late position/when last to act, so that if on the turn the callers check to you again and you haven't improved, you can check it back. This way – if the play succeeds – you can see the river for 'free' because of your flop bet.

### Freerolling

See 'redraw'.

### Full-ring

A game with usually nine or even ten players. As opposed to: 'shorthanded'.

### Grinder

A person who makes his money by playing poker with an edge. Usually has a bit of a negative connotation, where grinders are perceived to be 'tight', 'nit', 'percentage' players.

### Gutshot

Inside straight draw (4 outs maximum). As opposed to: Open-ended straight draw (8 outs maximum) or wraparound straight draw (20 outs maximum).

### Heads-up

When there are just two players left in a hand. As opposed to: 'multiway'.

### Hit-and-run

When you quit a game (almost) right after winning a big pot.

### Hot and cold

With no further betting. That is: Assuming a 'computer simulation' type of situation where two or more hands go all the way to the river, and where the possibility of betting each other out of the hand is ignored. A way to compare players' chances of winning, and to determine their 'expectation' in a hand. As in: 'I turned out to be a clear favourite over his hand hot and cold – but unfortunately, I decided to lay down my hand against his bet.'

### Ill-coordinated

When there are not many draws possible. Examples of ill-coordinated flop would be Q♠-7♥-2♦ or K♣-8♥-3♠ where it would be hard, if not impossible, for players to have a good draw. As opposed to: Flops like 10♣-7♥-5♥, where *many* draws are possible. Also known as 'non-descript'.

### Implied odds

When you figure to make a lot of money/be in a clearly +EV situation later in the hand, usually expecting to more than make up for any slightly –EV calls that you may have made earlier. For instance, if you can catch a good flop, turn or river, or if you are able to get yourself in another favourable situation – for instance one where you could get paid off handsomely because of 'surprise value', or where you could profit from a scare card by bluffing your opponent out. As opposed to: Negative or reverse implied odds, where you are more likely to *lose* a lot of money on the later streets than to win lots of money – or where for instance any wins would be fairly small, yet any losses could be *huge*.

## Isolate

As in: 'To isolate someone'. When you bet or (re)raise, sometimes while holding just a rather marginal hand, in order to get the pot heads-up between you and a weak or predictable player whom you can easily outplay/make money from.

## Knowing where you stand

Having a good view on the relative value of your hand, not just based upon the quality of your own holding, but just as importantly taking into account the actions of your opponents and the texture of the board.

## LAP

A loose/aggressive player. Someone who plays a lot of hands, and who tends to play them aggressively. Related to 'bully' and 'maniac'.

## Limp

Calling the initial bet in an unraised pot.

## Lockout

When someone improves his hand on the turn in such a manner that you will be drawing dead on the river – making it entirely irrelevant whether or not you improve *your* hand there. Usually when you are drawing to straights and/or flushes, but then your opponent fills up on the turn.

## Locksmith

A very tight, 'rock'-like type of player who would only voluntarily put in money into the pot with high-quality holdings (before the flop), and with big hands/big draws (after the flop).

## Loose-aggressive

See 'LAP'.

## Loose-passive

Someone who often calls, but who does not bet or raise very often. Loose-passive players (LPPs) are often referred to as 'ideal opponents', as they will pay you off when they are trailing/losing, but they won't push their edge when *they* are in the lead. (Unfortunately, you will find very few LPPs in pot-limit Omaha games, especially at the higher stakes.)

## Main pot

The 'first' pot, the pot in which the (first) all-in player belongs. Say if other four people are in a hand for $500 each, and you are all-in for $200, then you will be playing for the main pot of 5 x $200 = $1,000, while the remaining 4 x $300 ($500 – $200) will go into a side pot, $1,200 total. The all-in player cannot win any money from this side pot. He can only win the money from the main pot – the pot to which he has contributed.

## Make moves

Playing tricky, and basing your decisions on other factors than just the quality of your own holding. For instance, things like position, the texture of the board and characteristics of the opponents you are facing. Someone is said to 'make a move' when he is deliberately making a play that the quality of his cards does not warrant, usually by making a bluff, attempting to bet someone out of the pot, or trying to bet the best hand out of the pot while holding just the second-best one – in an attempt to remain in the pot with the third-best hand.

## Maniac

An extremely (over)aggressive player, who often bets and (re)raises when his cards clearly don't warrant it. Related to 'bully'.

## Money favourite

When you may not be an absolute (>50%) favourite to win the pot, but you still have a positive expectation in the hand. For instance, when you have an equity of more than 25% in a four-way pot.

## Multiway

1. As in 'multiway pot': When there are more than two players contesting the pot – say, not like a heads-up situation.
2. As in 'multiway hand': A hand that has more than one way to win – say, something like two pair + open-ended straight draw instead of just the two pair.

**Nit**

A tight, boring player with no flair. Someone who hardly ever gambles, who rarely if ever buys a round of drinks, and who doesn't like to tip. Usually a winning player, but not a very popular one.

**Non-descript board**

See 'ill-coordinated'.

**Nut-peddling approach**

A strategy where you don't bluff or even semi-bluff very often, and where you don't take many chances. A strategy where you are patiently waiting to complete your (usually high-quality) hand, hoping to get paid off.

**Nut potential**

When the cards that you hold (possibly, though not necessarily, in relation to the flop) give you opportunities/possibilities to end up with the nuts on the river. Usually, the more 'nut potential' a hand has, the better – especially in multiway pots.

**Offsuited**

See 'rainbow'.

**Outplay**

A situation where you are playing on a higher level than your opponent, and where you are able to use your better skills to lure him into making the wrong decisions.

**Overlay**

A situation where you have, or could have, a 'positive expectation'. Related to 'EV'.

**Overplay a hand**

Overrate a hand slightly, and as a result play it more strongly than its actual strength would warrant.

**Picking up a pot**

Winning a default pot by making a standard bet of anywhere from half pot to full pot. Usually when there has been no action yet, and thus the chances are that no one has enough of a hand to call or even raise.

### Play the player

Basing your decisions on characteristics and specific weaknesses of your opponent, rather than on the strength of your actual cards.

### Position

Where you are seated relative to the button. Usually, the closer you are to the button, the better. Also important is your position relative to the pre-flop raiser, and position that you have or don't have on your 'target', the person you are trying to break. In all cases, you usually want to have last action, meaning that you *first* can see what your opponents do, and *then* you can decide your own best course of action – based on *their* actions.

### PFR

Percentage of the time that you make a pre-flop raise (as opposed to folding or calling).

### Protecting a hand

Betting or raising in order to make worse and/or drawing hands pay to improve over your hand.

### Protection

When you are all-in and players with more chips than you make large bets or raises. This could lead to a situation where other big stacks/potential winners of the hand could get bet out of the pot. If this happens, not only will they be bet out of any potential side pots, but also they will also be bet out of 'your' main pot. Because this improves your chances of winning while you didn't have to invest any extra money for it, you are said to have obtained 'protection'.

### Rainbow

1.  A flop with three different suits, or even a turn with four different suits.

2.  A starting hand consisting of four different suits, meaning that one can never make a flush.

### Rake

The amount of money that the (online) cardrooms take out of every pot. Usually 5% with a cap of $3 or so.

### Rakeback

When a site gives back/refunds a certain percentage of the rake that their customers have paid. Sometimes an illegal action taken by third parties/affiliates, but just as often simply a means for sites to reward their loyal customers and/or to attract new ones.

## Redraw

1. When first your opponent hits a good card on the turn to improve over you, but then you catch a good card on the river to regain the lead and win the pot after all.

2. When two players have the same (currently winning) hand, either on the flop or on the turn, but one of them has a draw to a bigger hand. For instance, two players have both made the nut straight on the turn but one of them also has the nut flush draw to go with it. In this case, the person with the extra outs is said to have the 're-draw' here. In fact, he would be *freerolling*, as he is certain to get half the pot, yet if he hits one of his redraw cards, he will win the entire pot. Example: In a pot with $2,000 in it, where 8 out of the remaining 40 cards would improve the freeroller, he would split the pot 32/40 = 80% of the time, and win the entire pot 8/40 = 20% of the time – for an average (extra) profit of $400, free of risk. Especially in situations with deep money, the freeroll is one of the most profitable situations in PLO, even if you only have a few freeroll/redraw cards.

## Represent (a hand)

Betting your hand in a certain way so that, in combination with the board cards, your position, your image and your pre-flop actions, this bet of yours basically says: 'I've got two aces', 'I have a flush', etc. When you use these bets to convince your opponents that you have a certain hand when in fact you don't, you are 'representing' that hand/that range of hands. Please note that these plays can only work against *thinking* players – people who try to figure out by your betting, your tendencies and the texture of the board, what you probably hold. So, never try to represent a hand against people who think only about their *own* hand.

## Reverse implied odds

See 'implied odds'.

## Runner/runner

See 'backdoor'.

## Sandbagging

An old term for check-raising, where you first check to try and let the people behind you do the betting for you, to then raise when the action comes back to you.

### Scare card

A card that could very well have helped your opponent and/or that could have completed his draw(s). A card that is perceived as potentially dangerous in the eyes of the lead bettor. After the betting round on the flop or turn, he figures his opponent for having a draw or a weaker made hand than this. But now (because of this scary turn or river card) he knows that his opponent's hand could have improved over his own holding.

### Second hand low

When you first flat call a bet or raise while holding a very big hand – say, something like aces before the flop. You feign weakness by just calling, hoping that someone behind you will (re)raise, so that you can then come over the top with a massive reraise. A shrewd and advanced way to maximise your winnings on a hand.

### Semi-bluffing

Betting or raising on the flop or turn with a hand that is unlikely to be currently best – most likely you are pushing a draw – with the goal of making everybody fold. Yet if you do get called, you know that you still have some or even a lot of outs to *improve* to the best hand.

### Shallow money

When the sizes of the stacks are small in relation to the size of the blinds/the size of the pot, meaning that you will be all-in in just very few betting increments. As opposed to: 'Deep money'. See also 'betting leverage'.

### Shorthanded

A game with anywhere from two to six players. As opposed to: 'full-ring'.

### Short money

See 'shallow money'.

### Side pot

A second pot that is created in addition to the main pot. (Note that these terms say nothing about the *size* of the pot; the side pot can be many times bigger than the main pot.) A pot that is contested only by the bigger stacks in the pot, not by the all-in player who can only win the main pot.

## Single-suited

See 'double-suited'.

## Slowplay

When you play a very big hand in a much more passive way than could be expected based on its strength. Usually done in order to lure other people into the pot and/or to 'not scare the customers'.

## Software programs

Computer programs that could help you improve or analyse your (or your opponents') poker game and also your results.

## Speculative holdings

Hands that do not hit/catch any good flops very often, but that if they *do* hit could make you a lot of money.

## Stop bet

A small bet that could prevent someone else of making an (unwanted) bigger bet, and that could lead to you reaching the turn or river cheaply.

## Stop raise

A small raise that could prevent someone else of making an (unwanted) bigger raise. Related to 'stop bet'.

## Swings

See 'fluctuation'.

## 'Target'

The person in your game that you are trying to break; the weak player whose money you are after. As in: 'Having isolated my target before the flop with a small reraise, I knew that if he didn't catch any part of the flop, the pot would be mine.' Also known as your 'prey'.

## Tell

Giveaway. Something other than the actual betting usually, that indicates how strong or weak your opponent's hand probably is. Common tells: 'Acting strong means being weak', 'Glancing at chips means intending to play/holding a strong hand'.

### Tight-aggressive

Someone who plays very few hands, but who often bets and raises on the hands that he *does* play in order to push his edges. As opposed to: 'Loose-passive'.

### 'Tightass'

A very tight player, someone who is involved in very few hands. Negative term for a 'rock'. Related to the (also negative) term 'nit'.

### Time collection

When the house doesn't make its money by taking a certain amount out of every pot (rake), but rather charges a fee for every 30 or 60 minutes that the players are in a game. Common way to charge players in high-stakes brick and mortar games.

### TPTK/Top Pair Top Kicker

When you have paired the top card of the board and hold the best possible side card to go with it. A typical hold'em term, one that usually implies a decent or even good holding. In Omaha, TPTK is usually not worth all that much though. Also, if in Omaha you had the hand top pair + best sidecard, you would talk about top pair + *multiple* kickers, simply because you've got four holecards instead of just two.

### Tricky

Someone who plays in a very deceptive manner. Someone who often doesn't have the hand he represents, or who often plays his hands quite differently from the way most people would play it. As in: 'Knowing he is a tricky player, I knew that his check didn't automatically mean that he had nothing.' As opposed to: Straight-forward.

### UTG/Under the gun

First to act after the blinds, which is usually considered to be the worst possible position in the betting. UTG+1 = second to act after the blinds, UTG+2 = third, etc.

### VPIP

Percentage of the time that a player has voluntarily put chips into the pot.

### Weak-tight (Tight-passive)

Someone who plays very few hands, but who does not push his edges/play aggressively enough on the few hands that he *does* play. A term with a rather negative connotation, one that implies: 'OK, so he may be decent in his hand selection, but still he is not much of a player.' As opposed to: 'loose-aggressive'.

## Wraparound straight draw

Better known as just a 'wrap'. Indicates that you have a premium straight draw like Q-J-8-7 on a board 10-9-x, where you have the flop 'surrounded'. (Any K, Q, J, 8, 7 or 6 would give you a straight – not necessarily the nut straight, but still a straight.) Nowadays in Omaha, all hands that are clearly more than just an open-ended straight draw are usually called wraps, even when technically speaking that may not be the case. In addition, hands like J-10-9-x on a flop Q-8-x are called 'inside wraps' because you don't have the flop cards surrounded, but the flop cards have *you* surrounded.

# Further reading, useful websites and tools

## Recommended PLO books and writers

When it comes to PLO books, I would recommend most books by Bob Ciaffone, simply because he usually gives good and solid information, and very well-written on top of that. Stewart Reuben has written quite a bit about the game as well (in one book even together with Ciaffone), and some of his stuff is actually quite good. Having played in one of the toughest PLO games in the world – the one in the Vic – and having performed quite well there with a rather loose style of play, Mr Reuben's works often offer a good deal of insightful information. However, his writing style can sometimes be quite hard to follow and, perhaps more importantly, he talks about extremely deep-money games – games that have become almost non-existent in the shallow-money Internet age. So, simply imitating Mr. Reuben's strategies in the games that most readers will probably perform in (Internet games or brick and mortar games with a cap on the maximum buy-in) is an almost certain recipe for disaster.

Other Omaha writers usually write more about limit than about pot-limit (or about Omaha/8 instead of Omaha high), for instance Michael Cappelletti and Steve Badger. And then of course there are some books that have one chapter or section on pot-limit Omaha. This is the case for instance in *Super/System 2* (the Lyle Berman section) and also in *Championship Omaha* (the section by T.J. Cloutier). In both cases, I am not overly enthusiastic about the results. For more information why I feel like this, simply check out the 'Book Ratings & Reviews' section on my site www.rolfslotboom.com, where I have rated all the important poker books, good and bad alike, so you may find some useful guidance there.

All in all, I would recommend Bob Ciaffone as a PLO writer, and to a lesser degree also Stewart Reuben. The book they co-wrote (*Pot-Limit and No-Limit Poker*) is probably one of the best books on big-bet play, even though (again) there is just one chapter about PLO. This chapter was written by Stewart Reuben, who (as in his *How Good is your Pot-Limit Omaha?* book) has a rating system for his quizzes that I don't like at all. However, the information he provides is quite good. The same thing with Ciaffone's *Improve Your Poker* – not a lot about PLO, but what's there is of more than decent quality. (In both books there is a lot of information that may not be *specifically* about PLO, but that is very useful for this game nonetheless. So, don't just read the PLO sections; read the entire books.)

Another book, Bob Ciaffone's *Omaha Poker,* has just been released as a 21st century edition. Even though some people seem to think that this is *the* book on PLO, I believe it is only moderately good. Most of all, I think the book is way too thin for a 'definitive' book, with discussion of way too many games, structures, ideas, etc. Even the relevant PLO section has just 36 pages. But the information that *is* provided is of very high quality, like his evaluation of starting hands, his chapter on percentages and the twelve PLO tips – together, they account for probably the best PLO information that has been released in print so far. A final recommendation is for Stewart Reuben's *How Good Is Your Pot-Limit Omaha?*, albeit with all the words of caution that you can read in the review on my site.

# Recommended PLO sites and tools

In all honesty, you can probably find as much good PLO information for free online, as you can by buying the various poker books. Web sites with good PLO information include:

## www.bet-the-pot.com

In particular, the forum and article sections of this site have some good information, more than anything because of the work and efforts of Felonious Monk.

## www.winningonlinepoker.com

In the Omaha section, you can find lots of good PLO information.

## www.cardplayer.com

This site has lots of good PLO articles in the archives, written either by Bob Ciaffone or by me. (And occasionally by some other writers as well, for instance Daniel Negreanu and Phil Hellmuth.) Also, there are some decent/insightful discussions in the Omaha forums, albeit not all that frequently.

## www.twoplustwo.com

Often has decent discussion in its Omaha forum, even though there may be just six or seven regular posters who *really* know a lot about PLO.

## www.internetpokerpro.blogspot.com

The blog of one of these posters from Two Plus Two, where he discusses some interesting hands/situations that often involve PLO. The quality of the replies is sometimes quite good.

## www.twodimes.net

This site had already been mentioned before in this book. It is *the* source for PLO simulations and hand match-ups.